T0173979

IT Development in Korea

This book investigates the contextual factors that led to Korean society becoming "broadband heaven"—the most wired nation in the world—by scrutinizing the historical contexts surrounding the Korean Information Infrastructure (KII) project (1995–2005), which aimed to establish a nationwide high-speed backbone network, as well as its later evolution, which involved redesigning the public infrastructure.

The book details the hidden mechanisms and the real elements of building the "broadband heaven": the global constraints conditioning its telecom policies, the dense state–capital linkages, and the bureaucratic desire for social control. It draws on the state-in-society approach to analyze the deformations caused by the symbiosis between the state and big business in implementing the rosy vision of the broadband network. This book provides insights into how to formulate future telecom policies along much more democratically participatory lines, while restraining the overwhelming power of the telecom oligopolies and conglomerates. It stands alone as a comprehensive study of the recent East Asian model of IT development, written specifically to examine Korea's socio-historical mechanisms for promoting physical speed and broadband mobility.

This book will be important reading to anyone interested in Korean Studies, Information Technology and I.T. Development.

Kwang-Suk Lee (이광석 李光錫) is an assistant professor in the Graduate School of Public Policy and Information Technology at Seoul National University of Science and Technology, Seoul, South Korea; and Honorary Visiting Fellow at the University of Wollongong, Australia.

Routledge advances in Korean Studies

IT Development in Korea

A broadband nirvana?

Kwang-Suk Lee

Routledge
Taylor & Francis Group

LONDON AND NEW YORK

First published 2012
by Routledge
2 Park Square, Milton Park, Abingdon, Oxon OX14 4RN

Simultaneously published in the USA and Canada
by Routledge
711 Third Avenue, New York, NY 10017

Routledge is an imprint of the Taylor & Francis Group, an informa business

© 2012 Kwang-Suk Lee

British Library Cataloguing in Publication Data
A catalogue record for this book is available from the British Library

Library of Congress Cataloging in Publication Data
Lee, Kwang-Suk.
IT development in Korea : a broadband nirvana? / Kwang-Suk Lee.
  p. cm. – (Routledge advances in Korean studies ; 25)
  Includes bibliographical references and index.
  1. Information technology–Social aspects–Korea (South) 2.
  Communication and culture–Korea (South) 3. Technology and state–
  Korea (South) I. Title.
  HM851.L446 2012
  303.48'33095195–dc23

                                                          2011024482

ISBN: 978-0-415-58746-4 (hbk)
ISBN: 978-0-203-15269-0 (ebk)

Typeset in Times
by Wearset Ltd, Boldon, Tyne and Wear

To my parents, in gratitude for their patience and love

Contents

Figures

Tables

Acknowledgments

This book had its origins in a doctoral research project in the Department of Radio, Television, and Film at the University of Texas at Austin. The completion of this book would not have been possible without the assistance of many people. Above all, I would like to express my sincere gratitude and appreciation to my supervising faculty member, Sharon Strover, for the strong support and guidance she provided throughout the long journey of my doctoral research. Her guidance during and beyond my doctoral research has been formative to my academic development. I also wish to express my deepest gratitude to Joseph Straubhaar for his scholarly supervision, warm guidance, and constant encouragement. I am also indebted to Philip Doty, who has been always a strong supporter and actually saved my academic life when I was at a most difficult juncture in transitioning to my current field of study. David J. Phillips has been my teacher and friend since the beginning of my master's degree, the most difficult period of my study and of my life. Laura Stein gave me insightful comments on my writing and always assessed my academic abilities to be greater than I felt them to be at the time.

Intellectual nourishment also came from an extended community of friends and colleagues who have helped along the way, whether knowingly or inadvertently. At risk of making any accidental omissions, I would like to thank the following people for their support at various stages of my research and writing: Paik Wook Inn, Won Yong-jin, Choi Young Mook, Cho Hyun Suk, Lee Wonjae, Oh Byoungil, Moon Tae Soon, Lee Dong Yeon, Kim Chang Nam, Yoo Sun Young, Paik Won Dam, Kang Nae Hui, Lee Ki Hyung, Lee Sang Gil, Ryoo Woong-Jae, Jeon Gyu Chan, Lee Young Joo, Kim Yeran, Kim Seojoong, Park Jin Kyu, Harmeet Sawhney, Robin Mansell, Charles Ramirez Berg, Park Han Woo, Jin Dal Yong, Katina Michael and MG Michael, Brian Martin, Richard Howson, Andrew Whelan, Yenn Lee, Jo Dongwon, and Hong Sung-Il.

Further, I was very fortunate to receive considerable help in the midst of my research project from colleagues whom I met in the 2006 Summer Doctoral Program at the Oxford Internet Institute at the University of Oxford. Another stroke of good fortune was finally to meet Dan Schiller, who had served as a reader advising my doctoral research at the 2007 National Communication Association (NCA) Doctoral Honors Seminar, held at the University of Colorado at Boulder: unexpectedly, in 2011, I again received good advice on my research from Dan when he invited me to give a public lecture in the speaker series at the University of Illinois at Urbana-Champaign.

Scholarly research presentations resulted in valuable clarifications, and I am grateful for invitations proffered by David Marshall, Karsten Weber, Shalini Venturelli, Yeo Shin Joung, Dan Wedemeyer, Milagros Rivera, Kim Shin Dong, and Rachel Brooks to present research at the University of Wollongong, the Universität Bielefeld, the American University at Washington, DC, the University of Illinois at Urbana-Champaign, the University of Hawai'i at Manoa, the Asia's Future Foundation, and the University of Surrey, respectively.

I count it a privilege to have been employed as an Australian Research Council Postdoctoral Research Fellow, and now as an Honorary Visiting Fellow at the University of Wollongong, Australia, conducting a four-year research project (2010–13) entitled *A History of the Internet in Australia and the Asian Pacific*. It is a pleasure to thank Gerard Goggin, Mark McLelland, and Haiqing Yu for the generosity and care they have extended to me academically and personally. I would especially like to express my deepest thanks to Mark for guiding me in how to survive Australian academic culture, even though I have had not much time to enjoy it before moving to a new position in Korea.

My special thanks should be given to my old friend and tutor, Wesley Weed. Without his critical comments and editing work, I could not have brought this book to life. I also want to give my heartfelt thanks to the interviewees of this study, especially Na Seong-Wook, a senior researcher at the National Information Society Agency. Despite their busy schedules, they willingly gave of their time for the interviews and shared their ideas and policy visions with me. My gratitude also goes out to the friends and colleagues whom I met during my years at UT–Austin and who have always encouraged me to continue in my post-doctoral research in Australia and overseas, especially Brian Yecies, Shim Ae-Gyung, Hwangbo Young Hee, Vicki Crinis, Gabriel Garcia, Kim Hee-Young, Chang Joonsoo, Kim Sarah, Joe Sanchez, Cha Sunah, Shin Chang Won, Kwak Kyong Soo, Yi Kyung Yong, Kang Seung Ho, Ha Seung Tae, Moon Sun Young, Wei-Ching Wang, Nobuya Inagaki, and Fabio Ferreira.

I would like to thank my father and mother, who have supported me spiritually and financially as I followed this path of study, and my wife and son, Kyong Rae and Seung Jun, who have always reminded me of the truth about living and love as a family throughout the past thirteen years in Austin, Incheon, and Wollongong. Without their encouragement and patience, I could never have realized the completion of my book, so I offer my utmost gratitude to them.

Last but not least, I thank Stephanie Rogers and Ed Needle at the Routledge Asian Studies editorial team for waiting patiently for my overdue manuscript. I am grateful for their careful attention and assistance.

** Chapter 5 is reprinted, slightly revised, from Kwang-Suk Lee (2009). A final flowering of the developmental state: The IT policy experiment of the Korean Information Infrastructure, 1995–2005, *Government Information Quarterly*, 26(4), 567–76, 2009, with permission from Elsevier.

Abbreviations

ADSL	Asynchronous digital subscriber line
APEC	Asia-Pacific Economic Cooperation
APII	Asia-Pacific Information Infrastructure
ATM	Asynchronous transfer mode
BcN	Broadband convergence network
BIT	Bilateral investment treaty
BOK	Bank of Korea
CATV	Cable television
CCTV	Closed circuit television
CDMA	Code division multiple access
CEI	Committee for Educational Informatization
CK21	CyberKorea 21
C/S	Client-server
CT-2	Second-generation cordless telephony
DMB	Digital multimedia broadcasting
DRAM	Dynamic random access memory
DSC	Defense Security Command
DTV	Digital television
e-GTN	e-Government Telecommunication Network
EIS	Education Information System
EPB	Economic Planning Board
ETRI	Electronics and Telecommunications Research Institute
EU	European Union
FAIP	Framework Act on Informatization Promotion
FCC	US Federal Communications Commission
FDI	Foreign direct investment
FTTH	Fiber to the home
G-7	Group of 7 (Canada, France, Germany, Italy, Japan, the US, and UK)
GATS	General Agreement for Trade in Services
GDP	Gross domestic product
GICC	Government-wide Integrated Computing Center
GII	Global Information Infrastructure

GNI	Gross national income
GPS	Global positioning systems
HSDPA	High-speed downlink packet access
ICT	Information and communication technology
IEEE	Institute of Electrical and Electronics Engineers
IMF	International Monetary Foundation
IP	Internet protocol
IPTV	Internet protocol television
ISDN	Integrated services digital network
ISP	Internet service provider
IP-USN	Internet Protocol-Ubiquitous Sensor Network
IPv6	Internet protocol version 6
IT	Information technology
ITU	International Telecommunication Union
JSC	Joint Struggle Committee for Human Rights in Information Society and Against the NEIS
KADO	Korea Agency for Digital Opportunity and Promotion
KAIT	Korea Association of Information and Telecommunication
KAM	Knowledge Assessment Methodology
KBS	Korean Broadcasting System
KCC	Korea Communications Commission
KCIA	Korea Central Intelligence Agency
KDI	Korea Development Institute
KERI	Korea Electrotechnology Research Institute
KII	Korean Information Infrastructure
KII-G	Korean Information Infrastructure-Government
KII-P	Korean Information Infrastructure-Public
KII-T	Korean Information Infrastructure-Testbed
KISA	Korea Internet and Security Agency
KISDI	Korea Information Society Development Institute
KMTS	Korea Mobile Telecom Service
KOREN	Korea Advanced Research Network
KORUS FTA	Korea–US Free Trade Agreement
KT	Korea Telecom
KTF	KT Freetel
KTU	Korean Teachers and Educational Workers Union
LAN	Local area network
LCD	Liquid crystal display
LG	Lucky Goldstar
LMDS	Local multipoint distribution service
MBC	Munhwa Broadcasting Corporation
MIC	Ministry of Information and Communication
MCT	Ministry of Construction and Transportation
MEHR	Ministry of Education and Human Resources
MMDS	Multichannel multipoint distribution service

MoC	Ministry of Communications, old name of MIC
MOGAHA	Ministry of Government Administration and Home Affairs
MOTIE	Ministry of Trade, Industry, and Energy
MPLS	Multi-protocol label system
NAFTA	North American Free Trade Agreement
NBIS	National Basic Information System
NCA	National Computerization Agency, old title of NIA
NEIS	National Educational Information System
NGO	Non-governmental organization
NHRC	National Human Rights Commission
NIA	National Information Society Agency
NIEs	Newly Industrialized economies
NII	National Information Infrastructure
NIS	National Intelligence Service
NSL	National Security Law
OECD	Organization for Economic Co-operation and Development
OEM	Original equipment manufacturers
PC	Personal computer
PCS	Personal communications by satellite
PDA	Personal digital assistant
PFC	Priority foreign country
QoS	Quality of service
RFID	Radio frequency identification
SONET	Synchronous optical network
UBcN	Ultra Broadband convergence Network
W-CDMA	Wideband code division multiple access
WEF	World Economic Forum
WiMAX	Worldwide interoperability for microwave access
xDSL	a number of standards in DSL (digital subscriber line), known collectively

Introduction
South Korea as broadband heaven?

[T]o the degree that large industry develops, the creation of real wealth comes to depend less on labor time and on the amount of labor employed than on the power of the agencies set in motion during labor time, ... [a power that] depends rather on the general state of science and on the progress of technology, or the application of this science to production.

(Marx, [1939] 1993: 704–5)

Developmental states become consistent with neoliberalization to the degree that they facilitate competition between firms, corporations, and terrestrial entities and accept the rules of free trade and rely on open export markets. But they are relatively interventionist in creating the infrastructures for a good business climate. Neoliberalization therefore opens up possibilities for developmental states to enhance their position in international competition by developing new structures of state intervention (such as support for research and development).

(Harvey, 2005: 72)

As the class power of an ascending fraction of capital increased, the corporate chieftains of informationalized capitalism pressed new demands on the state, and the government responded by documenting, elevating, and projecting these [ICT] policy preferences domestically and internationally. Widely hailed as a return to the supposed natural logic of the free market, therefore, accelerated commodification was anchored for strategic purpose by the state.

(Schiller, 2007: 39–40)

Internal and external reality: a Janus-faced South Korea

Over the last several years, many South Koreans have been flattered by descriptions of their country, in the news media and elsewhere, as a kind of "broadband heaven." Since the early 2000s, the Korean informatization index, which is based on surveys by international institutions such as the Organization for Economic Co operation and Development (OECD) and the International Telecommunication Union (ITU), has showed Korea on a sharp curve rising up into the first tier of information wealth within a short time span. American and European journalists have appraised the broadband infrastructure-driven IT growth in

Korea as one of the most successful government-led projects of modern times. For instance, the *New York Times* described Korean society as the realization of "America's broadband dream" (Belson & Richtel, 2003), and *Fortune* magazine glorified Korea as "leapfrogging the US to become the planet's pacesetter in high-speed Internet" (Lewis, 2004). Recently, the *Economist Intelligence Unit* (2011) put Korea at the top of those countries set to benefit from the roll-out of improved broadband infrastructure. Paul Wolfowitz, the former president of the World Bank and a well-known neo-conservative, visited Seoul in 2006 and praised South Korea as a "world IT leader." A scholars' conference even formulated new terminology describing Korea as moving from the status of a "newly industrialized economy" to that of "a newly advanced economy"—an economy employing growth strategies in a less exploitative and more market- and technology-driven manner that transcends the catching-up growth model (Mahlich & Pascha, 2007: 2). Thus the Korean government has succeeded in getting high praise from the outside world, and has persuaded other countries that pervasive broadband, actively subsidized by the government, will increase industrial efficiency, create e-businesses and jobs, improve global competitiveness, and increase household income.

Academic scholars have focused mainly on the causal factors that have contributed to Korea becoming the most wired nation in the world—a vigorous and effective government-led policy, the introduction of competition into the telecom market, the cultural attitudes of the Korean people, a dense and urbanized population, cooperative relationships among the public, private, and R&D sectors, and so on. In contrast to the state-driven IT plans in Asian countries, many point to the failure of the US model, where the telecom infrastructure has been evolved in a very decentralized way since the mid-1990s, quite unlike the state-sponsored "centric" model in Asian countries such as Korea. The failure of the market to achieve widespread broadband Internet access in the US, as well as the subsequent debate about "Net neutrality" (e.g., PBS, 2007, October 18), make it clear that the US policy approach of a "bottom-up" or "polycentric" model (Sawhney, 1993) for interconnecting the infrastructural network—one that limits federal policy interventions and leaves users at the mercy of telecom conglomerates—has delayed US citizens' having equal access to broadband Internet. Such analysts would see the active implementation of the Obama administration's broadband plan as a relatively late but appropriate drive toward realizing the public interests of the Internet. This drive is a push towards the goal of escaping the market failure caused by the incumbents in the US telecom market. With the recent focus on national broadband plans in the major advanced countries (see Table I.1), state interventionism in Korea's IT development is once again in the spotlight. The governments in advanced countries would like to learn how to establish domestic broadband infrastructure effectively, so as to further twenty-first-century state-guided developmentalist policy schemes like those in Korea.

Many Western observers have emphasized the cultural specificities of Korean society to explain the successful story of the "digital nation," especially those of metropolitan Seoul. They point to the nationwide diffusion of physical and virtual hypermedia spaces, such as the culture of the "PC-bang" (Internet café), online computer game rooms, and Cyworld, a popular web-community site, as examples of the Korean users' "demand-pull," through which the government's rapid supply/push of information infrastructure was completed. American and European IT-related business journals and TV documentaries have given rosy and even sensational news coverage of Koreans' hyper-social culture greatly affecting how people connect in virtual space, transforming the nation into the "most connected and Net-addicted country on Earth" (Taylor, 2006; see also, Herz, 2002; BBC, 2010; PBS, *Frontline*, 2008, 2010). Others have noted the living conditions of urbanism, and the fact that most Koreans reside in apart-ments or multi-dwelling units, as an advantage for broadband development. It is said that the geographical density of the population was the main reason that Korea became a digital nation so rapidly: specifically, that the facility-based telecom service providers saved an enormous amount of networking costs by ter-minating their fiber optic lines in central telecommunications exchanges or main distribution frames (MDFs), leaving apartment builders usually responsible for the "last mile" to each household.

Others have pointed to the IT policy promotion of past civilian presidents: undeterred by the budget reductions resulting from the Korean financial crisis of 1997, the government's main drive was to construct high-speed broadband mobility and connectivity across the country. After the country had passed through the long dark tunnel of military regimes and transitioned to civilian gov-ernment in the mid-1990s, South Korea's government-led broadband infrastruc-ture plans were quite successful in shifting market conditions into a new economic system.

These analyses of the factors responsible for the birth and growth of a "digital heaven" represent only certain aspects of "the Korean Way": most analyses fail to notice the Janus-faced nature of Korea's IT success—they ignore the govern-ment's attempts at hyper-panoptic social control, the vulnerable condition of online human rights, the chronic cronyism between the state and the IT-involved conglomerates, the rise of online activism against the "neo-authoritarian" civil-ian government, and other realistic conditions of a neo-liberal market state. The incorporation of Korean information technology into a new capitalist mode of production, and into bureaucratic mechanisms designed to regulate each Korean citizen, is the dark side of Korea's "broadband nirvana." The interventionist role the government has played in the process is far from the normative role of the state as a public mediator guaranteeing citizens' equal rights; such a government should defend citizens' freedom of expression and information rights against predation.

The neo-liberal conditions of a digital nation

It is not widely known internationally that, as of 2010, Korea has the highest suicide rate among OECD countries, at 31 per 100,000, as well as the lowest birth rate. The suicide rate is not only much higher than that of the US (11 per

100,000), but even higher than that of Japan (24 per 100,000). A rapid increase in the suicide rate has been noted as an ongoing trend in Korean society since the late 1990s (Statistics Korea, 2010)—the period when the government promoted the arrival of "affluent society" on the material bases of consumerism and broadband Internet culture. More evidence of Korea's social ills has been emerging continually: for instance, as of 2011, the happiness index for Korean teenagers was the lowest among the 23 countries in the OECD. As of 2010, Korea was also ranked second lowest in social welfare spending among OECD countries.

Far from the myth of IT growth stimulated by a "broadband heaven," the conditions of workers in Korea are extremely insecure: among OECD countries, they have the longest working hours—2,256 hours per year and 45 hours per week, as of 2008 (OECD.StatExtract, 2011). This number is more than 100 hours longer than the next longest-working country, Greece (2,116 hours). If we further consider the material conditions of Korean workers—overworked, stressed, threatened, and always situated within "institutionalized precariousness" (Bourdieu, 2003)—simply noting that they work the most hours in the developed world falls short of describing their insecure working conditions. According to Bourdieu (2003), such a "dual economy" is made up of an enormous industrial reserve army—"a sub-proletariat with no employment prospects, no future, [and] no plans" (30–1)—on one side and a small privileged minority of secure workers with a regular wage on the other. The "zombie-like" sub-proletariat (see Shaviro, 2002), always vulnerable to being laid off and not renewable after their labor power is consumed and exhausted, consists mostly of the younger population in Korean society. In Korea, this zombie sub-proletariat is now dubbed the "KR880,000 *won* Generation"— the younger generation earning a net pay of about US$650 per month (Seo & Kim, 2009). Young Korean workers suffer from continually precarious job positions as temporary staff or contract workers, being trapped at the bottom of the pay scale, and thus embittered by their broken dreams, despite their elite educations and careers. While in the global market the *Chaebols*[1]—Korean-style family-owned multinationals such as Samsung and LG—are reaching the apex of the consumer electronics industry, their workers and young Koreans are still captives in the early era of industrial capitalism. The mega-corporations have accumulated ever-increasing profits through more worker exploitation and the appropriation of surplus value by using semi-permanently institutionalized precarious and insecure conditions for workers. Indeed, the introduction of the casualization of employment is planned as "part of a *mode of domination* of a new kind, based on the creation of a generalized and permanent state of insecurity aimed at forcing workers into submission, into the acceptance of exploitation" (Bourdieu, 1998: 85, emphasis in original).

The statistics that give an inside view of Korean society have received far less notice than the IT growth stories about Korea. Above all, while the broadband Internet has become a crucial communication medium promoting freedom of socio-political expression in Korea, online space is also becoming an electronic dungeon patrolled by the "neo-authoritarian" government due to its anxieties about online users' freedom of expression. In 2009, when Frank La Rue, a UN Special Rapporteur, visited Korea, he noted the "ironic" aspects of Korea's IT development, including its advanced broadband Internet: "It is crucial to protect and promote the right to freedom of opinion and expression in cyberspace paralleling technological advancement in South Korea" (People's Solidarity for Participatory Democracy [PSPD] news site, 2009).

This book arose from concerns about the little-known and widely ignored dark side of Korean IT development. The present writer began to think about why these Janus-faced conditions have been gradually increasing since the mid-1990s, and which undemocratic trends during the government-led broadband installment projects have eroded the health and the potential of advanced IT in Korean society. As a starting point, this study explores the decade-long telecom policy plan, the Korean Information Infrastructure (KII) project (1995–2005). The KII project aimed to establish a nationwide high-speed backbone network and has become the basis for the present technological advancement in Korea. In fact, this IT master plan concretized the civilian governments' desire to incorporate Korea strongly in world IT economies, as a means of surviving the dog-eat-dog market competition of the new world order of capitalism in a digital age.

A Korean-style "information superhighway"

In South Korea, the rapid construction of national roads and railways under the military regimes of the 1970s and 1980s was a typical case of state interventionism, aimed at promoting industrial economies that were lagging behind the West. The highway and railway infrastructures were closely tied to the government's project of economic modernization, to save on the costs of transporting goods and services and to speed up the mobility of the labor population. For the same reasons, the national construction of electronic backbone networks has become appealing to the government as the engine of economic efficiencies and growth. Beginning in the mid-1990s, the Korean civilian governments launched their master plan to construct the nationwide telecommunications superhighway project, the KII plan. The Korean government's information backbone network project was originally modeled after the US "information superhighway" plan of 1993, and was further developed by Japan's "Pilot Model" and the EU's "Euro-ISDN" in 1994.

To establish a nationwide information superhighway along the lines of the National Information Infrastructure proposed by the Clinton administration in the US, the Korean government invested public funds of US$6.2 billion over 11 years, with the expenditure of US$16.5 billion from the private sector. The Korean government has celebrated the synergistic effects of the KII—chiefly, the bureaucratic efficiencies brought about by the technological rationalization of interconnecting public institutions electronically, and the growth of the new IT-related economic market. In other words, the implementation of the KII project was viewed at the time as a vehicle for promoting e-governance and IT business. In contrast to the Korean government's public investment in establishing the national backbone networks, the US information superhighway project depended

Table 1.1 Public broadband infrastructure plans

Country	Public investment (amount)	Policy goal	Penetration target	Speed target
Australia	AU$43 billion	Creation of the National Broadband Network (NBN) plan (2009–18)	90% of all homes and businesses connected by fiber optic lines	100 Mbps for 90%, 12 Mbps for 10%
China	CNY2 trillion	Broadband plan under China's twelfth Five-Year Plan (2011–15), "Broadband China Optical Network City" project (2010–12)	30 million homes in 2011 100 million (80% of population) by 2015	8 Mbps or higher
Japan	JPY185 billion + 500 billion	u-Japan policy package + "e-Japan strategy 2015" Promoting the nationwide development of wired and wireless broadband infrastructure	Broadband: 100% in 2010 Ultra-high speed: 90% in 2010 93% by fiber optic cable by 2015	1 Gbps (fixed) and 100 Mbps (mobile) by 2015
South Korea	• **Gov: KRW440 billion** • **Telcos: KRW29 trillion (KII, 1995–2005)** • **KRW1.3 trillion (UBcN, 2008–13)**	• **Building of the Korea information infrastructure (KII, 1995–2005)** • **UBcN (further KRW 32.8 trillion from the private sector)**	**50–100 Mbps service to 14 million residents by 2012 (1 Gbps service by 2013)**	**Fixed: 1 Gbps (max), Mobile: 10 Mbps (avg)**
Singapore	SGD 750 million	Build the Next Generation National Broadband Network (NGNBN)	Open the fiber optic network to all service providers	100 Mbps – 1 Gbps
Finland	Gov: €66 million Municipalities and EU: €66 million	To offer high-speed broadband services to end users in sparsely populated areas	More than 99% of population	100 Mbps

Country		Plan		Speed
Italy	€800 million	New-generation networks throughout the country by 2013	99%	4 Mbps
Portugal	€125 million	• Construction of more than 1,000 km fiber optic cable backbone (€34 million) • Fiscal incentives as part of the stimulus package (€50 million) • Increase broadband Internet access in schools (€61 million)	1.5 million homes connected by fiber optic cable	100 Mbps in 2010
Sweden	Gov: 50% (SEK 4.4 billion)	• the Broadband plan (2001–07): deploying broadband to rural areas lacking access • World-class high-speed broadband (2009–13)	99% in 2008, 40% by 2015, 90% by 2020	100 Mbps
United Kingdom	£830 million	"Digital Britain" plan (2009) & "Britain's Superfast Broadband Future" (2010) • Getting isolated and rural areas onto the broadband grid	Countrywide by 2015	Average speed of 50 Mbps
United States	US$7.25 billion	National Broadband plan (broadband.gov): • The expansion of broadband service in rural, unserved, and low-income areas, improving mobile broadband access	At least 200 million households connected to 50–100 Mbps by 2020	50–100 Mbps 1 Gbps for public institutions

Source: OECD (2010) and each government's website.

entirely on private sector efforts. Due to the lethargic response to the policy initiative by the private sector, the US has lagged behind in establishing a national broadband network. State-led supply policies for national telecommunication networks have succeeded only in a few countries which had a strong policy plans led by an interventionist state—countries in which the telecom incumbents conformed to the governments' master plans.

Recently, we have observed an age of digital convergence in which advanced countries such as the US, England, Finland, and Australia, as well as East Asian countries, are developing national backbone infrastructures by replacing aging copper lines with fiber optic cables, or by integrating the wireless and mobile Internet networks on the technical basis of landline Internet protocol (IP) architecture, as Table I.1 shows. The recent tendencies toward renovation of national electronic infrastructures among the advanced countries reflect a new stage of IT applications in the global market, one in which the "next-generation" high-speed broadband Internet is increasingly an essential network for revitalizing the recessive phase of global economies, as well as for promoting citizens' opportunities to enjoy freedom of speech and information use. The KII project has been considered as a precedent for state-guided Internet infrastructure policy plans, including the Obama administration's broadband initiative, the Australian government's National Broadband Network (NBN) Plan, and other advanced countries' public broadband infrastructure investment plans.

Political elites in Korea see the KII project as a very successful story of state interventionism following the Korean economic crisis of 1997. Many scholars view the KII as the "second phase" of the Asian economic miracle: the first phase involved Asia catching up to the West in the industrial economy, while the second phase involves Asia becoming a leader in IT fields. The present writer, however, invites readers take an ambivalent view of the state-guided KII plan, a view that will be largely sustained throughout this book: while it is obvious that the KII was a successful case of government-driven IT policy during the last phase of a strong state, it is equally clear that the interventionist policy has burdened Korean society with new emergent social problems. To disclose the latter inconvenient truth, the present book describes and analyzes contextual factors of the project, such as the structural mechanisms and politico-economic processes that conditioned the KII during the period from 1995 to 2005. The purpose of this examination is to observe the real-world determinants that conditioned the social code of technology in a newly industrialized economy.

First, this book challenges the optimistic view of the ostensibly successful IT project, focusing instead on the hidden mechanisms for implementing the KII project—the external constraint of global capital, the state–business linkages and the sacrifice of other stakeholders in order to create or maintain those links, and the bureaucratic desire for control over society.

Second, interventionism in East Asian states has usually been explained by their dense linkages to the private sector in economic policies. In the case of the KII project and post-KII broadband investments, however, this book contributes to exposing the state's covert desire to expand its control over the citizen, in addition to the publicly stated desire to promote the shift from an industrial economy into the new economy.

Third, this book considers state-driven public IT infrastructure investments such as the KII and post-KII projects as complex events, in which three entities—the state, the domestic conglomerates (the *Chaebols*), and global capital—collide at once in the process of the spatial re-zoning of the nation. In this book, spatialization based on networked mobility is seen as a kind of stimulus for uniting the interests of the state and of large capital in a common project. The KII is thus a significant case study for examining the new spatial patterns of state power and accumulation, based on the national IT infrastructure.

Finally, the developmental state theories, which explained in glowing terms the East Asian economic miracle, have been tarnished by the financial crisis of the East Asian states in the late 1990s. Despite the decline in popularity of such theories, however, this book rereads the old developmental arguments anew, and rethinks those arguments in the light of the state-led KII project and its subsequent phase in Korea.

Rather than boasting of the synergistic relations between government leadership and the strategic restructuring of telecommunications brought about by the KII, this book focuses on the threefold aim of the KII project and its subsequent infrastructural broadband projects: enlisting South Korea as an Asian hub of global capitalism (boosting economic growth), supporting the domestic conglomerates (buttressing the so-called *Chaebols*, the Korean form of crony capitalism), and normalizing "social control"[2] through nationwide networked mobility (maximizing bureaucratic efficiency). This book further discusses how, after the completion of the basic infrastructural broadband investment for the KII in 2005, the current administration of Myung-bak Lee (2008–present) has reinforced the KII and post-KII convergent networks as an electronic arena for the neo-liberal IT market, as well as for the "neo-authoritarian" control of e-space.

This book describes in detail the deep structure of the relationships between the state and the big capital directly involved in implementing the KII project, investigating how they entered into alliances with each other, how they excluded the agendas of other stakeholders, and how they articulated their own interests as they related to implementing the project. Moreover, it investigates how the technical effect of the nationwide telecom backbone network has tended to facilitate the invisibility and neutrality of power, and allowed the government's reach to become ubiquitous and omnipresent, based on electronic and high-speed transmission capacity and networked mobility. This book reveals, thus, how the Korean government's desire for technological rationalization through the KII and post-KII plans became the material grounds of the electronic backbone networks that are currently furthering capitalist accumulation in Korea.

Overview of the book

The primary question of this book is this: What were the major driving forces that conditioned the public broadband infrastructure project (the KII) during the period of 1995 to 2005 in the newly industrialized economies? This primary question leads to the following sub-questions: What were the relevant policy decisions concerning the KII project, and how did global factors affect those decisions (Chapter 3)? What kinds of symbiotic relationships between governmental and business entities have developed through the KII and post-KII investments (Chapter 4)? How was the Korean government's desire for social control articulated and realized in establishing the infrastructural broadband plans (Chapter 5)?

Based on these three main sub-questions, the book offers a model of the forces that influenced the implementation of the KII project historically. Figure I.1 graphically represents the factors that were analyzed in order to answer the overarching question of the book, which investigates the major driving forces in the KII project and their influences on the post-KII phases of broadband development.

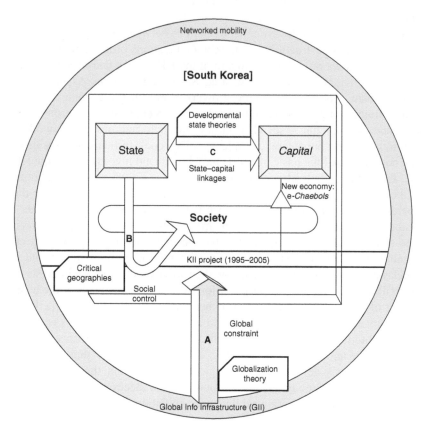

Figure I.1 Overview of the research design.

Notes
* e-*Chaebols*: Korean conglomerates, such as Samsung, LG, KT, and SK, incumbents in the new IT sector, as well as in the traditional manufacturing sector.

Figure I.1 depicts the following structural conditions: as background to the investigation of the driving forces conditioning the KII project (1995–2005) and its subsequent phases (2005–present) of broadband development, Chapter 1 summarizes the theoretical backgrounds for examining a Korean-style public broadband infrastructure plan: the theory of globalization, state theory (especially the developmental state theories concerning East Asia), and critical geographies. Employing these three theoretical approaches, this book explores the major contextual factors conditioning the KII project in Korea: the global constraints conditioning the East Asian states' telecom policies (globalization theory), the dense state–capital linkages in the East Asian states (developmental state theories), and the bureaucratic desire for social control (critical geographies). This book uses globalization theory to consider the active role of the state as an agent of local and global corporations; it upgrades developmental state theories to criticize the deformations caused by the close liaisons between the state and big business during the IT project; and it uses critical geographies to scrutinize the friendly symbiosis of state power over the citizens and social control based on flows and speed.

Chapter 2 surveys the history of state-led physical and virtual infrastructures in modern Korea and situates the broadband infrastructure plans (the KII and post-KII convergent networks) within past governments' infrastructure projects, such as highway, railway, and communication networks. This chapter observes how, in the dynamics of capital accumulation, the private sector needs constant spatial reconfiguration through the building of infrastructures; thus, the past state-led infrastructure plans are historically closely linked to the birth of the information infrastructure plans. This chapter traces the historical and geographical processes of installing the physical and IT infrastructures throughout the country, from the colonialist era (1910–45) through the post-Korean War period (1953–62) and the military dictatorships (1963–92) to the civilian governments (1993–present). Chapter 2 situates the IT infrastructure project (KII) not only within the succession of past administrations' infrastructure plans, but also within the response of the Korean government and business interests to the new digital mode of capitalism.

Chapter 3 analyzes the dominant pattern of capitalism in the early 1990s as an attempt to transform each country's economic structure into a digital mode of production. Point A in the diagram shows the influence of the new material conditions of network-based global capitalism, and the external constraints it imposed on the Korean policymaking processes historically related to the KII project. This chapter examines the external factors that led South Korea's government to design the KII project. It focuses on the global–local dynamics of structural adjustment to global constraints seen in the government's construction of the KII, which was designed, implemented, and evolved into the post-KII convergent networks during the period of the civilian governments (1993–present). Chapter 3 examines the strong trends of localization in the processes of economic globalization (global networked mobility), trends seen most clearly in the active role of the Korean state as an agent of local and global capital.

In regard to globalization theory, this chapter confirms a hypothesis that even the denationalizing force at the global level also feeds the localizing mechanisms of the economic sphere in a nation, as well as of the socio-cultural sphere.

Chapter 4 shows how the Korean state, the rapidly growing telecom duopolies, and the *Chaebols* have become deeply interpenetrated by means of state financial support, the organizational collaboration between these entities, and a hegemonic consensus.[3] Point C in Figure I.1 represents how the state has constructed a new relationship with the *Chaebols* through the KII and post-KII projects, one that is far from that of the military regimes' authoritarian and interventionist state which dominated the *Chaebols* in the past. In contrast to the private sector development exemplified by the US information superhighway initiative in the early 1990s, the Korean government was at the forefront of directing the KII project and the post-KII infrastructural policies aimed at building a nationwide high-speed broadband backbone network. Chapter 4 surveys how the "developmental state" model—a term referring to the centralized economic development of the East Asian states—was employed in South Korea by the authoritarian state under the military regimes. It then looks at how the developmental mechanism of Korea during the KII and post-KII projects was challenged by contextual factors such as market liberalization, the growth of the domestic conglomerates, and the social democratization that began to occur in the mid-1980s, which led to the transition from military to civilian governments in the early 1990s. This chapter then shows how the state, rather than asserting its dominance over business entities with regard to the KII plans, served primarily to mediate conflicts between the private sector and the relevant public agencies. Theoretically, this chapter aims to read critically the developmental state theories that failed to perceive the dark side of the symbiosis between the state and the *Chaebols*. By situating the state within class and society (the state-in-society approach), this chapter examines the evolutionary phases of the state's power from the military regimes to the civilian governments, phases which have been influenced chiefly by two factors: the emergence of Korean civil society and the e-*Chaebols*' growth in the market.

Chapter 5 focuses on how the KII and post-KII architectures function as virtual networks which enhance the government's disciplinary and surveillant power over its citizens. Point B includes the bureaucratic desire of government elites to control the citizens through spatial re-zoning, such as the regulatory use of dispersed digital networks. Chapter 5 discusses how, along with the ever-expanding state intervention in the economy, the state's desire for control is closely related to a shift in the state power from coercive discipline to a digital grid of control at the institutional level. Point B represents how the nationwide electronic network has embedded in itself the positive techniques of institutional power. This chapter examines how the techniques of power were gradually transformed from a centralized and hierarchical model into a distributive and dispersed network model, based on the flow, speed, and mobility of the KII and its evolving convergent broadband infrastructure networks. Theoretically, this chapter supports Gilles Deleuze's thesis that today's society has become increasingly based on digital technology, which is used for the reproduction of power systems—an idea summarized by his term "control society"—while never abolishing the conditions of disciplinary suppression by state power over the citizens. As a case study of the new techniques of social control based on the electronic infrastructure, Chapter 5 examines the policy debates over the nation-wide introduction of the National Education Information System (NEIS) which first erupted in 2003. The NEIS is a nationwide database system aimed at managing more than 350 pieces of personal information about each of the eight million students in Korean primary and secondary schools, through a central server computer operated by the Ministry of Education and Human Resources (MEHR). This policy initiative could not have been conceived without the material existence of the KII. Chapter 5 concludes by examining the NEIS as an example of the state's continuing bureaucratic desire to manage the citizens' data electronically, and also as an example of the newly emerging direction of surveillant control brought about by the government's collusion with e-*Chaebols*.

Finally, relying on the analysis of the previous chapters, Chapter 6 summarizes the book's findings on the IT mode of Korean society: no "broadband nirvana", but rather a dearth of democratic decision-making processes in building a broadband future. The national backbone network plans such as the KII, sustained by government subsidies, have enhanced the national IT indicators and elevated Korean society into the first tier of global IT development (a shift of the Korean economy from the export-oriented industrial system to a knowledge-based one), but this final chapter concludes that the legacy of developmentalism practiced by the military juntas has also left its mark on the KII and post-KII broadband projects. In conclusion, it offers alternatives to guide public policy towards a fuller realization of democratic participation from below, along much more socially interventionist lines.

1 The political economy of networked mobility

A theoretical overview

Some theoretical considerations: globalization, the state, and space

The theoretical framework undergirding this book is the political economy of networked mobility, which explains power as "a form of control" in the production, distribution, and exchange of electronic mediated communication (e.g., Mosco, 1996). To grasp the essence of power embedded in a national project of infrastructural construction, the political economy approach insists that an analysis must be firmly rooted in the wider social and global context. Specifically, it looks at the structural factors that establish such patterns as government regulation and intervention favoring capital, the concentration of ownership and market monopoly by both foreign and domestic large capital, capital accumulation based on the uneven development of geographies, and the swelling wave of privatization, commercialization, and deregulation. The theoretical framework of political economy encourages us to question and critically assess the essential components of how the world order of contemporary capitalism continues to expand its scope through networked mobility. This leads to increasing geographical and social gentrification, commercialization, and the transformation of information and communication technology and its cultural outputs into mere market commodities, rather than contributing to the common welfare and the lives of citizens.

To investigate the empirical case of the nationwide information infrastructure project in South Korea, this chapter explores the following theoretical approaches situated in the political economy of networked mobility: the theory of globalization, state theory (especially the developmental state theories concerning East Asia), and critical geographies. First, the theory of globalization aims at elaborating on the structural metamorphosis of capitalism, from the old system of imperialism to the dispersal of power throughout the world market under the new system of Empire. The theoretical approach used in this book situates Korea's information and technology growth within the universal structure of networked global capitalism, and reveals it as striving to enlist the local as an active part of the new global network. Second, developmental state theories for interpreting the "economic miracle" in East Asia are intended to evaluate specific mechanisms of East Asian states' interventionism, both for regulatory control and for economic imperatives. These developmental state theories help us to understand how authoritarian states such as South Korea's have been able to successfully catch up to high-tech industrialization. Third, critical geographies allow this book to consider space as an expansive source of the state's bureaucratic and economic power, which has been sustained by reconstructing its infrastructural bases. Critical geographies' insight that space is inseparable from the social power intersecting it enables us to uncover the hidden layers of the spatial reconfigurations that the state and large capital have actively implemented. On the basis of the three theoretical approaches discussed in this chapter, later chapters examine the major contextual factors conditioning South Korea's KII project: the global constraints conditioning the East Asian states' telecom policies (globalization theory), the dense state–capital linkages in the East Asian states (developmental state theories), and the bureaucratic desire for control (critical geographies).

The new conditions of globalization: a global networked mobility

This theoretical section undertakes first to make a brief sketch of globalization theories, especially focusing on the new material conditions of globalization that the worldwide electronic network of capital has constructed virtually.[1] The virtual geography of globalization, based on mobility and connectivity, signifies a shift in the power of capital, and forces local states to affiliate with or integrate into the new world system which Hardt and Negri (2000) have described as "Empire," the replacement for classical imperialism. The survival of local regions, they argue, depends largely on their close links to the global electronic conduits of capital. Under the new conditions of virtual geographies, inequalities of development and underdevelopment are complicated by whether an entity is "plugged" into or "unplugged" from the worldwide electronic web of global capitalism (Castells, 2000a). This section will investigate the new global order of electronic Empire by tracing the development of globalization theories—a series of critical theories extending from classical imperialism to the current discussion of Empire, via dependency theories in Latin America, the world system theory, cultural complexity theory, and the global-local nexus theory.

Looking back to the age of imperialism

The term *globalization* and related terms such as *global system*, *global economy*, and *global culture* have been used since the mid-1980s, in both popular and academic literature, to describe the "temporal-spatial compression" of the physical world (Harvey, 1989). New information and communication/telecommunication technologies are viewed as linking distant localities into one globalizing world, in a synchronous time zone that goes beyond real territories. The speed and mobility generated by electronic networks become indispensable for creating the physical conditions of globalization, tying together the world as a whole. Popular futurists have optimistically characterized a globalizing or united world: Fuku-yama (1992) depicts globalization as the last triumph of capitalism and its market economy, and Friedman (2006) writes of a flattening and fiber optic global world, while Gates (cited in Gatlin, 1999) refers to friction-free capital-ism, which creates new opportunities for all countries to participate in global competition. Meanwhile, critical scholars see globalization as the result of the imperialist expansion of the industrialized countries and multinationals, sans col-onies (Magdoff, 2003). In this view, advanced technologies offer support for absorbing the surplus generated in the so-called "Third World," thus undermin-ing its technological, political, economic, and cultural viability. In the mid-19th century, Marx predicted a global move toward unconstrained capitalist expansion:

> All that is solid melts into air. ... The need of a constantly expanding market for its products chases the bourgeoisie over the whole surface of the globe. It must nestle everywhere, settle everywhere, establish connexions every-where. ... In one word, it creates a world after its own image.
>
> (Marx and Engels, [1848] 1998: 38–40)

> The more production comes to rest on exchange value ... the more import-ant do the physical conditions of exchange—the means of communication and transport—become for the costs of circulation. Capital by its nature drives beyond every spatial barrier. Thus the creation of the physical con-ditions of exchange—of the means of communication and transport—the annihilation of space by time—becomes an extraordinary necessity for it.
>
> (Marx, [1857] 1973: 524)

Confronting the age of imperialism in the nineteenth and early twentieth century, a revolutionary Marxist like Lenin ([1916] 1969) saw the colonialist mechanism of dominance in terms of the rise of monopoly and the export of capital abroad. Luxemburg ([1913] 2003) posited the birth of imperialism in the capitalist need for surplus outlets in non-capitalist formations; Baran ([1957] 1968) saw imperi-alism as arising from an American capitalism dominated by monopolies: since these are incompatible with growth and technological innovation, he thought that the only way to escape the monopolistic state of stagnation was by exporting capital, which helped to absorb surplus from underdeveloped countries like those in Latin America. These Marxist scholars' studies of imperialism contributed to establishing the theoretical framework that describes capitalism as always needing to expand the lifespan of monopolies in the advanced countries at the cost of non-capitalist or underdeveloped countries.

In a similar way, from the late 1960s to the late 1970s, critical scholars who looked at Latin America developed so-called *dependency theories*, which deline-ated how large businesses reconfigure the new order of capitalism and reproduce the unequal relations between states. For instance, Andre Frank (1969) saw "underdevelopment" in Latin America as largely controlled by US monopolies. Frank attempted to explain a continued failure of "development" in Latin America, even in the era of decolonization, and viewed the capitalist system as divided into a *center* and a *periphery*. Similarly, Amin (1974) described a chain of *metropolis–satellite* or center–periphery structures using the concept of "accumulation on a world scale." Wallerstein (1979) extended Amin's dual system to the hierarchical division of the capitalist "world system" as a totality divided into three tiers of states: those at the core, those at the semi-periphery, and those at the periphery. Related to the economic status of the peripheral countries, Cardoso's (1973) "associated dependent development" and Evans' (1979) "dependent development" were further examinations of the limited scope of development in the Third World, which suggested that "partial" development or growth can be accomplished under the general conditions of dependency. These dependency theories were devoted to explaining a value chain of accumulation on a global scale, unequal development among states, and the destructive effects of multinational capital to the Third World. They failed, however, to anticipate the East Asian form of state-interventionist "development," in which states become relatively free of the structural constraints of dependency.

Scholars working in the political economy tradition view the global expansion of capitalism as linked to the microelectronic revolution and networked flows of information, communication, and culture, and to the flows of industrial and financial capital. Research in this tradition has been centrally concerned with the integrated contribution of digital information and communication to the operation of global monopolies, and with trans-border data flows (Schiller, 1981, 1984; Hamelink, 1984). Examining the international traffic of media content such as film and TV programs, Guback (1984) offered an analysis of the film business that viewed the state as its active supporter in both the national and the international arena. Employing the classical view of imperialism, Varis (1984) regarded the dominant flows of US television programs as similar to the export of commodities in general, rather than as "cultural" output to be "interpreted" and "decoded" by the audience.

A significant theme in research on the international political economy is how the global activities of transnational media and telecommunication industries are freer from the regulatory barriers of other countries than those of industries in the classical sense. This theme has led to such critical topics as the monopolistic global media system and the cross-border flows of media outputs (e.g., Herman & McChesney, 1997), the homogenizing effects of media contents on indigenous cultures (e.g., Tomlinson's [1991] discussion of "cultural imperialism" in the critique of global capitalism), and the reorganization of global electronic communications on behalf of capital's demands (e.g., Castells, 1996; Golding, 1996; Mosco, 1996; Schiller, 1999, 2001). These approaches, however, were based on a rather simple dichotomy of dominance and subordination in the global economy, which failed to take into consideration the complex and heterogeneous flows of technology, information, culture, and people across borders.

Whose hybridity or complexity?

Critiques of Marxist economic reductionism, which had a tendency to focus on a shift towards a single united world economy, have arisen first from the problem that globalization can no longer be understood by simple center–periphery models or as a single one world-system. One kind of critique arises from a "loose" structure thesis, which emphasizes the relative independence of "socio-cultural" factors in the local setting when subjected to a globalizing force (e.g., Robertson, 1990). This critique is based on the theoretical presumption that there are fundamental "disjunctures" between economy, culture, and politics. Appadurai (1990) argued that we need to differentiate the manifold spheres of international interaction in terms of "ethnoscapes" (descriptions of the flows of peoples), "technoscapes" (of technology), "finanscapes" (of money), "media-scapes" (of media contents), and "ideoscapes" (of ideologies). Sreberny (2005) extended the analysis of globalization to the multi-dimensional spheres of global culture, including map-making and nation-building, the export of religion, the institutionalization of Western-style education, administration as a "professional imperialism," colonial languages, the "pleasure periphery" produced to serve travel and tourism, and the transfer of technology.

These analytical divisions of "globalization" into multi-layered mini-globalizing processes have resulted in an awareness of the "non-linear, fractured nature of cultural globalization" (Ang, 1996: 154)—the so-called "hybridity" of global culture—in contrast to the replication of uniformity by economic globalization. Some empirical studies, for instance, focus on the independent consumption patterns of TV audiences, which are greatly affected by the "cultural proximity" created by such factors as local culture, language difference, local market strength, and other cultural variables (Straubhaar, 1991). These studies were largely based on the successful story of multinational channels such as Televisa (Mexico) and TV Globo (Brazil) in Latin America as a counterweight to worldwide cultural standardization by global media outputs (Sinclair, 1999).[2] Defenders of cultural localism note the "loose" relation between structure as a globalizing power and the local as having relative autonomy—a dialectical relation that is conditioned by the "slightly higher" weight of the former on the latter (Straubhaar, 1997: 6).

The research, particularly on Latin America in terms of cultural proximity, reveals globalization as a web of "hybridity," "complexity," or "mélange" (Pieterse, [1995] 2005; García Canclini, 1997; Straubhaar & Hammond, 1998). These new approaches view uneven, asymmetric, and even "unpredictable" links in the global–local nexus as salient in the present phase of globalization. They aim to negate the dualistic and hierarchical framing of the world in terms of dominant and dominated, colonizer and colonized, and center and periphery, and to engender more fertile possibilities that allow us to see globalization "from below" (i.e., the local)—specifically, to ground critical globalization studies in praxis (e.g., Kellner, 2002; Robinson, 2005). Viewing globalization as complex and hybrid enables us to see many deviations from a rigidly "prefigured" path of a globalizing force into a one-world system (Straubhaar & Hammond, 1998), and to perceive socio-cultural complexities as supporting cultural sustainability and participatory democracy in the local or the periphery.

In contrast, rather than seeing the politics of "hope" or the "Third Way" in global complexity, some scholars approach complexity as the art of legitimating the scope of global capitalism. For instance, Urry (2005) divided the global system into two main forms, "global networks" and "global fluids" (245–9): while global networks are predictable, calculable, routinized, integrated, and standardized (as in global enterprises), global fluids are autopoietic, rhizomatic, and decentralized (as in world money, social movements, the Internet, the anti-globalization movement, international terrorism, and so forth); it is the latter that accounts for the aspects of global complexity and hybridity. It is significant that Urry described globalization as "pools of order that heighten overall disorder" (249). His viewpoint is analogous to Hall's (1991) perspective on global economic and cultural power, which is always "wanting to recognize and absorb [cultural] differences within the larger, overarching framework" (28). Hall argued that global power never attempts to obliterate differences or complexities: "it operates through them, it has to hold the whole framework of globalization in place and simultaneously police that system: it stage-manages independence within it [...], without absolutely destroying what is specific and particular" (28–9). Hall described the "decentered" power of globalization as absorbing the differences of the local; similarly, Urry described it as "mobile power" (249): it is based on "speed, lightness, distance, weightlessness," crossing over both global networks (the universalizing power) and global fluids (the complex localities). In fact, mobile power achieves new and intricate relations between global networks and global fluids. Globalization is thus "like putting together a jigsaw puzzle: it is a matter of inserting a multiplicity of localities into the overall picture of a new global system. ... The 'local' should be seen as a fluid and relational space, constituted only in and through its relation to the global" (Morley & Robins, 1995: 116–17).

These new approaches to the intertwined dynamics of the global–local nexus revive the more holistic and pessimistic vision of a "global state" or "market state" that modulates the local differences over its global network system, a system of "Empire." The next section examines the structure of Empire in order to situate the historical–geographical condition of Korea's informatization in relation to Empire's global networks.

The "smooth world" of electronic Empire

As promoted by the Reagan administration in the US and Margaret Thatcher in Britain from the early 1980s onwards, neo-liberal public policy has engaged in commercialization (from state regulation to market regulation), liberalization (from monopoly regulation to competition), privatization (selling off state enterprises), and transnationalization (global and local expansion of transnational or multinational corporations), subsidized by the "constitutive" role of the state (e.g., Mosco, 1996; Murdock & Golding, 1999; McChesney, 2004). Neo-liberalism aims to reconfigure global society through the operations of national and international business powers, thus going beyond the classical claims of the laissez-faire market operated by the "invisible hand." Harvey (2003, 2005, 2006) defines neo-liberalism as the concept of "accumulation by dispossession": it designates an active role of the state which releases a set of public assets for deregulation, privatization, financial liberalization, and the commercialization of cultural and historical assets that were once in the public domain. To optimize conditions for capital accumulation, market-friendly public policy is essential in the neo-liberal state system, which typically causes cut-backs in welfare provisions, health care, public education, and core social services. At the same time, it produces market incentives in the form of tax breaks, the provision of infrastructure at state expense, and the opening of local markets known as "structural adjustment" to global forces (Harvey, 2006: 23–6). The state constitutes the rules under which the market exists, and thus "deregulation" is only a name for shifting from overt government regulation to regulation by the market structure enabled by the state (Horwitz, 1989). The state provides national and international incentives for preferred corporate behavior, which is promoted by an "intrinsic" logic of policymaking (Hills, 2002: 12).

Under the neo-liberal order of chaos, global power has been transformed from a center–periphery system to a complex and dispersed system of global–local nexus, and worldwide capitalist power integrates local differences within a globalizing force by means of digital technology and its electronic networks. For example, Hardt and Negri have suggested the holistic vision of a global society of control crossing over national boundaries. According to them, we have entered into the new age of "Empire," in which "rule has no limits" and "encompasses the spatial totality" of the globe (Hardt & Negri, 2000: xiv). The establishment of a global society of control "goes hand in hand with the realization of the world market and the real subsumption of global society under capital" (332). In the immanent and ubiquitous condition of global control by capital, it is meaningless to demarcate geographical zones as center and periphery, North and South, First World and Third World: "The geography of uneven development and the lines of division and hierarchy will no longer be found along stable national or international boundaries, but in fluid infra- and supranational borders" (335). This vision of a hybrid totality goes beyond the above-mentioned multi-layered global–local nexus thesis, and argues for a global web structure of control by capital over the "space of flows." Under these conditions, the sovereignty of nation-states has declined, and the network of Empire becomes a description of the physical conduit for contemporary global power. The fundamental sources of modern capitalist power are dependent upon both connectivity and mobility. This book is interested in the electronic infrastructural conditions for current global capitalism, and uses such descriptions as the "electronic global Empire" or the "e-Empire" (Raley, 2004) or the "information Empire" (Poster, 2004). These terms are used to designate a new global power which has modulated its worldwide control through media and electronic networks. The complex pyramid of global power has been built on "access to the means of transportation and the resulting freedom of movement" (Bauman, 2000: 10).

The principal strategy in the exercise of power has become extraterritorial and unbounded. The rejection of any territorial confinement means that for the use of power, it rarely matters now "where the giver of the command is" (11), since power has become dispersed, de-centered, and even hybridized—what Hardt and Negri have called the "smooth world" of Empire. Taking into account these ubiquitous traits of the power of capital, we need to observe the virtual geographies of the invisible web of global flows, and how it enables the concrete redefining of the new global system. The fluid and liquid space is embodied by a global conduit of electronic networks: transcontinental networks such as submarine cables, ship-to-shore wireless, broadcast radio and shortwave wireless, telephone lines, and worldwide business and Internet networks. A fabric of electronic networks has been created to help abstract intellectual properties such as financial capital, electronic business data, and entertainment content to move about quickly on a planetary scale. Contemporary capitalism is reshuffling local geographies so as to facilitate the national and global expansion of capital, by increasing and channeling the mobility of people, money, goods, and information.

Table 1.1 describes the virtual phase of capitalism in the age of globalization. This table shows the technological and physical layers that enable the expansive mechanisms of power to operate through physical and virtual geographies, as well as through the uneven geography of segregations and disparities that lead to social disintegration and the furtherance of class divisions. New complex hierarchies are being reconfigured, with metropolitan and global cities as command centers and nodal points, "technopoles" as research and development (R&D) centers, and the global telecommunication infrastructures as the conduit of capital and information. "A new geography of centrality and marginality" (Sassen, 2005) is being drawn, not so much by national boundaries as by these virtual geometric representations of power. In sum, the unequal mechanisms among localities depend on whether they have plugged into, switched on, and connected themselves to the virtual geographies of mobility.

Table 1.1 The virtual topography of globalization

ICT layers in virtual globalization	*Physical layers in a globalizing space*
Digital information (bits and bytes)	Immaterial labor, information commodities
The circuit of electronic networks	National and international ICT backbone Infrastructures
Nodal points, exchanges, communication hubs	Informational cities, global cities, command and control centers (Headquarters of transnationals)
Servers, databases	Technopoles, new industrial districts (milieus for innovation)
Technical standards	Supranational institutions for intellectual property rights

Summary: the dynamic global–local nexus

This section has briefly surveyed the genealogy of globalization theories, focusing especially on Marxist interpretations of capital accumulation on a global scale. In the first stage, critical scholars investigated the absorption of surplus by colonialist expansion to non-capitalist states, and next by the export of capital to underdeveloped countries. In the second stage of globalization studies, scholars considered the "underdevelopment" or "dependent development" of the Third World, especially Latin America, with a dualistic structure of center–periphery and North–South. These dependency theories and world system analyses of globalization supposed a rigid hierarchical structure of the globalizing force over the local. Scholars' recognition of hybridity and complexity in globalization has led some to view the flexible and multiple statuses of the local as relatively free from the dominion of global capital. Others, however, have argued that these hybrid and complex traits should be regarded as the sign of global capital's ability to absorb such local differences. This argument is largely dependent on seeing the global–local nexus as an intricate web structure.

Globalization as Empire upgrades these global–local debates with the concept of a global society of control. Hardt and Negri have argued that the current digitized patterns of a globalizing force, which the electronic networks make possible, are able to absorb differences and complexities across the world through "modulating networks of command" and "insinuation." Thus, Empire no longer designates the Pax Americana or the "triad" of economic powers, but rather denotes the interconnected web of the world market. The worldwide web structure becomes "mobile power," the overarching regulatory control of global capital. The new "hypermobile" power is able to "lay an abstract space over concrete territorial configurations" (Morley & Robins, 1995: 75) and construct a global space of control by weaving hyperspace electronically. The present study uses this theoretical approach, but also considers the active role of the state as an agent of local and global capital. The next section, therefore, reviews the state-led role of establishing industrial accumulation and global networked mobility.

The developmental state theories of East Asian growth and their limits

Confronting East Asia's economic "miracle" during 1970s and 1980s, a group of social scientists in the West turned away from the neo-classical, market-centered views and dependency theories, and developed alternative interpretations for the new phenomenon. The academic field known as *developmental state theories* rapidly grew to explain how the state's interventionist role in the four "Asian Tigers"—Hong Kong, Singapore, South Korea, and Taiwan—allowed these countries to successfully catch up with the industrialization of the West. Although the Asian financial crisis of the late 1990s, which represented a harbinger of global instability, diminished scholarly interest in developmental state theories, it is obvious that even after this economic turmoil, a strong tendency toward state interventionism in the economy has survived in East Asian states, and the interventionist state has partly succeeded in promoting the national information economy—while simultaneously creating massive new labor market insecurities, the intensification of inequality, and exploitation (Burkett & Hart-Landsberg, 1998; Pirie, 2006).

This section first reviews the main arguments of developmental state theories, especially those dealing with state–capital relationships and state autonomy issues, then points out these theories' shortcomings in interpreting the contemporary conditions of the East Asian states. Finally, it maps out a research design for examining the role of the state in Korea's electronic superhighway plans of the 1990s and 2000s.

The revival of the role of the state

The first state theories developed to explain the economic miracle in the East Asian states began with a critique of two theoretical camps: the neo-classical or market-centered approach, and dependency theories (e.g., Haggard, 1990). On the one hand, the dependency theorists are devoted to explaining a value chain of accumulation on a global scale (a chain of "metropolis–satellite" or "center–periphery" structures), unequal development among states, and the destructive effects of multinational capital to the Third World, but they failed to anticipate the East Asian form of state-interventionist development, in which states become relatively free of the structural constraints of dependency. On the other hand, the so-called "market-centered" approach—which has been rapidly disseminated by such international economic institutions such as the World Bank and the International Monetary Fund—closely ties East Asia's economic growth to the rise of market idealism in post-socialist societies. The neo-classical arguments are based on the idea that East Asia's success is in line with market-based outcomes, but that nonmarket mechanisms, such as extensive government interventions in markets, have generally failed to improve economic performance, and that government's role should be the minimal one of providing a safe environment for the market. From the neo-liberal perspective, "governments are likely to do more harm than good, unless interventions are market friendly" (World Bank, 1993: 10). The market-centered view rarely confronts the fact that the East Asian states create and command the (new) market. A failure to understand the Asian quality of these states is parallel to the economistic approach evident in Marxist-Leninist exegeses, which often regard the state as merely a reflection of the class structure and mode of production as a whole.[3] Developmental state theories, therefore, were also a theoretical rebuttal of the economistic tendencies of Marxism. Skocpol (1979), a prominent non-Marxist statist, challenged the economic reductionism in both the neo-classical view and the economistic approach of Marxism. She conceived of states as "administrative and coercive organizations—that are potentially autonomous from (though of course conditioned by) socioeconomic interests and structures" (14). She viewed the state as an agent of social and political change. In Skocpol's analysis, the basis for the potential autonomy of state action originates from the maintenance of social order and its involvement in an international network of states (30–1). Her state-centered perspective has become the most often cited epistemological basis for the developmental state model, especially her view of state autonomy, which sees the state as insulated from, and even above, society.

In short, the first developmental state model was a reaction both to dependency theories and to the neo-classical perspective: in contrast to the former, it encouraged scholars to rethink "development" in the Third World, since it is apparent now that "partial" development or growth in the Third World can be accomplished even under the general conditions of global capitalism. In contrast to the latter, the developmental state model brought the state back into the analysis of economic development in East Asia. State-centered studies considered the state as relatively autonomous, and created by the need for a bureaucratic, rule-enforcing apparatus. Taking this thesis of "state autonomy," developmental state theorists focused mainly on the "strong state" (Myrdal, 1968: 898), which is relatively independent from social and economic interest groups, and which imposes obedience to state policy.

The role of a strong state in late industrialization was originally introduced by Gerschenkron (1962). In his three different categories of industrialization patterns, he described Russia in the late nineteenth century as an "extremely backward" country, in which the state directly mobilized financial resources and created new heavy and chemical industries, sheltered behind tariff walls, to allow Russia to catch up to two different industrial models—that of Britain (advanced) and of Germany ("moderately backward").[4] Gerschenkron (1962: 7) argued that differences in the speed and character of industrial development across countries were, to a considerable extent, the result of the application of different institutional instruments and patterns. An equivalent to Gerschenkron's schema for "extremely backward countries," the East Asian developmental state model was first suggested by Johnson (1982, 1987) to explain the institutional role of the state in organizing the economic activities of private firms. Johnson (1982: 20–1) first differentiated between the "developmental" orientation of the East Asian states, especially Japan, where state involvement enabled rapid recovery after World War II, and the "regulatory" one in the US. While the US-style regulatory state concerns itself with the rules of economic competition, the East Asian developmental states concern themselves with substantive matters, such as which industries ought to exist, and which industries are no longer needed. In the developmental mode of the Asian states, Johnson saw "the commitment by political elites to 'market-conforming' methods of intervention in the economy" (1987: 141). Johnson regarded the developmental regime in East Asia as "soft authoritarianism," since it was based on a coercive political–bureaucratic elite, autocratic power and political repression, and oppressive labor policy, through which the states drove the private sector toward the goal of economic growth. In her analysis of the Korean case, Amsden (1989) went a step further than the autonomous state model offered by Johnson, arguing that the state autonomy in Korea was almost absolute in planning late industrialization, disciplining private firms based on their performance, and controlling the opposition to growth from unions and civil rights movements. Wade (1990a: 24–9) added the "governed market" (GM) theory, which highlighted the bureaucratic power of the Korean and Taiwanese governments to "manage" or control their national markets, rather than following or conforming to their demands.[5] Shin (1998) described how the governments in Korea have supervised, and even disciplined, the business entities:

> The series of economic plans in South Korea has constituted the major source of industrial transformation and economic growth. ... The state ... selected several industries as strategic sectors and gave them protection from excessive competition among domestic as well as foreign enterprises. The state provided financial subsidies and supports and scrutinized their economic performance. It controlled the number of competing enterprises in the market by restricting entry and production capacity and [by] frequent state-led mergers of private firms.
>
> (8)

In summary, the models of the first developmental state school (e.g., Amsden, 1989; Haggard *et al.*, 1994; Wade, 1990a, 1990b; White & Wade, 1988) emphasized the autonomous power of the state in leading the industrial transformations of the East Asian economic "miracle." According to these theorists, the strong developmental states created a set of strategic industrial policies in high-tech sectors, aimed at creating the long-run wealth of their nations. The obvious features of the strong East Asian states made the first developmental state theorists believe firmly that the East Asian states acted in complete autonomy. A new group of statists responded critically to this concept of the state, as a set of institutions commanding power and discipline over society and capital. Those developmental state theorists, designated as *neo-statists*, have shifted their focus to examining the densely interconnected linkages between the state and business.[6]

From total state autonomy to state–business linkages

Neo-statists pay close attention to the blurring demarcation between state and society, without ignoring the leading role of the state over business in East Asia. Evans (1995) was a leading scholar pioneering this new statist trend. With his concept of "embedded autonomy," Evans tried to reinterpret state autonomy in the following two directions: First, although these states were sufficiently autonomous and sovereign to formulate their own goals (the state's internal structure), their autonomy was also embedded in specific social links (state–society relationships). In Evans' analysis, South Korea, as one of the typical developmental states, was a case of establishing successfully cooperative links between political bureaucrats and industrial elites at the institutional level.

The developmental state was, Evans said, different from the "predatory state," such as Zaire in Africa. The predatory state usually exercises a strong top-down power without institutionalized negotiation with social groups, and thus "has little capability of transforming the economy and social structure over which it presides" (Evans, 1995: 45). Borrowing Mann's (1988: 5) categories of state power, we can say that the state elites in Zaire possessed "despotic power" (top-down predation of a strong state upon society) but weak "infrastructural power" (capacity of the state to penetrate society and to implement political decisions throughout the realm).[7] To the first statist school, state autonomy was the capability of the state to wield "despotic" power with little interference from interest groups, giving the state a high degree of flexibility in the formulation and implementation of policy.

The earlier statists rarely noted the "infrastructural" capacity of the state, which refers to its increasing ability to coordinate society's resources and allocate them to desired ends. In contrast, Evans' neo-statist perspective affirmed Mann's thesis that despotic power is a source of state weakness, whereas state strength is derived from a developed degree of infrastructural power. Applying Mann's concept to the case of Korea, one can say that the political elites before the early 1990s were both "despotically and infrastructurally strong," at least in the state–business linkages. In other words, one can say that, without the state's "embedded autonomy," or "infrastructural power," vis-à-vis business, the developmental path in Korea could never have emerged, and the country would have fallen into the predatory condition of despotic power. According to Weiss and Hobson (1995: 7), state strength increases with effective infrastructural power (the developmental state), whereas state weakness ensues under the exertion of despotic power (the predatory state). Therefore, whether a state is a predatory or a developmental one depends on the extent of the "embeddedness" of a state's autonomy.

According to Evans (1995), Korea was a prototypical case of a developmental state, which created dense linkages between bureaucratic elites and industrial capital. In such linkages, Evans noted, the state usually performs four different roles: formulating and enforcing rules (the role of "custodian"); playing out the generic role of regulator (the role of "demiurge"); assisting emergent entrepreneurial groups (the role of "midwife"); and protecting local entrepreneurial groups from global changes (the role of "husbandry") (12–14). Weiss (1998) viewed state autonomy as more limited in its relationship to the private sector. Weiss' model of state–business relationships reflected the increased economic power of Korea's family-owned conglomerates, the *Chaebols*, a power almost equivalent to that of the state.[8] The state–business linkages were highly "selective" and "mutually dependent." Weiss' so-called "governed interdependence" (GI) theory noted that both the state and the dominant private sector were equally strong in their autonomy. GI refers to "a negotiated relationship, in which public and private participants maintain their autonomy, yet which is nevertheless governed by broader goals set and monitored by the state" (38). Introducing such relational terms as "mutual dependence" or "interdependence" between public and private entities, Weiss' GI theory expressed a much weaker view of state power than Evans' "embedded autonomy" did, and focused on the growth of highly concentrated business power. Nevertheless, Weiss (1998: 49–53) took into account the centrally "coordinated" and "governed" quality of state power over industry. In Korea, for instance, the coordinated capacities of the state were exemplified by highly qualified bureaucrats, the intelligence-gathering network for up-to-date knowledge about production conditions in priority sectors, and the Economic Planning Board (EPB), a super-ministry insulated from the market.

In sum, whereas the earlier statists looked at the East Asian "miracle" by focusing on the disjuncture between the state and society, and the dominance of the state over society, the neo-statists explored this economic success by focusing on the dense linkages between the state and the private sector. Even the neo-statists, however, pointed to the "state-induced deliberate shifting of the industrial structure towards higher technology, higher value-added products" (Weiss & Hobson, 1995: 150). In fact, despite their varying emphases on the state–industry linkages, it is clear that both the old and new statists agreed about the state's dominant role in the East Asian economic miracle. From the beginning, developmental state theories were intended to describe a technique for "the rise of 'the rest'" (Amsden, 2001) in the world market, based on the historical experiences of the East Asian states as late industrializers.

Debunking developmental state theories as a recipe for growth

This section describes some theoretical shortcomings in developmental state theories. The critique will be beneficial in clarifying the material conditions of the state in Korea. First, *the developmental state theorists' arguments were essentially looking for a recipe for success and growth.* Whether their approach was based on the autonomous power of the state or on state–business linkages, both the old and the new statists focused on the incredible performance of "growth" and "catching up" in the East Asian economies. To detect the recipe for success, the statists concentrated excessively on how the state performed its role as coordinator, and what kind of industrial policy it used in collaborating with the private sector. This developmental logic could lead to the argument that dictatorship and exploitation should be endured in order to achieve developmental activities of effective planning and economic growth. What is often ignored is that capitalist growth is accompanied by intense exploitation (see Hart-Landsberg, 1993). The state theorists' tribute to East Asian growth ignores the "tendency toward deformation" that occurs with rapid growth under conditions of extreme state intervention—a deformation which includes such phenomena as the unequal conditions between major cities and other areas of the same country, environmental destruction, repressive labor control, crony capitalism, and corruption. The statists fail to interrogate the problems of development in itself.

Second, *the developmental state theorists overlooked the possibility that the developmental states in East Asia could descend into being predatory (or rent-seeking).*[9] At the very least, it is clear that the symbiotic relationships between the state and big business in Korea have been damaging to civil rights, social welfare, and distributive justice. For the developmental state theorists, these symbiotic relationships—specifically, those between the authoritarian state and the *Chaebols*—rarely become problems if the two actors serve to limit the extent of rent-seeking and corruption, and pursue aggregate growth by means of the state's dense "embeddedness" in the powerful conglomerates.[10] The developmental state model shows how the crony linkages of corruption between government and business can develop into an engine for economic growth. It pays little attention, however, to the destructive linkages of corruption and rent-seeking between the actors—linkages between the political power of developmental dictatorships and the monopolistic power of privileged capital. The dominant blocs of the state and monopolistic capital benefit each other exclusively, denying the citizens' need for participatory democracy and distributive justice. In short, a bias toward the positive dynamics of state–business linkages is one of the weaknesses of the developmental state theories.

Third, *developmental state theories tend to reduce state–society relations to simple state–business linkages for economic growth.*[11] Koo (1993) precisely identified the missing piece of developmental state theories:

> [T]he East Asian literature confines its focus to the interplay of the "developmental state" and the market, more or less separate from the broader context of civil society. This narrow economistic approach results in a tendency to exaggerate the autonomy and strength of the East Asian state and to interpret economic growth in isolation from other political and social changes. An obvious danger of such an approach is a reification of the concept of the state, as often found in many stylistic accounts of the East Asian developmental states.
>
> (7)

Koo further maintained that the state-centered approach overstressed the independent role of the state at the expense of societal forces, while it ignored how "the state is embedded in society" (5).[12] Koo was much more inclusive in his approach to society, going beyond the traditional orthodox Communist view of "state monopoly capitalism" as a simple reflection of class relations rooted in the mode of production. Migdal's (1988, 1994, 2001) "state-in-society" approach shares common ground with Koo; from the socio-centric perspective, states cannot be properly understood without looking at social contexts, at the various socioeconomic determinants of politics (Migdal *et al.*, 1994: 2–3). According to Migdal (1994: 9), patterns of domination within states are determined by key struggles spread throughout a society's multiple arenas of domination and opposition. In contrast, the developmental statist theorists, despite their analysis of the dense state–business linkages, failed to look at the multitudinous layers of social contexts. The present study views the state not as a monolithic unity of command that simply represents uniform citizens, but as the "material condensation" or "institutional ensemble" balancing a relation of forces among classes (Poulantzas [1978] 2000: 35–46; Jessop, 1985: 336–9). The degree of state autonomy thus depends on the specific social and class conditions, and the field of class struggles in a given society (see Jessop, 1982: 12–24; 1990: 24–47; Cho & Kim, 1998: 130–1; Lee, 2003: 27–31). The state-in-society approach, whether used by Marxist or non-Marxist state theorists, asks us to extend the state–business linkage approach to consider the state as situated within socioeconomic contexts and class tensions. Jessop (1982) gives us a clear-cut description of how to perform a theoretical analysis of a state: it must examine "not only [a state's] economic determinations but also those rooted in the distinctive organization of the state as well as in the social division of labor between officialdom and people" (30).

Finally, *one of the theoretical problems in state-centered approaches is that they seek the engine for growth in a state's "endogenous" property, focusing on domestic state–business linkages and the leading role of a strong state in boosting the national market.* This myopic view overlooks how external factors, such as the changing global economic system of capitalism, affect the local government and economies. The survival of the developing countries depends largely on their close links to the global electronic conduits of capital. Without fully examining such external constraints as the new conditions of global geographies, we are unable to fully understand the changing developmental mode in the East Asian states. The statists thus failed to take into account the reconfiguration of transnational capital, and the vulnerable conditions of the East Asian states and businesses.

Summary: the state-in-society approach

While developmental state theories contributed to tracking state dominance in the economic transformation and growth in East Asia, they failed to perceive the deformations caused by the symbiosis between the state and big business. Further, these theories were unable to describe both the class and social conditions within which the state is situated, and ignored the external factor of global capitalism, which greatly constrains the autonomy of regional governments and economies. By perceiving the state as wholly situated within class and society, the state-in-society approach critically supplements the weak or missing links of developmental state theories, going beyond the theses of unfettered state autonomy (espoused by the old statists) and those of the close liaison between the state and business (espoused by the new statists). Moreover, both the old and the new statists have tended to overestimate the state's role in sustaining capital accumulation. They have failed to see that the major function of the state is to preserve the stable cohesion of various classes in a given society, through repression and concession (Gramsci, 1971: 206–76; Poulantzas, [1965] 2008: 98–100).

The present study views the state's autonomy as largely based on two sources of power. One is the state's relative autonomy in establishing policies that influence industrial development. The other is the state's bureaucratic capacity to embed its control in society at large and in citizens individually, which is exactly what is designated by Mann's term "infrastructural power." The latter derives from the autonomous power of the state continually to develop new bureaucratic techniques to control society. As the next section illustrates, the re-zoning and policing of space exemplifies the introduction by the bureaucratic elites of a more pervasive and omnipresent technology for social control. The state-in-society approach enables us to explain why the state tries incessantly to rearrange the forces of social classes, and to insert its bureaucratic desire for control into policy plans, such as those for Korea's national information superhighway.

Critical geographies: the state–space–capital links

This theoretical section investigates concept of "spatialization" in critical geographies, which explains the process of re-zoning that stratifies and concentrates the power of capitalism over physical and virtual geographies (Mosco, 1996). The present study applies the theoretical perspective of critical geographies to analyzing the empirical case of the Korean electronic superhighway project, as it relates to the drive toward spatialization. This drive has two sources: one source stems from the bureaucratic desire for control by the developmental state over society, an institutional desire that is closely related to increasing the state's "infrastructural power" (Mann, 1988) over society. Using Foucauldian concepts such as disciplinary societies and "governmentality," the present study examines how the techniques of power in contemporary states are gradually transformed from a centralized and hierarchical model into a distributed and ubiquitous network model through virtual spatialization, the so-called de-territorialization of political power. The other source of the drive toward spatialization is the need of large capital to metamorphose itself into the knowledge-based mode of production. To East Asian states, spatial reconfiguration also signifies the economic capacities for the developing countries to achieve "functional" positions as nodal points in the global networks of Empire. The spatial reconfiguration of domestic territories by capital is the developmental states' strategic plan for survival in the age of digital capitalism.

In short, this section examines how spatial re-zoning facilitates the state and large capital in obtaining their goals of control and accumulation, respectively. Before entering into the topic, let us begin first with the concept of space as the geographical medium through which socio-economic power is administered and controlled.

Space as social power and "flows"

Spatialization—spatial configuration by market need, segmentation of places, and spatial policing around class, gender, and race—produces complex spatial geometries of power (Dodge & Kitchin, 2001: 36). Harvey (1989: 226) noted that those who define the material practices, forms, and meanings of space, together with those of money and time, define certain basic rules of the social game. Harvey (1996), in his investigation of the historical transitions of capitalist geographies, described the capitalist reshuffling in space with the concept of "flexible accumulation" by "time–space compression." Different from the place-adhesive recognition of space as something fixed, his viewpoint extends space as an expansive source of capitalist power, which has been sustained by reconstructing its geographical bases.

Space is not wrought out of thin air but rather is socially constructed and mediated through the interplay of human beings striving to control political, economic, cultural forces. Space, therefore, is inseparable from the social power intersecting it. As Soja (1996) put it, we are "first and always historical–social–spatial beings, actively participating individually and collectively in the construction/production of histories, geographies, societies" (73). In Soja's concept of the "trialectics of being," the human body has been always located within the interplay between space and socio-historicality. A linkage to the socio-historicality of space indicates that space should be understood as grounded in the social and historical struggle to control places. In this respect, space as social power is a connotative texture that underlies the physicality of places. If space signifies "a system of containers of social power" (Harvey, 1989: 237), any struggle to reconstitute power relations is a struggle to reorganize their spatial bases (238). In this respect, space is not the passive host for the reifying society, but rather a malleable container that allows its reconfiguration (Fabijancic, 1995).

Many critical geographers have investigated the spatial reconfiguration wrought by capitalism, such as the global expansion of capital markets in order to ameliorate over-accumulation with a "spatial fix" (Harvey, 2001). This can be interpreted as spatial reorganization and geographical expansion, facilitated by innovation in physical infrastructure—as well as re-territorialization and de-territorialization for controlling increasingly and bewilderingly complex flows of capital. Flexible spatialization corresponds to "lay[ing] an abstract space over concrete territorial configurations" (Morley & Robins, 1995: 75). Lash and Urry (1994: 13–17) also noted that, through the rapid circulation of subjects and objects, time and space "empty out" and dissolve into the spatio-temporal ether. Space is directed especially to channeling the mobility of people, money, goods, and information. Thus space is becoming increasingly "process-oriented" (Castells, 1985: 11–15) and more "fluid" and "movement-driven" (Urry, 2000; 2007).

When the spatial conduit of electronic communications becomes the material infrastructure of contemporary power, "the space of flows" is more dominant in our economic, political, and symbolic life than "the space of places" (Castells, 1996: 412). Space as "flows" reproduces a hierarchical network of social classes in terms of disparities among regions, locales, cities, and nations. The "space of flows" approach is a useful method for reading the inner mechanisms of power, and also the uneven geography of segregations and disparities that leads to social disintegration such as class divisions (Hepworth & Robins, 1988).

In Figure 1.1, the second spatial layer "interpreted" by the state and large capital designates the inner or real mechanism of spatial enforcement, in contrast

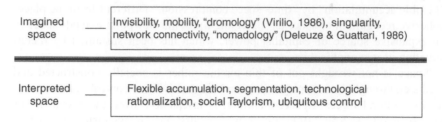

| Imagined space | ___ | Invisibility, mobility, "dromology" (Virilio, 1986), singularity, network connectivity, "nomadology" (Deleuze & Guattari, 1986) |

| Interpreted space | ___ | Flexible accumulation, segmentation, technological rationalization, social Taylorism, ubiquitous control |

Figure 1.1 Two different layers of spaciality.

to the cognitive effects of electronic space in the first layer of "imagined" space. In other words, whereas *imagined space* refers to the reconfiguration of physical space based on mobility and speed, *interpreted space* depicts the actual dynamics of the fluid and mobile space affecting the structural system of capitalism.

State–space–capital

Foucault ([1979] 1991) defined *governmentality* as the art of exercising power on things, in other words, the scientific management of population and the constitution of political economy. He described the power shift in eighteenth-century Europe as a shift "from a regime dominated by structures of sovereignty to one ruled by techniques of government" (101). This concept illuminates how Korea's power systems have developed the regulatory mechanism of a science of knowledge. Foucault's concept of governmentality presents the ubiquitous mechanism of the exercise of rule as far more than simply its direct discipline or use of violence. The management of population or statistics is used more toward shaping the "general" conditions of the population than toward directly managing its individual bodies. This section examines the new phase of institutional control over society in terms of spatial reconfiguration in the electronic age.

Free-floating control

In his "postscript on control societies," Deleuze ([1990] 1995) contrasts Foucault's concept of *disciplines* with the concept of *controls*. According to Deleuze, the "disciplinary societies" of the eighteenth and nineteenth centuries should be differentiated from the kind of society we have today. He describes today's societies as control societies, and sees them as superseding the disciplinary societies Foucault talked about. Deleuze's division of societies into these two periods—one of discipline and the other of control—reflects the digitization of information in modern society and its use for the reproduction of power systems. He sees control societies as based on digital technology, while disciplinary societies are based on analog technology. Digital technology facilitates free-floating control and continuous flows of information between databases without spatial-temporal restraints, while analog information has the logic of "confinement" and of "moldings" that are broken up into physical cells and molds such as factories and prisons, where monitoring is performed from a physical watchtower. Under digital conditions of control, Deleuze observes, the masses become floating samples and data. Gandy (1993) notes that personal information is "produced through the monitoring of behavior, and not the behavior alone" (76). Just as workers' actions in a workplace are managed by employers and consumers in everyday life are identified, classified, and evaluated by private corporations, all through the so-called "panoptic sort," what new technologies enhance is the ability to digitize, collect, sort, and control the activities of citizens in the public space (Gandy, 1993). In this respect, digital technology becomes a new means for modern power to escape from the confinement of barriers, fences, and borders into the free-floating control of flow, speed, and mobility.

In a move similar to Deleuze's distinction between disciplinary societies and control societies, Bauman (2000) divides capitalist modernity into two phases using the concepts of "solidity" (analog, in Deleuze's terminology) and "liquidity" (digital). Bauman observes that the pyramid of power has increasingly been built on "access to the means of transportation and the resulting freedom of movement" (10). He notes that the principal strategy in the exercise of power has become exterritorial and unbounded. He regards the "melting of solids" in the current capitalist system as the "revenge of nomadism over the principle of territoriality and settlement" (13). This rejection of any territorial confinement means that for the use of power, it rarely matters now "where the giver of the command is" (11). Bauman's metaphor of "liquid" power is useful in conceiving of a dispersive, de-centered, and even neutralized power. This wide dispersion of power techniques makes it easier to conceal the goals of control. As Foucault ([1976] 1990) said, "power is tolerable only on condition that it mask a substantial part of itself" (86). Accordingly, power seeks to make "all things visible by becoming itself invisible" (Foucault, 1980: 71; also see Foucault, [1975] 1995: 187). The invisibility of power has been greatly increased by the dispersed and "value-neutral" techniques of high-tech panoptic devices such as radio frequency identification (RFID) chips, electronic bugs, geographic positioning systems (GPS), wireless tracking techniques, and other fine-grained data-mining software. These devices have been accompanied by new hegemonic values that persuade people to embrace a "digital sublime," and thereby have gained consensual acceptance of the devices throughout society.

Social power today is articulated in "flows," the purpose of which is the ubiquitous control of space. In other words, the mechanism of social control is "translated into a proliferation of new repressions in space and movement, undergirded by the ubiquitous *armed response*" (Davis, 1990: 223, emphasis in original). As applied to urban areas, "fortified" or "carceral" are terms that seek to describe a new stage of deregulatory social control, one that involves policing urban space through pervasive and ubiquitous mobility, augmented by new spatial tracking, sensing, and location technologies such as RFID and GPS (Davis, 1990; Soja, 1996; Body-Gendrot, 2000; Crandall, 2010).

M. G. Michael and Katina Michael (2010) describe this "carceral" phase of power relations with the concept of "überveillance"—"the sum total of all types of surveillance and the deliberate integration of an individual's personal data for the continuous tracking and monitoring of identity and location in real time" (10). Under the digital conditions of "überveillance," therefore, mobile tracking is most usefully viewed both as a new experiment in power enforcement and as one of the spatial designs of power in the wireless world of "flows." Elliott and Urry (2010) depict this "überveillant" phase as a digital "Orwellian-ization" of self and society, in which there is essentially no movement without digital tracing and tracking (150).

When power has difficulties in integrating the liquid, free-floating, and dispersed practices of surveillance into its library of databases, however, power's regulatory mechanisms are likely to be incomplete (Poster, 1990). Thus modulation of power on a large scale is impossible without interconnected networks. Raley (2004) notes that interconnected networks make up "modulating networks of command" (125). Although Raley's research focused on the current shift of the global capitalist system, in other words, on "societies of 'imperial' control," the concept of "modulating networks of command" is quite useful for analyzing the new techniques of control. Raley explains the modulating system of power as "a loose assemblage of relations characterized by ... flexibility, functionality, mobility, programmability, and automation" (Galloway, 2001: 132). The technology permitting such an assemblage is the electronic network, which "abstracts human bodies from their territorial settings and separates them into a series of discrete flows" (Haggerty & Ericson, 2000: 605). The loose but integrated communication network is the "instrumental facilitator" of power (Raley, 2004: 135). Raley concludes that the new mechanism of power need not necessarily operate through domination, subjection, and imposition, because it now operates through insinuation, which is a modal switch of power and consists of hosts accepting, rather than rejecting or being forced to accept (135). When the spatial conduit of electronic communications becomes the material infrastructure of contemporary power, modulation and assemblage become the technical standards of common protocols or codes that link the free-floating data of individuals, groups, and classes.

Space–capital linkage

As discussed previously, the importance of networked mobility for transnational capital at the global level explains why South Korea's government and business sectors are urgently struggling to incorporate the country into the electronic mode of capitalism, so that it can achieve a functional position as one nodal point in the global network. For instance, during the Japanese occupation of Korea in World War II, Japanese military imperialism forced Koreans to build a national road and railway network across the Korean Peninsula to give the imperialists access to the vast markets of Manchuria (see Chapter 2). The current colonialist project, however, will not need the violence of physical mobilization to subordinate the local under its global order. To obtain membership to global society, Korea must construct information infrastructures across the entire country, and plug itself into the electronic networks of economic globalization. Survival in the age of digital capitalism depends on local abilities to function as a part of the broader web structure of the global market.

The electronic telecommunication network has become the material infrastructure of contemporary capitalism, allowing the products of immaterial labor to be disseminated beyond local boundaries. Terms such as "cybernetic capitalism" (Robins & Webster, 1999), "digital capitalism" (Schiller, 1999), and "fast capitalism" (Agger, 2004) denote the deepening reliance on the virtual dynamics of capitalism, shaped by technological innovation. These terms suggest a new stage of capitalism in which the flows of capital, labor, commodities, information, and images achieve a global reach, and in which they can be produced and consumed almost instantaneously.

Virilio (1997: 119–45) described how the incessant desire of large capital has been promoted by speed and mobility. Fundamental sources of modern capitalist power are dependent upon both electronic connectivity and mobility. The nationwide and worldwide infrastructural technologies thus have made it possible for media giants to establish powerful distribution and production networks (McChesney, 1999). For instance, Hills (2002) examined the initial phase of the historical struggle between the US and Britain for domination of international telecommunications from the mid-nineteenth century to World War II. He noted the major role of the communication infrastructure as a colonialist power resource and conduit— the transcontinental network consisting of submarine telegraph cables, ship-to-shore wireless, broadcast radio and shortwave wireless, and telephone lines. Regarding regional patterns of spatialization, Schiller and Mosco (2001) described the economic function of telecom network lines in the regional integration across the North American continent that culminated in the North American Free Trade Agreement (NAFTA). These networks account for the geographical reconfiguration of Mexico and Canada by means of the continent-wide network lines of US-based telecom businesses. Such virtual networks are an expanding source of capitalist power that enables optical flows of intellectual properties embodied in financial capital, electronic business data, and entertainment content.

Based on the political economy of postindustrial spaces, Mosco's (1999) concept of "spatial convergence" is also useful for describing "the coming together of related businesses that form networks of firms in the same physical place" (105). Mosco investigated how, facilitated by state and city governments, the densely high-tech space of the convergent computer, communication, and cultural sectors in Manhattan functions as a local center of power. He considered this convergence, nested in one place, to be a new form of media and telecommunication concentration. "Spatial convergence" suggests a way to understand recent trends in urban entrepreneurialism, such as the techno-city projects which aim to create ideal future cities, incorporating digital technology and communication networks in leading Asian IT countries like Hong Kong, Singapore, South Korea, and Taiwan.

At least in Korea, spatial convergence, or the so-called techno-city project, not only supports the government's urban renewal projects motivated by the IT industry, it also allows the domestic *Chaebols* and telecom oligopolies to enter into the new profitable market of urban entrepreneurialism through private joint ventures with international companies. The specific state–capital linkage greatly contributes to breaking through the current state of stagnation in the domestic IT market. In other words, national and metropolitan policy, based on the developmental strategies of techno-cities in Korea, has been organized as a force compliant to neo-liberal market forces led by the *Chaebols*, national and international telecom oligopolies, and the interventionist state, for the purpose of boosting national IT economies.

Both the "space of flows" of capital weaving together the global–local nexus and the 'spatial convergence' within specific places (such as New York or some Asian cities) enable us to view the expansive mechanisms of power through both physical and virtual geographies.

Summary: the flexible control of space by the state and capital

Space is an active expression of both state power and capital power, and socioeconomic power today is articulated in "flows", the purpose of which is the flexible control of space. The materialist perspective on space deserves further exploration as a tool for analyzing the social domain in which communication technology is applied. The Korean electronic highway project is most usefully viewed both as a new experiment in power enforcement and as one of the spatial designs of power in the wired world of flows. The shift in the exercise of power from places to flows in space explains why broadband communication technology, which was enacted on the basis of placelessness, has been subordinated into modern power structures. To use Foucault's ([1975] 1995) words, a "power of writing" or "documentary techniques" on bodies has been constituted as another component of the power mechanism of discipline (189–92). A "panoptic" vision of power allows us to understand networked mobility as an updated documentary technique for managing citizens' bodies through the space of "flows." Further, power structures as "flows" change the "writing" performance with the technologically advanced IT devices, so as to reduce the antipathy of individuals to structural control. Networked mobility by means of electronic spatialization facilitates the invisibility and neutrality of power, and allows a "micro-power" to become ubiquitous and omnipresent. While networked mobility gives us physical freedom from spatial restraints, it may be grounded in the ubiquitous power to manage a social system. Electronic spatialization thus strengthens the dominant motive of control as well as the efficient regulation and segmentation of bodies as social classes. In the present study, a critical angle on the friendly symbiosis of digital space as "flows" combined with state power is crucial to analyzing the systematic management of Korean citizens in a local domain, along with spatial reshuffling based on the infrastructural broadband networks for the purpose of flexible accumulation of capital.

2   From a physical infrastructure to a virtual infrastructure in modern Korea

[S]peed in transport and communication has practical political and economic uses: it not merely confirms the authority of the ruling elite but makes it possible for them to exert more effective control over distant territories, tributaries, and markets. From the eighteenth century on, power and speed became the chief criteria of technological progress, along with quantitative productivity. ... [T]he power complex today is preoccupied only with acceleration; and cannot concede that it may be necessary, for the preservation of life, to reduce the tempo, to alter the direction, or to bring a profit-making but dangerous process to a halt.

(Mumford, 1970: graphic section I-4)

There is no linear increase in fluidity without extensive systems of immobility. The latter include wire and co-axial cable systems, the distribution of satellites for radio and television, the fiber-optic cabling carrying telephone, television and computer signals, the mobile phone masts that enable micro-wave channels to carry mobile phone messages and the massive infrastructures that organize the physical movement of people and goods.

(Urry, 2007: 54)

Geographical reconfiguration and national infrastructure

As the background for investigating the major driving forces that conditioned the birth of the Korean Information Infrastructure (KII) project in the early 1990s, this chapter describes South Korea's historical and geographical processes of installing physical and IT infrastructures throughout the country. The chapter will look at the following time periods: from the colonialist era (1910–45) through the post-Korean War period (1953–62) and the military dictatorships (1963–92) to the civilian governments (1993–present). From the early 1990s onward, the addition of spatial mobility by configuring the physical infrastructure (such as power lines, railroads, highways, and telephone lines) to that of the virtual infrastructure (such as electronic optical backbone networks and mobile telephony antennas) represented a new stage of economic mechanisms in Korea. This chapter focuses on how, in each era, the government's plans to install a national infrastructure have been closely tied to its economic goals: 1) The Japanese colonial government mobilized Koreans to build the physical infrastructure across the peninsula, in order to reach the enormous Chinese market during the early twentieth century; 2) the military regimes renovated the national physical infrastructure in order to subsidize the domestic heavy and chemical industries under the banner of industrial modernization; and 3) the civilian governments sought to construct the national IT infrastructure (KII) in order to foster new actors of the digital age and enlist Korea as an Asian hub of global capitalism. This chapter discusses how the Korean spatial re-zoning, based on virtual geographies, was a driving force both to promote an information economy and to achieve a "functional" position as a nodal point in the global networks. The state chose the development of a virtual infrastructure (KII) as the strategic plan for survival in the digital mode of global capitalism.

Overview of South Korea

A brief overview of South Korea will be useful before discussing the historical development of the national infrastructure in South Korea. The Republic of Korea (commonly known as South Korea) is on a peninsula that lies between China to the west, Japan to the east, and the Democratic People's Republic of Korea (also known as North Korea) to the north. North Korea is a nation of 24.5 million people in a mostly mountainous area, with a land mass of 120,538 square kilometers, or 74,899 square miles (CIA, 2011). North Korea shares a border on the north with China and, for a few miles on the northeast, with Russia (Jeong, 2004). South Korea's only land border is with North Korea, along the 38th parallel. South Korea includes major cities such as Busan (or Pusan, 3.5 million), Incheon (or Inch'ón, population 2.6 million), and Gwangju (or Kwangju, 1.4 million).

In 2010, South Korea's population was 50.51 million, with a land mass of 99,720 square kilometers, or 61,963 square miles. The capital city, Seoul, is its biggest metropolitan city, with a population of 10.3 million. Out of the total South Korean population, the economically active population is 24.4 million. As of 2009, the gross domestic product (GDP) was $833 billion, and the per capita gross national income (GNI) was $17,175 (World Bank, 2010; Korea Culture and Information Service, 2010). The Korean economy relies on the export of industrial products such as semiconductors, automobiles, ships, consumer electronics, mobile telecommunication equipment, steel, and chemicals. Politically, South Korea is a republic, which elects a president to a single five-year term by direct popular vote. Since the launch of a republican system of government in 1948, South Korea has benchmarked the Anglo-Saxon political traditions emphasizing the balance and division of powers among the executive, the legislature (the unicameral National Assembly), and the judiciary.

Historically, an independent Korean state or collection of states has existed almost continuously for several millennia. From its initial unification under the Silla dynasty in CE 676 through the Goryeo (918–1392) and Joseon dynasties (1392–1910), Korea existed as a single independent country. The next section surveys the development of the national infrastructure from the late nineteenth century, a period when the Korean state confronted the Western nations' technology and "civilized" power.

Geographical rescaling under the Japanese colonial rule

In Korea, the development of communication in the modern sense can be traced back to the end of nineteenth century. At that time, the issue was centered on the ideal of *Dongdoseogi*,[1] which was directed at maintaining East Asian values while adopting Western technology. Embracing Western technology, especially a communication infrastructure, was considered to be a path to modernization. On November 18, 1884, in an endeavor to escape the pre-modern age of the Joseon dynasty, young reform-oriented politicians launched the *Woo Jung Chong Guk* (the Directorate General of Postal Service) for the first time, and released the first Korean stamp, the so-called *Moon-wi*, which was used for mail delivered between Seoul and Incheon. This postal service, however, survived for only three weeks, because on December 8 of the same year the reformists' coup d'état (the *Gap Sin Jung Byun*) failed to unseat the royal family (*Korea Post*, 2006). Nevertheless, the royal family could not stem the advancing tide of Western technology. In 1885, the Joseon dynasty established a central telegraph office and began the first telegraph service in Korea, between Seoul and Incheon. The telegraph service was extended to link Seoul to Eujoo (a Korean city bordering Manchuria) and then to Busan (currently the second largest city and the biggest port city of South Korea) with the technical assistance of American and British engineers, respectively. In the same year, railroad service linking Seoul and Incheon was also launched, and in 1896, intracity and intercity telephone service began (Kim, 2002; IEEE Region 10, 2006).[2]

Despite the Joseon Dynasty's pragmatism in voluntarily importing Western technology, following the *Dongdoseogi* philosophy, after the outbreak of the Russo-Japanese War in 1905, Japanese troops seized Korean telegraph and telephone networks by occupying Korea's central telegram office. With the Japan–Korea annexation treaty in 1910, Korea entered into a period of forcible Japanese occupation (1910–45), and between 1910 and 1919 the Japanese colonial government expanded the existing telecommunication networks to nearly the entire peninsula. It also created its own telegram bureau, as well as the Joseon Postal Shipping Co., which monopolized the wartime postal service between the Japanese mainland and colonial territories (KADO, 2007). In 1927, the colonial government launched a national radio broadcasting station in Korea to justify their imperialist warfare in Asia, under the aegis of a "Greater East Asia Co-Prosperity Sphere," a slogan suggesting that Japan would lead a geographical bloc of Asian nations set free from Western powers (Yang, 2006).

The Japanese colonial government invested substantially in the construction of Korean infrastructure, with more than 67 percent of total government expenditure from 1911 to 1938 going to transportation and communication sectors such as roads, railways, and the postal system (Kim, 2006). The colonial government mobilized Koreans to build a national road and railway network across the

Korean peninsula, but rather than connecting Korean cities based on regional needs, it reconfigured the national geographies according to Japan's imperialist desire. S. Minobe, one of the Japanese imperialists who governed the Bank of Joseon, describes vividly the role of railways in creating the market value for colonialism, and the role of the Korean peninsula as a gateway to further riches:

> Its easy access to the most promising markets in the world, China, Manchuria, and Siberia, is in itself a great economic asset. A railway line now connects this once "Hermit Kingdom" [Korea] with the heart of Europe, passing through the whole of northern Asia, the economic possibility of which no one can fathom, while by another line the peninsula is connected with China and its numerous cities offering immense tradal [*sic*] prospects.
>
> (Bank of Chosen [= Joseon], 1920: 5)

To fulfill this function, the Japanese colonialist government constructed a military infrastructure that crossed the peninsula vertically, focusing on the South-to-North axis (from Busan–Seoul–Pyongyang–Shinhwju onward to Manchuria and China) in order to transport munitions, soldiers, commodities, and natural resources.

Korea regained its independence following Japan's surrender in 1945. After World War II, a Republic of Korea was set up in the southern half of the Korean Peninsula while a communist government was installed in the north (the Democratic People's Republic of Korea [DPRK]). The first elections in Korea were carried out on May 10, 1948, in the areas south of the 38th parallel, and Syngman Rhee was elected as the first president of the Republic of Korea. Meanwhile, north of the 38th parallel, a communist regime was set up under the leadership of Kim Il-sung (CIA, 2011). During the Korean War (1950–53), the US and UN forces fought alongside South Korean soldiers to defend South Korea from DPRK attacks supported by China and the Soviet Union. After massive casualties on both sides, an armistice was signed in 1953, dividing the peninsula along a demilitarized zone at about the 38th parallel.

The Korean War destroyed almost two-thirds of the nation's productive capacity. Throughout the 1950s and the early 1960s, a massive inflow of foreign aid, mainly from the US and the UN, was a significant source for sustaining the postwar national economy and reconstructing national infrastructures such as energy facilities (19 percent of US aid and development loans went to this sector of the economy), manufacturing (26 percent), telecommunications (3 percent), and transportation (28 percent) (Mason *et al.*, 1980). Despite a reconstruction program massively funded by foreign aid,[3] Korea's economy and major information and transportation infrastructures were still devastated and in chaos. Furthermore, the split of the Korean peninsula into two countries completely bisected the national backbone infrastructures that had previously allowed flows of transportation and communication to cross the entire peninsula.

In sum, the Japanese colonialists forcibly reshaped the peninsula as a base for imperialist troops—through the expropriation of land for military use, the seizure of Korea's transportation and communications facilities, and the exploitation of concessions in agriculture, forestry, mining, and fisheries (National Assembly, 2006). Although the peninsula was liberated from Japanese occupation in 1945, shortly thereafter the Korean War substantially damaged the nation's transport and communication facilities such as railroads, highways, and ports and harbors. With the help of foreign aid, the reconstruction of the infrastructure proceeded up until the early 1960s, but did so very slowly.

Physical infrastructure as the means of industrial modernization

From the time of General Cheong-hee Park's coup d'état, which precipitated more than three decades of military rule,[4] the major concerns of the ruling regimes were economic independence from foreign debt and a total disciplinary control of society. This has been described as "developmental dictatorship," focused on the dual aims of economic development and political control. The Park administration (1963–79), the first in a line of military dictatorships, had ambitions to escape Korea's Third World status and to promote industrial modernization, especially by constructing transportation and information infrastructures across the nation.

The Park regime built the major backbone transportation infrastructure—the national highway and railway system—to promote its export-oriented industrialization policy. Several major backbone highway and railway lines were built, such as the 24-kilometer (15-mile) Kyong-In expressway linking Seoul and the satellite city of Incheon in 1968, the 425.5-kilometer (264-mile) Kyong-Bu highway line between Seoul and Busan in 1970,[5] and the railway line transporting commuters from Seoul to Incheon in 1971. Overall, in 1966 the total length of roads in Korea was 28,144 kilometers (17,488 miles) with a concrete pavement rate of five percent, whereas in 1971 the total road length was 40,635 kilometers (25,249 miles) with a concrete pavement rate of 14.2 percent (Kim, 2005). The transport infrastructures were closely tied to the regime's project of economic modernization, to facilitate speedy flows of goods and services and to maximize workers' mobility between Seoul and its satellite cities.

The earliest computerization policy in Korea was directed primarily at gathering and storing information about citizens so it would be immediately available to both the national and the local authorities (see Chapter 5, discussing the combinative effect of the national ID system, which already existed for identifying each Korean, and the resident computer databases, which enabled the government to centralize all the information). Mandated in the January of 1975 by Park's order of administrative computerization, this computer database system facilitated the government's control by sorting out citizens' profiles at the national level (NCA, 2005a). The purpose of the Basic Plan for Administrative Computerization, which the government implemented between 1978 and 1987,[6] was to introduce personal computers into each government agency and to transform public archival documents holding information about citizens into electronic databases. The Park regime used the computer system as no more than a technical tool to supplement the bureaucratic control of the citizens' data. The computer system enabled the regime to accumulate 140 different pieces of personal profiling information, including detailed personal data such as permanent and current addresses, military records, criminal records, political activities, photographs, family relations, and all ten fingerprints (see Chapter 5).

It was in the 1980s that the subsequent military regime, that of Doo-hwan Chun, first conceived of information and technology as a new tool of bureaucratic efficiencies that could rationalize the organizational structures of the public sector through the use of a backbone network. In 1986, the regime passed the Act on Promotion of Computer Network Expansion and Usage to implement the National Basic Information System (NBIS), a national computerization project.[7] In the January of 1989, the NBIS Steering Committee (the interministry agency to resolve potentially controversial issues affecting several governmental departments) designed the Basic Plan for the NBIS (No. 93100–452). The government planned to construct five major information networks: the National Administrative Information System, the Financial Information System, the Education and Research Information System, the National Defense Information System, and the National Security Information System. The Chun regime desired not only to upgrade administrative systems through the NBIS, but also to promote an electronic network as a national infrastructure to enhance economic efficiencies, especially the financial flows. Nevertheless, the first state-led investment plan for building an electronic network failed to reach its goals, for reasons such as a decrease of government funding in the final phase of the NBIS, a failure to boost IT demand from the private sector, and the lack of a nationwide broadband backbone network.

The NBIS project prompted a rapid increase in computer use and in interministry electronic networks, going beyond telegraph and telephone service. In the early 1990s, despite the stated goals of using IT development to increase bureaucratic efficiencies, the government invested very little in the IT sector, only 3.8 percent of the total GDP. The overall IT index of Korea at that time was also far behind that of the advanced countries, and even behind those of Taiwan and Singapore (MIC, 2005).

The birth of the Internet in Korea

The beginning of the Internet in Korea was first driven by some academic scientists in the early 1980s, who were eager to affiliate Korea with the international electronic networks. The "System Development Network" (SDN), often described as Korea's first Internet system, was launched on May 15, 1982. For the first time, the SDN interlinked three computer servers—those of the Department of Computer Science at Seoul National University, the Korea Institute of Electronics Technology (KIET, now ETRI), and the Korea Advanced Institute of Science and Technology (KAIST) via the technical capacities of the TCP/IP network, which consisted of two nodes with a 1200 bps bandwidth (Chon *et al.*, 2007). The SDN was mostly used for network research and education research, and interconnected with several countries in Asia,[8] as well as Europe and North America. In July

1986, the .kr domain was registered as the official domain name of the country code named Korea, and in 1988, the Academic Network Committee was founded to systematically regulate domestic Internet use. Parallel to the launch of the SDN, commercial communications service for PCs using bulletin boards and text-based interface—such as Chollian and Hitel—also proliferated in the 1980s. This type of online network, using PC communications, operated as a separate service independent of the Internet until the mid-1990s, when regular PC network users were able to connect to the Internet using commercial networks. KORNET, operated by Korea Telecom (KT), launched its first Internet service in 1994 (KCC & KISA, 2010), and thereafter, with the government-guided installment of high-speed backbone infrastructures such as the KII and post-KII convergent networks, Korean society entered into a new phase of Internet development.

To sum up, the Japanese colonialists considered the Korean peninsula to be the base camp from which to launch their thrust into Manchuria and China. The postwar governments were desperate to rebuild destroyed facilities with the help of foreign aid and grants. The military regimes strove to modernize the national economy through constructing a nationwide transport infrastructure, thus saving on the costs of transporting goods and services and increasing the mobility of the labor force. In turn, the civilian governments have built the nationwide electronic backbone networks as an engine of economic efficiencies and growth in the digital mode of capitalism. During the 1970s and 1980s, the Korean "economic miracle" was accomplished through the state's strong interventionist and export-oriented policies, based on the labor-intensive industries. In this period, the driving force behind the state-led development of physical infrastructure was the military elites' desire to improve transportation and communication efficiencies, in order to catch up to the advanced economies. Further, under a military regime, the NBIS was the first policy plan in which an electronic network was designed to enable economic efficiencies as well as bureaucratic ones, although it failed to achieve either of those goals. Since the civilian governments (1993–present) took power, their focus has been actively directed towards establishing a virtual infrastructure as the material basis for the economic growth, which would permit faster flows of capital and information at the national level.

The birth of the nationwide electronic backbone network

The military regimes that ruled Korea from the 1960s to the early 1990s were focused entirely on economic development policies that promoted heavy and chemical industry, and the construction industry. Using interventionist, government-driven economic policies, the country was escaping the underdevelopment typical among the developing countries. Korea's per capita gross national income (GNI) was less than US$100 from 1945 up to the early 1960s, but had increased to US$7,000 by 1991, when the sixth Five-Year Economic Development Planning (EDP) was completed, to US$11,400 by 1995, and to US$16,000 by 2005—the latter two being the years when the KII project was launched and completed, respectively.

Figure 2.1 shows how two major economic forces—industrial modernization and the digital economy, respectively—coincided with an increase in the national income during the first period, from 1962 to 1991, and the second period, between 1993 and 2005, even though the financial crisis of 1997 put a downward spike in the sharp rise of the growth curve. Since the launch of the civilian government in the early 1990s, the Korean economy has been losing its privileged export status based on low-wage labor in textiles and heavy industry due to the emerging digital economy, the limited world market, and greater competition in low-tech products.

As shown in Figure 2.2, up through the early 1990s, low and medium-low technology products accounted for 56 percent of Korea's exports. By 2004,

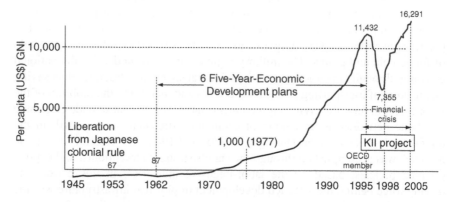

Figure 2.1 National income growth, 1945–2005 (source: Kim [2007]).

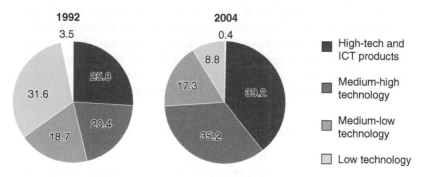

Figure 2.2 Composition of Korea's exports (source: data from OECD [2007: 49]).

Notes
1. High-tech & ICT products include aircraft, spacecraft, computers, office products, semiconductors, electronic valves, radio, TV, communication equipment, and optical instruments;
2 medium-high technology covers electrical machinery, chemical products, motor vehicles, home appliances, and machinery equipment;
3 medium-low technology covers shipbuilding and repairing, coke and petroleum, rubber and plastic products, and basic and fabricated metal products; and
4 low technology covers textiles, apparel, footwear, food, beverages, tobacco, wood, and paper products.

however, low and medium-low technology products had shrunk to just over 26 percent of Korea's exports, while high-tech and ICT products accounted for more than 39 percent. The stagnation of the Korean export-oriented economy, which had been based on heavy industry, reflects the changing patterns of international trade, which evidence an increasing share of high- and medium-technology products (OECD–World Bank Institute, 2000).

The World Trade Organization, the World Intellectual Property Organization, and the information superhighway plans in the advanced countries all prompted Korean officials to rethink their plans for economic growth. The state-led KII electronic infrastructure plan was an active response by the civilian government to the challenges of the new environment, as it sought to expand Korea's economic growth from the traditional factory systems, cultivated during the military regimes, into the new digital sphere. After Young-sam Kim took office as the first democratically elected civilian president, the civilian government retained its desire to upgrade the transportation infrastructure. As the highway system built under the Park regime was no longer able to support the heavy traffic it had spawned, the civilian government built a high-speed rail link between the two biggest metropolitan cities, Seoul and Busan. Despite the financial crisis of 1997, the main drive for unrestrained economic growth was to mobilize the citizens towards high-speed physical mobility and connectivity throughout the country (e.g., Kim, 2006; Jin, 2005). For instance, in 2004, the state-owned national railway monopoly, Korail, built a high-speed express railway line from Seoul to Busan at a total cost of US$16.3 billion, with heavy involvement from France's Train à Grande Vitesse (TGV), Alstom, and the French transportation engineering firm Systra. Its transport speed of 300 kilometers (186 miles) per hour is more than 100 times faster than that of the first railway in Korea.[9]

Connectivity was also important in terms of communication systems. Under the Kim administration, the Ministry of Communications (MoC) was asked to draw up an IT policy program for building a "New Korea" in 1993. The Korea Information Society Development Institute (KISDI), one of the government-funded IT-related think tanks, released a policy report entitled "A New IT Policy Direction for the 21st Century," which suggested developing the IT sector as a survival strategy for the nation. This "new IT policy" supplied ideas later incorporated into the Korean Information Infrastructure project. The same year, the Kim administration issued its "Five-Year Plan for a New Economy" (No. 93100–380: MoC, 1993, July), a plan intended to integrate Korea into global capitalism. In this plan, the government officially designated IT as crucial to economic growth. To develop a national IT-intensive economy, the plan included government support for the asynchronous transfer mode (ATM) switching system to create local autonomy for the telecom equipment industry, and provided a basic plan for the construction of a nationwide backbone network (MoC, 1993: 25–27). Based on this plan, the government roughed out the "Basic Plan for the KII" (No. 93100–452, 1993) and finally announced the "Master Plan for the KII" (MoC, 1994), which was to be implemented in three phases.

To emphasize its new role of directing IT policy at the national level, the MoC was renamed the Ministry of Information and Communication (MIC) in 1994, at which time it also absorbed the IT-related administrative functions of the Ministry of Commerce, Industry, and Energy, the Ministry of Science and Technology, and the Korean Overseas Information Service. The master plan for the KII was legally supplemented with the 1995 "Framework Act on Informatization Promotion" (FAIP, Act No. 4969). The Korean government's basic information policy was oriented toward setting up economic "efficiencies" in the national and global market. By encouraging the *Chaebols* to launch into the new IT sector, the FAIP was used to provide sources of profit for them to increase their market share with the formal support of the Korean government, primarily through building the backbone of a national high-speed broadband network.[10] The FAIP designated how the government's various policy measures could be used to promote private investment.[11] The FAIP meant, therefore, that the government would directly intervene at the policy level in the nascent market of IT industries, and encourage them to restructure themselves toward IT competitiveness in both the local and the global knowledge market. The ostensible purpose of the FAIP was to prescribe government support for making the public IT investment seen as necessary to the success of the KII plan. The Act was intended to provide a stable, secure source of public funding from government investment and loans, the telecom incumbents' financial contributions, dividends from shares of the state-owned Korean Telecom (KT), and the frequency allotment charges. The FAIP designated the methods and sources of public funding. This aimed to ensure that the policy failures of the final phase of the National Basic Information System (NBIS) plan, a nationwide computerization project from 1991 to 1996, would not be repeated. Under the military regime, the NBIS was the first state-led investment plan to integrate economic production and an electronic network, but it failed to reach its goal because of a decrease in government funding in the final phase and a failure to boost IT demand from private sector.[12]

The state-guided development of the KII project

The KII Planning Board was organized in the August of 1994 to assign the main roles of the project, such as designing the master plan, gathering public funds, and implementing network-related technology to each government agency. The Board consisted of six divisions, which included officials selected from the following: the MIC; the Ministry of Finance and Economy; the Ministry of Commerce, Industry and Energy; the National Computerization Agency (now the National Information Society Agency), and the Electronics and Telecommunications Research Institute (ETRI),[13] and the telecom companies Korea Telecom, Dacom (now LG Telecom), and Korean Mobile Telecom (now SK Telecom). The Planning Board[14] directed the main KII-related project from its inception until 1995, when its affairs were transferred into the Informatization and Planning Office[15] at the MIC (NCA, 2005: 64). No bidding process among the private telecom vendors for the KII project ever occurred; the Korean government granted exclusive rights in the construction of the KII-G backbone network to two facility-based telecom service providers: Korea Telecom (KT) was given a 70 percent share and Dacom a 30 percent share.

The KII project was subdivided into three separate networks: the KII-Government (KII-G), KII-Public (KII-P), and KII-Testbed (KII-T or KOREN—the Korea Advanced Research Network). The KII-G is a nationwide backbone network which interconnects more than 30,000 public administration and agencies and 10,000 schools using asynchronous transfer mode (ATM) switches, which had been developed in 1996 and began to be installed from 2001 onward, on high-speed fiber optic cables (155 Mbps–410 Mbps) in 144 metropolitan and small cities nationwide (NCA, 2004: 27). The KII-P, constructed by the private sector, is a home and business network for nationwide broadband access and high-volume data transmission (1.5–2 Mbps), encompassing more than 1,400 localities. The KII-T, also called KOREN, is a testbed network for the purpose of developing telecom devices and network facilities; KOREN also serves as a research network linking Korea with such Asian-Pacific networks as the Asian-Pacific Information Infrastructure and the Trans-Eurasia Information Network. A total of US$22.7 billion was invested to construct the KII network: the government invested US$6.2 billion in the major backbone networks (the KII-G), as public seed money to encourage the private sector's active participation, and the private sector expended US$16.5 billion for the "last miles" of the network (this figure includes the private sector investment in the KII-P, the commercial network, as well as in the KII-G, up to 2005, the year of the KII's completion).

To avoid redundant investment while installing the KII, the government mandated that KT install the fiber optic networks along the highways and Dacom along the railways (NCA, 2006: 63). The construction of the KII-G ensured that public agencies and educational institutions would subscribe to broadband service from the telecom service providers. Based on the stable rate of subscription from the KII-G, the private telecom sector was able to expand its broadband service into homes and businesses. By June 2003, the number of subscribers had reached 14 million households, and there was a nearly complete penetration level even in rural and suburban areas (NCA, 2003: 29–30). Both the KII-P and the KII-G broadband services promoted rapid private sector growth in IT production: for instance, IT-related revenue in 2004 was US$20.7 billion in e-commerce and US$78.7 billion in online securities trading (NCA, 2004), while total revenue in the infrastructure-related network industry was US$4.7 million (KAIT, 2004).

While the KII-G and the KII-P serve as governmental and commercial networks, respectively, the KII-T serves as the optimal high speed R&D and testbed network for research institutes and universities, for the testing of new telecom network technologies and applications developed by research centers such as the ETRI. To set the technological standards in the global market, the Korean government supported the ATM network switching technology implemented by the ETRI, and applied it to the backbone networks from the second phase of the project onward. While the three KII network structures were separately operated by the stakeholders—research institutions and universities, the government, and the private sector—they became closely linked to each other by the evolving processes of broadband technology from the KII-T to the KII-P by way of the KII-G (see Table 2.1). The KII-T contributed to the "creation" of new telecom network technology, the KII-G served as the "application" of technology tested by the KII-T, and the KII-P promoted the "diffusion" of network technology to businesses and homes.

Unlike the other two infrastructures, the KII-G was developed in three phases, based on the shifting of specific policy goals. The first phase of building a backbone network (1995–97) aimed at improving network connectivity among government agencies: the government first upgraded the intelligence and police network lines, which are part of the KII-G, and the optical networks interlinking these 4,000 agencies, and constructed the main backbone network connecting 80 call zones. Some metropolitan cities were interconnected to the optical broadband network with transmission capacities of 155 Mbps to 2.5 Gbps. In the second phase of backbone network completion (1998–2000), the nationwide optical infrastructure network (155 Mbps to 5 Gbps) was established, connecting 144 call zones with ATM-based switching technology. The third phase (2001–05) was an expansion or advancement of the second phase. As of September 2005, 32,000 public institutions were able to access the nationwide broadband service, and the ATM switching network was upgraded from 622 Mbps to 40 Gbps (NCA, 2006: 68–107). As shown in Figure 2.3, total

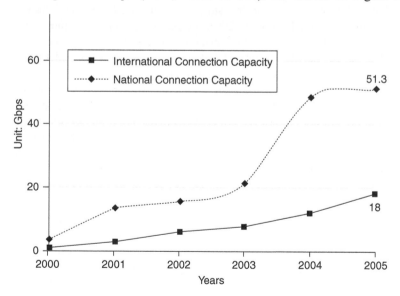

Figure 2.3 Traffic capacity of the Korean broadband network (source: data from NCA [2006]).

Note
"International connection capacity" is defined as the data-processing bandwidth in the domestic online nodal points that are linked to foreign countries' network lines.

Table 2.1 Korean Information Infrastructure (KII) project, 1995–2005

		KII-Testbed (KII-T) →	*KII-Government (KII-G)* →	KII-Public (KII-P)
Role of each infrastructure		Development and testing of technology	Application of technology	Diffusion of technology
Main user		Research institutions	Government	Home and business
Investor		Government and private sector	Government	Private sector
Main target		Testbed	Backbone	Access
Procedures	Budget	Government and KT	Government (reimbursement of budget from private sector)	Separately operated and implemented by telecom service providers
	Management	NCA (NIA)	NCA (NIA)	
	Network builder	KT	KT (70%), Dacom (30%)	
	Phase 1 (1995–1997)	2.5 Gbps between Seoul and Taejon	Built 80 call zones linking 14,955 public institutions (45 Mbps), US$157 million publicly funded	Fiber optic lines to high density buildings
	Phase 2 (1998–2000)	2.5 Gbps connecting five metropolitan cities	Connecting all 144 call zones including 28,686 public institutions and schools with ATM switches (155 Mbps), US$238 million publicly funded	30% of total household with ADSL and CATV
	Phase 3 (2001–2005)	40 Gbps optical Net	Linking 32,000 public institutions with ATM-MPLS high quality IP service (1 Gbps), US$338 million publicly funded	Over 20 Mbps service to homes

Source: compiled from NCA (2006), MIC (2004).

broadband connection capacity in Korea has improved to 51.3 Gbps at the national level and 18 Gbps at the international level, respectively.

In effect, the KII project became the material basis for creating a nationwide interconnection of government agencies and public institutions through the optical networks. As noted by an executive principal researcher of the National Information Society Agency (NIA), the KII project, especially, the KII-G, has contributed to "saving the cost of data usage by the government agencies and enhancing the civil service through the Internet-based system".[16] The successful story of the KII was due to "the efficient management of public investment led by the government."[17]

Evolution of the backbone networks after the KII project

The government offered incentives to the telecom service providers at the beginning of the KII-G project by putting up the initial public funding and also by partly subsidizing the subscription costs of the broadband services to non-governmental and educational institutions. This government assistance made it possible for the two dominant telecom service providers, KT and Dacom, to lower the subscription price for network use, thus creating a rising number of subscribers from public, non-profit, and educational institutions until the end of the project in 2005. As a new administration—that of Moo-hyun Noh (2003–08)—took power and the KII project came to an end, the government began to focus on how to keep the service price low after the network's completion. The government's plan was to introduce two emerging facility-based telecom providers, Hanaro Telecom and SK Networks, into the public information infrastructure market.

The government aimed to bring more market competition in price and service among the four providers and to take the initiative in negotiating subscription prices. Moreover, with the completion of the nationwide backbone network, the government began to shift its policy from the facility-based supply system to the service-based system, which it hoped would be improved by means of competition among service providers. As part of this shift in focus, in September 2005, the government divided the KII-G network into two network architectures: the e-Government Telecom Network (eGTN), which interconnects the 16,000 government agencies and local governments and institutions, and the National Information Service (NIS),[18] which provides the service to 15,000 non-governmental and educational institutions. This allowed NIS service users to negotiate subscription prices independently through a group contract with the telecom service providers.[19]

The division of the KII-G network into the eGTN and the NIS was intended to secure and renovate the core of the eGTN as the governmental network. Separation of the governmental network from the NIS was reaffirmed by the establishment of the Government-wide Integrated Computing Center (GICC) in the October of 2005. Through the Computing Center, the MIC planned to share information resources, secure interoperability, and optimize the governmental network by efficient management and operation. The GICC was the most significant project among the Noh administration's "31 E-Government Roadmap Tasks." It divided the information systems of the 48 government agencies into two separate computing centers: Center 1 is located in a government building in Daejeon, which houses 24 government agencies including the MIC, the MOGAHA, and the Korean Customs Service. Center 2 is located in another building, which houses another 24 government agencies, including the Ministry of Construction and Transportation, and the National Tax Service. The initiative to upgrade the e-government telecommunication network is intended to establish a total IT infrastructure exclusively for government agencies.

The KII-P, the private sector network, has also been evolving: in 2004 it became the Broadband convergence Network (BcN),[20] in which communication, broadcasting, and Internet all converged. To ensure that the electronic network infrastructure is up to date with the new convergent situation, in the February of 2008, the Myung-bak Lee administration (2008–12) finally shut down the MIC and distributed its remaining functions among other agencies (NIA, 2008): some functions for national informatization were transferred to the Ministry of Public Administration and Security; the ICT industry to the Ministry of Knowledge Economy; and the telecommunications regulatory affairs to the Korea Communications Commission (KCC), which is under the direct political influence of the president. With its extended scope of policy regulation, in January of 2009, the KCC announced plans to renovate the old BcN with the UBcN (Ultra Broadband convergence Network), which is ten times faster than the BcN (KCC & KISA, 2010). Scheduled to be completed in 2013, the UBcN, as of 2009, already operated with 50–100 Mbps level broadband services to 25 million wireless and 11.8 million fixed-line subscribers (NIA, 2010). The commercial broadband service providers, with the technical support of the KII-T, have developed a multi-stage plan for the UBcN, and also created a UBcN transmission network, which ensures Quality of Service (QoS),[21] security, Internet Protocol version 6 (IPv6),[22] and open service, while upgrading the wireless and fixed-line subscriber network and allowing the use of seamless UBcN service (NIA, 2007). Further, in 2009 the KCC announced the master plan for building the IP-USN (IP-Ubiquitous Sensor Network) so as to integrate the existing closed sensor network for disaster prevention, weather monitoring, and public building security with the UBcN, which is already being installed (KCC & KISA, 2010). It also aims to prevent any duplicate investments in related infrastructure such as u(biquitous)-IT, u(biquitous)-city, and other many sensor network related government plans.

To summarize, the 11-year state-led KII project has evolved into the post-KII networks such as the e-Government Telecom Network, the National Information Service, the Ultra Broadband convergence Network, and the IP-Ubiquitous Sensor Network, all of which were instigated by creating competition within the private sector. In the process of building a national Information infrastructure, the government, especially the MIC, took a leading role in setting out a coherent and comprehensive communication policy plan. Under the increasingly laissez-faire conditions of the current national IT market, Korean society is unlikely to see more state-led "robust" IT policy plans such as the KII project, because the state no longer has the power to intervene in the market in the same way that it once did.

The present chapter has surveyed the historical background of the KII project; the next chapter turns to an analysis of the global factors that conditioned the creation of the national backbone network.

3 Local telecommunications policy within the digital mode of global capitalism

The British governing elite saw the international telegraph infrastructure as a strategic resource to be used for the defense of empire, although the system was owned by private companies. Britain's competitors saw it as a monopolistic power resource that gave the empire control of information...

(Hills, 2002: 5)

After the "end of history," prematurely announced a few years ago by Francis Fukuyama, what is being revealed here are the beginnings of the "end of the space" of a small planet held in suspension in the electronic ether of our modern means of telecommunication.

(Virilio, 2000)

The novelty of the new information infrastructure is the fact that it is embedded within and completely immanent to the new production processes. At the pinnacle of contemporary production, information and communication are the very commodities produced; the network itself is the site of both production and circulation.

(Hardt & Negri, 2000: 298, emphasis in original)

Outline of the chapter

This chapter investigates the dynamics of the global–local nexus in South Korea's information and telecom infrastructure development. The goal of this chapter is to examine the external factors that led South Korea's government to design the Korean Information Infrastructure (KII) project. The chapter focuses on the global–local dynamics of structural adjustment to global constraints, seen in the Korean government's construction of the KII, which was designed and implemented during the period of the civilian governments (1993–present). *Global constraints* are those external forces that influenced the Korean government's policies and actions; the present study, however, views structural adjustment in Korea not merely as an aspect of globalization, linking localities into global processes, but also as the active expression of local autonomy. This chapter, therefore, investigates the strong trends of localization in the processes of economic globalization (global networked mobility)—trends seen most clearly in the active role of the Korean state as an agent of local and global capital. Relevant to globalization theory, this chapter confirms the hypothesis that even the denationalizing force at the global level also feeds the localizing mechanisms of the economic sphere in a nation, as well as the socio-cultural spheres. Since the late 1980s, the global constraints imposed on the Korean government have forced it to deploy new policy plans for domestic structural adjustment; these are explicit in the World Trade Organization (WTO) Agreement on Basic Telecommunications—which includes regulatory measures such as requirements of non-discrimination, regulatory transparency, and openness to international markets—and implicit in the information superhighway experiments of the US and Japan in the early 1990s. This chapter also explores the inner mechanisms of national sovereignty in terms of the government's KII project, which functioned as a safety valve to minimize these external pressures in advance and to create new conditions for economic growth, with the consistent support of the private sector. This chapter, therefore, examines the KII project as a unique state-led IT plan, brought forth by a compromise between international pressure for market liberalization and domestic pressure for economic reforms.

The digital phase of "catching up"

During the 1970s and 1980s, South Korea was largely successful in transforming itself from one of the world's poorest agrarian societies into a state of late-industrialization. At the beginning of the 1990s, the Korean government was once again forced to decide whether to remain a member of the second-tier countries under the digital mode of capitalism, or to find a way to make a leap forward. The government chose transforming the nation from a labor-intensive economy to a "knowledge-based" economy and *segyehwa* (globalization) as the foremost goals of state affairs (e.g., President Young-sam Kim's New Year's speech, Office of the President, 1995; President Dae-Jung Kim's inaugural speech, 1998).

To succeed in the second phase of "catching up"—the digital phase—the government noted how advanced countries such the US, Japan, and the EU had achieved economic reconfiguration by means of high-speed telecommunication networks, and benchmarked their changes based on the new economy (e.g., MoC, 1993, July; 1994). Moreover, increased international pressures for market openness in bilateral and multilateral negotiation settings, such as those with the World Trade Organization (WTO) and the International Monetary Foundation (IMF)—through its bailout program after the 1997 crisis—affected Korea's telecom companies by forcing the country to open its markets. This eventually led the Korean government to deploy new policy plans of "structural adjustment." The Korean Information Infrastructure (KII) plan was a result of these direct and indirect global pressures; a strategy to enable a nation-state to survive in the digital mode of global capitalism. The main goal was to interconnect the public agencies through a fiber optic electronic network, and eventually to gear up IT productivity and efficiency in the private sector through this network.[1]

This chapter accentuates the intertwining of global constraints and the Korean government's restructuring of the national economy through the KII policy experiment, which has essentially created the nationwide backbone network for government agencies and public institutions. To explore the dynamics of the global–local nexus in Korea, this chapter examines the influence of the new material conditions of network-based global capitalism, and the national tele-communications reforms imposed by WTO regulation. This chapter sees the contextual factors surrounding Korea's information superhighway project (KII) project through a localized prism. For instance, the WTO's influence on the Korean telecom market since the early 1990s, culminating in the 1997 WTO Agreement on Basic Telecommunications, is one of the external constraints that forced Korea to open its telecom market, and indirectly conditioned the state-led KII policy planning. This chapter details the dynamics of WTO regulations at the local level, such as their influence on the government-driven R&D plan to develop the asynchronous transfer mode (ATM) switching system for promoting the national telecom equipment industry. Further, this chapter also interprets the flurry of "wired" capitalism in the early 1990s as seeking to transform the capi-talist economy into network-based systems. The chapter regards the influence of global standards to reconfigure geographically in advanced countries, such as information superhighway policy experiments in the US, Japan, and the EU, as their "hegemonic" effect on post-industrialization at the local level.

This chapter posits these two globalizing patterns—externally imposed regu-lation and external examples—within the localized reform programs of the Korean government, and then situates the state-led policy drive to undertake the KII project as part of the structural adjustment in the national telecom market. The local response to global pressures resulted in the domestication of the global force in the local market. The chapter concludes that the KII project, over eleven years, was actively conducted on the basis of a model similar to that of the state-planned "catching up" of late-industrialization in the 1980s. This is very differ-ent from the governmental model in the advanced countries, where the government's role is largely that of an assistant of or mediator for the private sector. The irony, then, is that Korea's state-led information infrastructure plan has been dramatically more successful than the private sector-led plans of more advanced nations such as the US and Japan (see Figure 3.1).

As to the scope of the research, this chapter focuses largely on the state-driven policy plan for installing the backbone networks to facilitate administra-tive affairs, such as the KII-Government (KII-G), rather than on the KII-Testbed (KII-T) and the KII-Public (KII-P), which are separately operated and were developed by the government-funded research institutes and by the private telecom sector, respectively. To understand the significance of the KII in the Korean economy, it is necessary to look at the current state of informatization in Korea and how it attained a status that exceeds that of most advanced nations in a brief period.

A "newly advanced economy"?

At the forefront of the global IT competition, the Korean government recognized the importance of information and telecom infrastructure as the conduit of capital, services, and information (e.g., Chapter IV of the 1995 Framework Act on Informatization Promotion; FAIP). It saw that extensive and high-quality infrastructure reduces the effect of distance between regions, with the result of integrating the national market and connecting it to the global market. Due to the active involvement of the government in building the IT infrastructure since the mid-1990s, Korea's economic efficiency in infrastructure is ranked 16th out of 131 countries, on the basis of the global competitiveness index released by the World Economic Forum (2007). As shown in Table 3.1, Korea invested heavily in virtual infrastructure throughout the 1990s, an average investment of 0.8 percent of GDP in the first half of the decade, which more than doubled to 1.8 percent in the second half. Korea's investment rate in virtual infrastructure was almost double that of Hong Kong and more than five times that of Japan in the second half of the 1990s, when the KII project was being launched.

Another distinguishing feature of Korean investment is that a high percentage of funding came from the government in the form of public sponsorship. In many countries belonging to the Organization for Economic Co-operation and Development (OECD), the public share in investment was zero in the late 1990s. For Malaysia, Singapore, and the United Kingdom, the public share was five percent or less, but in Korea, between 25 percent and 48 percent of investment came from the public sector.

Despite its relatively low rank in GDP per capita among OECD countries, as of June 2010 Korea was ranked fourth, with 34 broadband lines per 100 households, far ahead of the US and Japan (see Figure 3.1; in 2004 Korea was ranked number one).

Further, according to the information and communication indicator index of the World Bank (2009), in which variables are normalized or rescaled onto an interval between zero and ten using the Knowledge Assessment Methodology

Table 3.1 Korean investment in information infrastructure during the 1990s

	Investment/GDP (%)		Public Investment (% of total)	
	Average 1991–95	Average 1996–99	Average 1991–95	Average 1996–99
Hong Kong	0.58	0.98	0	0
Japan	0.14	0.34	0	0
Korea	**0.80**	**1.85**	**48**	**25**
Malaysia	1.12	1.04	6	5
Singapore	0.35	0.57	38	4
UK	0.23	0.35	2	2
US	0.58	0.52	0	0

Source: OECD-World Bank Institute (2000).

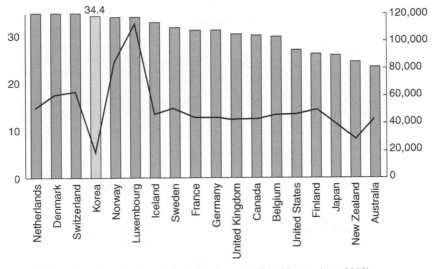

Broadband penetration (subscribers per 100 inhabitants, June 2010)
— GDP per capita (USD PPP, 2009)

Figure 3.1 OECD broadband penetration and GDP per capita (source: data from OECD [2010]).

Note
Broadband networks include all DSL lines, cable modem lines, fiber optic lines, and fixed wireless technologies such as satellite, MMDS, LMDS, WiMAX, and other fixed-wireless transport technologies.

(KAM), in the IT sector Korea comes very close to filling the "circle" within a spider chart reaching toward the maximum value of ten. This implies that it is better positioned in terms of the knowledge economy, except the low capacity of the international Internet bandwidth, compared to the normalized values of the G-7 countries and the average of the high-income countries. Among other indicators, the KII directly contributed to increasing values in the IT areas such as e-government services, Internet users and bandwidth, e-commerce, and Internet banking, as shown in the Figure 3.2 and Table 3.2.

For instance, as shown in Table 3.2, by reaching more than 16.4 million broadband Internet households out of a total population of 50.51 million as of 2009, the nationwide construction of the high-speed broadband network was physically complete.[2] With the extension of fiber optic cables into individual houses, isolated areas, and small islands, the major bottleneck in completing broadband networks, usually referred to as "the last mile,"[3] was overcome in the final phase of the KII project. The high-standard index of Information infrastructure is largely due to the Korean government's leading role in guiding IT development. In contrast to the rapid expansion of broadband Internet in Korea, the US has suffered from high prices and underdeveloped technology in its

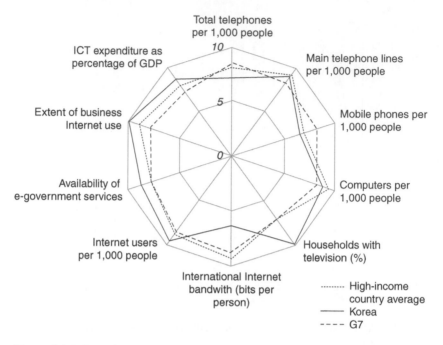

Figure 3.2 Information and communication indicator in South Korea (source: Author's
graphic based on data from the World Bank [2009] using the Knowledge
Assessment Methodology [KAM]. www.worldbank.org/wbi/kam).

Notes
Comparison group: 146 countries, type: weighted, and data: 2006–08.
High-income countries: 39 countries, including South Korea, which earned more than US$11,906 in
2008 Gross National Income (GNI) per capita.

broadband network, due to the monopolistic structure of the local telephone and
cable companies, which sought to protect old ISDN technology and delay the IT
infrastructure investment of the fiber optic lines (Bearn, 2004).

Most of the research on this subject has focused on the "broadband heaven"
created by the KII project (e.g., Picot & Wernick, 2007; Shin & Park, 2007;
Yang & Olfman, 2006; Frieden, 2005; Lee & Chan-Olmsted, 2004; Townsend,
2004; ITU, 2003; Han, 2003; Lee *et al.*, 2003; Jeong & King, 1996). Such obser-
vations have ignored the global–local nexus that forced the Korean government
to restructure the national economy in response to the changing mode of global
capitalism. Those IT policy studies that have mentioned the global constraints on
the KII project have tended to consider them a minor factor among various contextual elements, such as the active public investment, the Korean-specific col-
lectivistic culture, and the close public–private partnership (e.g., Lee *et al.*, 2009;
Lau *et al.*, 2005; Lee & Jung, 1998; and a series of IT-related policy reports
released in 2005 and 2006 by the National Information Society Agency [NIA]
and the Ministry of Information and Communication [MIC]). Some studies have

Table 3.2 Current status of informatization in Korea, 1998–2010

Category	1998	1999	2000	2001	2002	2003	2004	2005	2006	2007	2008	2009	2010
Broadband Internet subscriber (10,000 households)	1.4	37.4	401	781	1,041	1,118	1,192	1,219	1,404	1,471	1,547	1,635	1,722
Internet user (10,000 persons)	310	1,080	1,904	2,438	2,627	2,922	3,158	3,301	3,412	3,559	3,619	3,658	3,701
Internet usage rate (%)	–	–	44.7	56.6	59.4	65.5	70.2	72.8	74.8	75.5	76.5	77.2	77.8
Mobile phone subscriber (10,000 persons)	–	2,344	2,682	2,905	3,234	3,359	3,659	3,834	4,020	4,350	4,561	4,794	4,961
e-Commerce: Transaction volume (KRW trillion)	–	–	58	119	178	235	314	358	414	517	630	671	–
Internet Banking subscriber (10,000 persons)	–	–	409	1,131	1,771	2,275	2,427	2,674	3,591	4,470	5,260	5,921	–

Source: NIA (2007; 2010), KISA's Internet Statistical Information System (ISIS, 2011, http://isis.kisa.or.kr/).

examined how the external challenge in the mid-1990s led to the Korean telecom restructuring, and have chronicled the history of the US- and WTO-driven regulations and regulatory reforms in the Korean telecom market (e.g., Tcha *et al.*, 2000; Hyun & Lent, 1999; Hong, 1998; Cho *et al.*, 1996; Kim, 1993; Kim & Ro, 1993), but these studies have not focused on the KII project itself. The next section, therefore, investigates the factors that led to "the broadband nation" by scrutinizing the historical contexts surrounding the KII project.

Global pressure or national sovereignty?

The KII-driven IT growth in Korea appears to be a great story operated within its own local mechanisms; in the early 1990s, however, the global constraints on Korean bureaucrats were highly significant during the greatest phase of telecommunications liberalization. There were three external factors and three internal mechanisms led to the KII project: The external factors were 1) the US-led information superhighway initiative and its global extension by the Global Information Infrastructure (GII), 2) the Korea–US bilateral negotiations and the WTO regulatory system, and 3) the multinational telecom corporations. The three internal mechanisms that reacted to these external factors were 1) the interventionist role of the Korean government, 2) the telecom reform plans as a structural adjustment between 1990 and 1995, and 3) the government's desire for technological independence from foreign telecom companies. The state-led KII project thus arose from the dynamics of the interaction between global pressures and Korea's internal drives to escape technological dependency.

"Learning effects" from advanced countries

In the early and mid-1990s, one of the most important international influences on Korea was the advanced countries' rapid reconfigurations of their national infrastructures, based on electronic networks. For instance, a "Commentary for the KII Master Plan" (KAIT,[4] 1995) described external threats to Korean society as being largely derived from the rise of multilateral trade systems such as the WTO, regional economic blocs such as the NAFTA and the EU, and the IT infrastructure plans implemented by the US, Japan, and the EU. South Korea's national telecom policy, then, was at best an "unfiltered, imitative hybrid of policy measures borrowed from the advanced countries" (Kim & Ro, 1993: 485), such as the US, Japan, and the UK.[5] The global economic changes driven by the advanced countries had a "learning effect" upon the Korean government, to such a degree that it copied their policy programs.

In the US, the Clinton administration's Information Infrastructure Task Force (IITF, 1993) issued a report entitled "National Information Infrastructure (NII): An Agenda for Action," which was to be implemented by private sector leadership with the federal government's guidance. In a similar move, the Japanese government's Ministry of Posts and Telecommunications (now the Ministry of Internal Affairs and Communications) issued a report entitled "Reforms Towards the Intellectually Creative Society of the Twenty-First Century" (Telecommunications Council, 1994). Through the investment of JP¥50 trillion (equivalent to US$608.9 billion), the Japanese government planned to develop a "high-performance info-communications infrastructure" by 2010, so as to build an "intellectually creative society" as part of the economic shift from "conventional industry to new info-communications Industry" (TC, 1994: Section 1). Through this infrastructure plan, Japan expected to create a JP¥123 trillion (equivalent to US$1.5 trillion) multimedia market and 2.4 million new jobs (Igarashi, 1994).[6] Singapore's government in 1993 announced the "IT 2000 Vision" (Choo, 1997), which set forth an "Intelligent Island" program aimed at completing a national information infrastructure within 15 years.[7] In 1994 the British government issued a report entitled "Creating the Superhighways of the Future: Developing Broadband Communications in Britain," and in European countries such as Norway, Sweden, Denmark, and Finland, national infrastructure programs interconnecting the government agencies, educational institutions, and firms also became pervasive (Siochru, 2004).

These policy experiments emerging in the US, the EU, Japan, and Singapore influenced Korea at that time. Both the 1993 Basic Plan and the 1994 Master Plan for the KII specified "the new economy as the major motive for constructing the backbone networks" (MoC, 1994: 29) and urged "Korean society to pursue the new international trends toward network-based capitalism" (30). In a network-based economy, an infrastructure plan was essential to establishing an international market share (Jeong & King, 1996). Among the IT plans of the developed countries, the American NII initiative greatly influenced the launching of the KII project. The government officials interviewed by the present writer specifically mentioned the US government's lead in creating the network-based economy. For instance, one of the key actors in implementing the KII project noted that both the NII initiative, submitted by the US Vice President Al Gore, and the liberalization of the national telecom market, brought about by the bilateral negotiation between the US and Korea, motivated the Korean administration to plan the construction of the information infrastructure in the early 1990s.[8] Other interviewees from the NIA regarded the KII as "a voluntarily prepared government project benchmarking the US and Japan initiatives for the optical network"[9] or "a Korean-style NII project."[10]

During the presidential campaign of 1992, Bill Clinton first presented the value of the electronic backbone network for US economic growth:

> In the new economy, infrastructure means information as well as transportation. More than half the US workforce is employed in information-intensive industries, yet we have no national strategy to create a national information network. Just as the interstate highway system in the 1950s spurred two decades of economic growth, we need a door-to-door fiber optics system by the year 2015 to link every home, every lab, every classroom, and every business in America.
>
> (Remarks of Governor Bill Clinton in the Wharton School of Business, the University of Pennsylvania, 1992)

In their 1993 "Agenda for Action" report, Vice President Gore and the Secretary of Commerce, Ron Brown, offered a blueprint for the NII based upon a public–private partnership. The NII initiative sought to establish a "seamless web of communications networks, computers, databases, and consumer electronics that will put vast amounts of information at users' fingertips" (1993: 3). The NII initiative expressed the Clinton-Gore administration's desire to restore America's technological and economic leadership through investment in the nation-wide information infrastructure, and through promoting a more deregulatory climate in the national and international telecom market. Following up on the NII initiative, Gore expanded the administration's policy plan to a global scale by introducing the Global Information Infrastructure (GII) initiative at the first World Telecommunication Development Conference, in the March of 1994. The Conference, held in Buenos Aires, Argentina, signaled a new order of the world economy, in which everything would be connected by a grid of electronic networks. At this meeting, Gore called upon every nation to establish an ambitious agenda to build the GII, under the following basic principles: the encouragement of private sector investment, more competition, easy access to the network, a flexible regulatory environment, and universal service. World leaders incorporated these five principles into the International Telecommunications Union's "Buenos Aires Declaration on Global Telecommunication Development for the 21st Century" (ITU, 1994). In the May of that year, Japan also proposed the Asian Information Infrastructure (AII) initiative as part of the GII at the ITU meeting, in order to facilitate the regional bloc of the electronic network among the Asian countries (Igarashi, 1994: 17). In the February of 1995, the Group of Seven Nations' (G-7) Ministerial Conference on the Information Society, in Brussels, reaffirmed the main goals of the GII initiative led by the US administration.

The GII principles and the G-7 affirmation shared the WTO's regulatory principles on basic telecommunications, which focused on the openness of local telecom markets. For example, based on Gore's suggested GII principles, G-7 leaders proposed international principles of market liberalization, such as the promotion of interconnectivity and interoperability, developing global markets for networks, services, and applications, and protecting intellectual property rights (G-7 Chair, 1995). Despite differences in the scale and size of the local telecom market in developing countries, international pressures for network-based market liberalization, such as the GII initiatives and the WTO agreements led by the US administration (see the next section), forced the Korean government both to open its telecom market and to embrace the new world order of digital capitalism. The government was urged to conform to the US-led GII initiatives and the WTO agreements enacted in 1997 at the global level, and simultaneously to meet the benchmarks of Gore's NII project at the local level. In response to the US-led NII and GII initiatives, at the 1994 APEC Summit in Bogor, Indonesia, Asian countries, including South Korea, agreed to introduce the Asia Pacific Information Infrastructure (APII), for the purpose of promoting the free flow of information throughout the region (Kim, 2003). The Korean government actively responded to global pressures such as the WTO agreements by opening the domestic telecom market and by launching the KII project, as shown in the following section.

At the start of his presidency in 1993, the first civilian President, Young-sam Kim, popularized the discourse of "globalization" (*Shegyehwa*). His motto of a "New Korea" (*Sin Hanguk*) aimed to persuade people to voluntarily adopt "a market liberalization policy that was required by the 'globalization' of capital in order to become a member of the OECD" (Kang, 2000: 451). To become a member country of the OECD by 1996, the Korean government sought to be rapidly incorporated into multilateral trade organizations, such as the WTO system and the World Intellectual Property Organization (WIPO), in conjunction with a new liberal economic policy, the slogan of which was a "small but strong government." Thus in 1995, in his New Year's Message to the Nation, President Young-sam Kim offered the following advice to his people:

> On the threshold of the twenty-first century, the contemporary world confronts a new order. Along with a new year, the WTO system will be launched. This signifies an era of dog-eat-dog competition between nations and regions. A new era is coming when we must confront the unstable future of this new world. We should embrace the tide of globalization, reorganize our government to be "small but strong," and begin again from scratch. *Shegyehwa* is the only way we can interact with the outside world and move towards its center.
>
> (Office of the President, 1995)

President Kim's message about how Korean society could become a winner under globalization's law of the jungle was accompanied the government's active interventionist policy of redefining its developmental strategies with IT plans. Kim's rhetoric, which merged the "particular interests" of the private sector with the "general interest" of the nation-state, succeeded in persuading Koreans that these IT policies were necessary for their very survival in the unconstrained competition of a globalized world. One of the survival strategies in the age of globalization was a shift in the government's policy interest from industrialization to informatization. The government actually proposed its own vision of a cooperative Asia-Pacific Information Infrastructure (APII) at the Asia-Pacific Economic Cooperation (APEC) summit meeting held in Indonesia in 1994 (Embassy of the Republic of Korea in the USA, 2005), and it also issued the Master Plan for the KII the same year (MoC, 1994). Electronic networks became appealing to the government (e.g., see the public reports released by the MoC [1993, August; 1993, July; 1994]) because of the economic growth available if domestic capital were able to efficiently plug into the global and regional infrastructure networks. The government responded vigorously to the new mode of global capitalism by building the national broadband backbone network.

As Figure 3.3 shows, since Young-sam Kim's presidency, the government has raised investment in the IT sector in order to shift the nation from a labor-intensive industry to a knowledge-based one. In the 1990s, the amount of the government's telecom-related investment rapidly increased, except for the fluctuation during the 1997 IMF financial crisis. Korea's energetic state-led telecom investment was the response to a series of global influences, such as the early 1990s US-led flurry of construction of information infrastructure in various countries. Further, as discussed in the next section, it was a response to external constraints from the late 1980s up to the mid-1990s, such as the US' designation of South Korea as a Priority Foreign Country (PFC), which resulted in trade sanctions, the Uruguay Round of Multilateral Trade negotiations, and the WTO negotiations on basic telecommunications. During this period, the government not only began to install the nationwide infrastructure that would electronically interconnect government agencies and educational institutions, but also launched a national mobile telephony market. This allowed the *Chaebols*, Korea's family-owned monopolies, to take advantage of the "trickle-down" effect from the state-led IT boom.

The logic of the Global Information Infrastructure (GII) initiative was directed toward expanding access to foreign markets for America's high-tech companies and enabling global telecom conglomerates to attain "hegemonic" power, transforming the mode of capitalism. Behind the GII's rhetoric of one world interconnected by electronic networks lay the US-led WTO regulatory system establishing telecom liberalization as a universal policy—specifically, this impacted Korea by removing any trade restrictions to its domestic telecom market. The next section investigates the global influences of the WTO regulatory system on Korea's domestic IT policy.

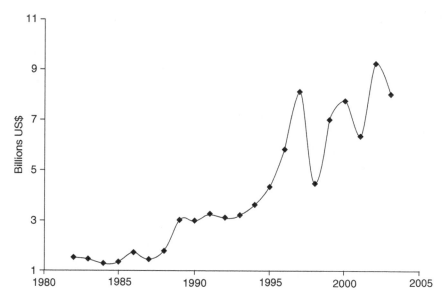

Figure 3.3 Annual government telecom investment until the completion of the KII project (source: Data from ITU [2005]).

The global regulatory system as an impetus for the KII project

Since the late 1980s, under the new network-based economic order of globalization, global regulatory institutions such as the Uruguay Round and the WTO have gradually become the new "global quasi-governments" (Hardt & Negri, 2004: 175). Korea was forced to prepare itself for a global challenge from the regulatory system of these quasi-governmental centers by integrating its local networks into the global electronic matrix. Most of those interviewed during the present study felt that the WTO regulatory system was a minor factor in the birth of the KII project, in contrast to the early 1990s' upsurge of information infrastructure projects in the advanced countries, which they saw as a strong motivator for the KII. In other words, they perceived a direct cause-and-effect relationship between two policy events—the American NII project and the KII project—and minimized the influence of outside pressures to liberalize the national telecom market. However, although the US-led NII and GII initiatives laid the ideological and material foundations for the KII project, the US government's trade sanctions and the WTO-based multilateral trade negotiations meant that, in order to join the global telecom market, Korea would have to open its national telecom market. It was this which drove the Korean government to accelerate building the national information infrastructure, so as to shield itself from being required to completely open its telecom market.

The KII arose out of the structural adjustment programs of 1990, 1994, and 1995, which the government launched in order to enhance the competitiveness of the national telecom market. Even though within the WTO framework, the government was forced to completely open the domestic telecom market to international competition, it granted two domestic incumbents, KT and Dacom, the right to build the nationwide information infrastructure, and thus protected the business rights for the KII-G project from foreign investors (the government had less control over the KII-P, since, as a commercial network, it was open to foreign investors). The KII project, thus, was the Korean government's most significant response to a series of global pressures such as the multilateral and bilateral trade negotiations of the 1990s (Figure 3.4 depicts global events and corresponding local adjustments since the late 1980s).

The first threat to the Korean telecom industry came with the trade sanctions imposed by the US Trade Representative (USTR) (Hyun & Lent, 1999).[11] The USTR designated Korea as a priority foreign country (PFC) in 1989, based on Section 1377 of the US Omnibus Trade and Competitiveness Act of 1988. That means the USTR would treat Korean telecom market as being in violation of a trade agreement under the Act, for which retaliation with trade sanctions was mandatory. The conflict centered on the anticompetitive practices of Korean telecom equipment and services; after ten rounds of bilateral negotiations between the US and Korea from 1989 to 1992, the Korean government agreed to lift investment restrictions on US value-added network businesses, beginning in 1994, and to open government procurement bidding at the level of the General Agreement on Tariffs and Trade (Hyun & Lent, 1999). During negotiations with

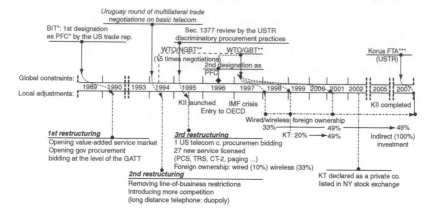

Figure 3.4 The Korean telecom market: global constraints and local adjustment (source: adopted from Frank [2007], Kim [2003, June], Hyun & Lent [1999], Lee & Jung [1998, November], and Cho *et al.* [1996]).

Notes
* Bilateral Investment Treaty (BIT) between the US and South Korea.
* Priority foreign country (PFC) applied by the US Section 1377 of the Omnibus Trade and Competitiveness Act of 1988.
** World Trade Organisation (WTO) Negotiating Group on Basic Telecommunications (NGBT/GBT).
*** Korea vs US Free Trade Agreement (KORUS FTA).

the USTR, the Korean government, in the July of 1990, announced the first telecom reform plan.

The government introduced Data Communications (Dacom)[12] as a second service provider into the international voice telephony market, previously served by KT as the incumbent and common carrier, and initiated competition in the radio paging market, which would be operated by SK Telecom and eleven local service providers. This reform aimed to enhance the competitiveness of the domestic telecom carriers by creating a limited competitive market. Further, as a result of negotiations with the USTR, the government agreed to abolish major regulations for the value-added service market, and partially lifted market entry barriers to the foreign investors.[13]

Since the early 1990s, another global pressure toward telecom liberalization stemmed from multilateral negotiations, such as the Uruguay Round and the WTO Agreement on Basic Telecommunication Services. The Uruguay Round of multilateral trade negotiations for the first time recognized services, especially telecom services, as an important item on the agenda of liberalization based on cross-border trade (Blouin, 2000). Through the Uruguay Round negotiations, the General Agreement for Trade in Services (GATS) was created in 1994, in order to promote the borderless flow of data in a new age of digital capitalism. At the end of the Uruguay Round in the May of the same year, to realize the GATS framework for telecom services through a more systematic regulatory power, the

Negotiation Group on Basic Telecommunications (NGBT) was created under the auspices of the WTO; this was extended in 1996 as the GBT. The long WTO/ GBT negotiations lasted until 1997, by which time 72 member states had finally agreed to open their basic telecom markets to foreign competition from February 1998 onward. The WTO/GBT agreements included specific commitments regarding market access and national treatment of foreign telecom service providers, as set out in the WTO agreement's regulatory codes, termed the Reference Paper. The Reference Paper aimed to further the actual market access of foreign investors, and to weaken the incumbents' control of local telecom networks (Blouin, 2000).[14] The WTO agreements ultimately brought basic telecommunications under an "internationally accepted enforcement mechanism" (Drake & Noam, 1997: 808). The WTO became a convenient forum through which the US-led foreign telecom carriers, who looked to foreign markets to create new business opportunities, legitimized a removal of major barriers to their entry into local telecom markets through a consensus about free trade (Cowhey & Klimenko, 2000).

To obtain membership in the OECD, the Korean government had to accept a wave of competition and liberalization of the telecom market during the early and mid-1990s, mainly forced by the WTO negotiations (Cho *et al.*, 1996). In June 1994, the government announced a second reform program to introduce more competition into national market. The reform plans included lifting the line-of-business restriction on wire-line and wireless service providers, creating one category of network service providers; introducing Dacom into the long-distance telephony market of KT monopoly; creating a duopolistic competition system in the mobile phone market between SK Telecom and Shinsegi Telecom; and allowing up to 33.3 percent of foreign ownership in the wireless service market. Nevertheless, the government was still hesitant to introduce full-blown liberalization in the national telecom market, and thus it authorized duopolistic competition in long-distance telephony, and a foreign ownership ceiling of only ten percent for telephone service.

In 1995, the USTR once again cited Korea's "discriminatory procurement practices," and the government was forced to allow one major US telecom company to bid in the 1995 procurement cycle (Hyun & Lent, 1999). Confronting the rise both of US pressures to liberalize and of a WTO-led new world order, the Korean government finally set forth a third reform plan in order to further open the telecom market. Unlike the two previous reform programs, the third reform plan was unanticipated and was carried out in a covert manner (Cho *et al.*, 1996). The third reform's timing—in 1995, three years ahead of the full-scale market opening required by the WTO pact—suggested the government's desire to minimize the impact of full-blown competition. The third telecom reform plan licensed 27 new service providers across seven service areas, including new types of telecom services such as PCS, TRS, CT-2, and wireless data communications (Hong, 1998), and also aimed to provide licensing rights for new, profitable IT services, both for potential entrants represented by the *Chaebols* and for national incumbents such as KT and Dacom. In addition, the third reform plan induced the private sector to join the KII project by offering the domestic incumbents special service licenses for services such as PCS, as well as by sponsoring the incumbents through seed money to build the nationwide fiber optic lines (Cho *et al.*, 1996).

In 1996, the USTR once again designated Korea as a PFC. The Korean government reacted strongly against the USTR, pointing out that Korea's trade deficit in the telecom equipment sector had increased since 1993, and in fact had reached a deficit of US$403 million by 1995 (Hyun & Lent, 1999). The US finally withdrew the PFC case without an agreement, and instead settled on a compromise within the boundary of the WTO/GBT agreements. From 1997 onward, pursuant to the WTO pact, the Korean government once again lifted the foreign ownership ceiling, this time to 49 percent in both wired and wireless services, and allowed the Korean company Hanaro to enter the local telephone service market, in which KT had been previously the dominant service provider (Tcha *et al.*, 2000). The Korean economic crisis of 1997 accelerated the government's liberalization of the national telecom market. The International Monetary Fund (IMF), through its bailout program after the 1997 crisis, urged the government to eliminate foreign ownership restraints in all areas. Under the pressure of the IMF bailout program and the WTO/GBT agreements, the government raised KT's foreign ownership ceiling to 33 percent in 1999 and to 49 percent in 2002, and completed the privatization of KT by 2002 (Jin, 2006).

Figure 3.5 shows the degree to which the WTO/GBT agreements have forced the government to increase the foreign ownership ceiling in the national telecom sector. Since the enactment of the WTO pact in 1998, foreign ownership has gradually increased, and during the period from 2003 to 2006 it reached the government's ceiling of 49 percent.

In the mid-1990s, therefore, knowing that the WTO pact would come into effect in 1998, the Korean government could foresee the difficulty of launching state-led IT policies once foreign investors dominated the national telecom market.[15] One could predict that foreign capital flooding into the telecom sector of a developing country would create a cascade of negative effects, such as an outflow of locally created profits, the pursuit of short-term profits, apathy to new IT-facility reinvestments derived from capital outflow, the destabilization of capital composition by international speculative capital, the destabilization of labor conditions, and potential national security problems arising from foreign ownership of basic infrastructure, as well as foreign capital's inertia to state-led IT projects such as the KII.[16] The KII project, which necessitated the collaboration of the private sector, was therefore an urgent task that the government had to complete before full-blown liberalization arrived. Pressure from the US and the WTO thus exerted an indirect but powerful influence on the KII project.

Escape from dependency through R&D: the broken dream

In the mid-1980s, Korea's telephony system had relied exclusively on costly telecom switches from foreign manufacturers. The three major "old" network

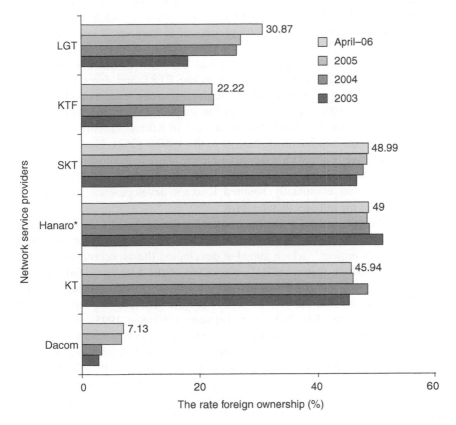

Figure 3.5 Foreign ownership in Korea's major network service providers since the global telecom liberalization (source: data from KERI [2007], MIC [2005, December], and Yahoo Finance [2006]).

Note
* The largest foreign shareholder of Hanaro Telecom was the AIG-Newbridge-TVG consortium, which owned 39% of the entire stock and thus had a controlling interest up until 2008, when the AIG consortium sold its stock to SKT.

equipment manufacturers—Alcatel (France), Lucent Technologies (USA), and Nortel (Canada)—then controlled almost half of the world telecom equipment market share.[17] To secure its own core telecom technology, the Korean government successfully developed a digital switching system called the Time-Division Exchange (TDX) through a ten-year state-led R&D project launched in 1986, and by 1990 the proportion of TDX switches within Korea had risen to 47.8 percent (Kim, 1993). For the Korean procurement market, the TDX switch became a shield providing technological independence from the transnational telecom conglomerates (Hyun & Lent, 1999). By the end of 1997, Korea had exported 3.7 million TDX lines to 26 countries, worth more than US$800 million (Lee & Jung, 1998). By 2003, KT, as the common carrier, was able to replace

76 percent of imported switches with domestically produced ones (Mani, 2007: 271). Korea thus became the tenth nation in the world to develop and export its own telephony switching system. The process of technological innovation that created the TDX switch has become the prototype of Korea's developmental mechanism.[18] This successful mechanism was based on structural cooperation between specialized R&D institutes, such as the ETRI, and domestic telecom manufacturers, such as Samsung and LG, under the strong leadership of the government. Castells (2000b) points out that "an emphasis on science and technology, and the upgrading of products and process in Korean industry, have been the obsession of the South Korean state since the 1960s" (252). This "obsession" is in fact indicative of the state's desire to escape being technologically dependent upon the advanced countries and their economic mechanisms. The desire to be independent has continually haunted Korea's developmental mechanisms since the time of the military dictatorships.

The collaborative model's success in creating the TDX led to its application to the next project on the government's agenda, the High Advanced Nation (HAN)/B-ISDN project,[19] which aimed at developing the asynchronous transfer mode (ATM) switch, then a critical component of the high-speed information network.[20] The government invested US$856 million in this project between 1992 and 1998. In fact, the HAN/B-ISDN project provided the technological basis for building the KII. Moreover, between 1991 and 1995—prior to the launch of the KII project—Korea had completed the development of optical transmission systems at the 155–565 Mbps and 2.5 Gbps levels, and between 1988 and 1994, the mainframe computers TiCOM I, II, and III. With the successful completion of the HAN/B-ISBN project, the government expected to improve Korea's telecom technologies up to the G-7 level, to create new telecom industries, and to construct a national backbone network.

The ATM switching technology was an advance on the TDX switch, both of which were heavily supported by the government's concessionary financing (Ingelbrecht, 1995; Lee & Jung, 1998). The government forecast the economic benefits of developing the ATM switching technology. First, the basic goal of the R&D investment was to escape technological dependency on foreign telecom equipment. As the national telecom service and equipment market was about US$60 billion in 1995, developing core technology was critical to protecting the national telecom market from the dominance of the foreign telecom industry. Second, the ATM switch, like the TDX switch, was anticipated to have spillover effects on the economy through its application to the KII project (Tcha *et al.*, 2000). Third, as with the TDX, the R&D collaboration on the ATM technology was effective in speeding up the circuit from investment to application. The government—specifically, the MIC—invested the funds, the ETRI was responsible for developing the TDX, the four major domestic telecom equipment manufacturers—Samsung, LG, Daewoo, and Hanhwa—produced the switches, and the wire-line incumbents—KT and Dacom—installed them in the process of building the backbone network. As an official at the National Information Society Agency commented,

In 1986, Korea entered into the age of universal service in landline telephony. At that time, the foreign-produced telecom equipment entirely dominated the national market. With the goal of promoting the domestic telecom equipment market, the government developed the first TDX switch by assigning enormous public funds to KT, then a state-owned company, and then KT assigned the R&D responsibility to the ETRI. The ETRI transferred the tested TDX technology over to Samsung and LG, both of which were involved in producing the TDX switch. The R&D collaboration in the TDX switch has historical continuity with the process used for developing the ATM for the optical transmission network.[21]

Due to the HAN/B-ISDN project developed by the ETRI, the domestic telecom manufacturers began producing ATM switches in 1996, and significantly increased their production rate in 2001 (phase three of the KII project) so that they accounted for almost 75 percent of public switching production in Korea (Mani, 2007). Most of the ATM equipment was used for building the KII rather than for export. The TDX was highly profitable, since an investment of US$133 million in the R&D produced total sales of US$6.3 billion, whereas the ATM switching system was relatively unprofitable, since an investment of US$200 million in its R&D led to total sales of only US$250 million. This result was dissatisfying, because the government was unable to make the ATM technology competitive in the foreign market, or to escape technological dependency on the transnational telecom conglomerates. An NIA official observed that, in contrast to the commercial success of the TDX switch,

> The ATM switch was limited to domestic consumption, and thus the [commercial] application was negligible. ... At that time, Korea was focused very one-sidedly on the development of the ATM switch, and, as a result, turned a blind eye to the [Internet-based] router equipment used for VoIP.[22]

Another NIA official was even more pessimistic:

> While the information infrastructure enhanced the citizens' access right [to digital information], the project to develop the core technology, the ATM switch, was an unsatisfactory policy to some degree. Because of the expansion of the Internet since the mid-90s, the dominance of the established telecom equipment manufacturers such as Lucent and other major foreign conglomerates has gradually collapsed, and the IP router equipment manufacturers led by Cisco have taken a lead in the world market. The new paradigm was unforeseen by our government. Under the present conditions of market control by foreign router equipment, the government terminated or downscaled R&D policy plans to develop core technology for the backbone network. At present, Cisco's advanced telecom equipment is completely dominant in the market. Meanwhile, Korea has developed only low-tech access equipment connecting a telephone base unit to subscribers.[23]

The director of the Presidential Advisory Council on Science and Technology, which was directly involved in the KII project from 1997 to 2000, also pointed out that "the Korean policymakers could hardly foresee the Internet architecture at that time [in the early 1990s] and thus regarded the ATM as the most advanced network switching technology."[24] Since 2002, however, the national telecom companies have "ceased to produce and install the ATM switch and have replaced many of the ATM switches with foreign IP-based router equipment."[25] Interestingly, a manager of KT's Network Engineering Department notes the WTO pact as a factor in the failure of the ATM technology:

> The opening of national telecom market [by the WTO pact] contributed greatly to giant foreign companies like Cisco entering into the Korean market and replacing our own ATM technology with the IP-based technology. This openness of the domestic market has resulted in it being overwhelmed by foreign advanced technology. … If Cisco had not existed at that time, Korea might have been able to develop the ATM as the core technology for major parts of the telecom equipment market.[26]

The story of the ATM highlights two problems: first, the shortcomings of the state-led R&D policy plans, in which the technocrats tried to set out a broad picture of development and technological innovation at the very beginning and did not build in enough flexibility to deal with technological shifts that may occur over a decade-long project;[27] thus the plans ended with a "broken dream" when the ATM technology was overtaken by the IP-based router. Second, the ATM story points out the difficulties that developing countries will always have in attempting to catch up to advanced ones, due to the head start the advanced countries inevitably possess.

Dialectics of external-internal constraints on the KII project

> [E]xternal causes are the condition of change and internal causes are the basis of change, and [...] external causes become operative through internal causes. In a suitable temperature an egg changes into a chicken, but no temperature can change a stone into a chicken, because each has a different basis.
>
> (Mao, "On Contradiction," [1937] 2007)

Although it has become a worn-out inscription on the gravestone of the demolished socialist systems of the last century, Mao's remark on the dialectics of external–internal causes surrounding the nation-state offers hints for untangling the external and internal constraints that conditioned the KII project. First, in regard to development of the national infrastructure by the civilian governments, this chapter has shown that the government launched the KII project under the "hegemonic" influence of IT policy plans elsewhere in the early 1990s, such as the US-led NII and GII initiatives. Even though the NII was strictly a domestic

IT initiative in the US, and not even a true policy, its effect on Korean telecom policies was powerful in both "symbolic" and "real" senses; in fact, the NII was seen as the ideal model for the future economy, a path for the Korean government to overcome economic recessions of the early 1990s. In addition, however, the MIC needed to respond to President Kim's rhetoric of globalization by setting forth an IT-driven policy plan, to catch up to the advanced countries' push to create the information superhighway. The government-led KII project was also in historical continuity with the series of economic industrialization plans under the military governments, as seen in the developmental strategies of the national infrastructure in each era, for the purpose of boosting national economies (see Chapter 2). The "economic miracle" created by these state-led industrial plans motivated the civilian government to seek to revive its economy, through an IT policy plan which emulated those of the advanced countries. From this perspective, "internal causes," such as the robust leadership of the government, were stronger than "external causes," such as the advanced countries' IT plans, which merely served as a model for Korea's efforts.

Second, it is clear that the US-led WTO agreements directly triggered the structural adjustments in the national telecom market. Meanwhile, by granting the licenses of the special telecom services under the third reform plan, the government motivated the incumbents KT and Dacom to become involved in launching the KII project, which itself became a growth engine for those companies, especially Dacom (see Chapter 4). To weaken the impact of foreign investment, the KII project was timed to launch prior to the advent of the full-blown opening of the national telecom market. The government wanted to protect the KII project from the rush of foreign investors, who tended to be uncooperative with state-led IT plans. In this case, however, the "external causes as the condition of change," represented by the US-led WTO pact and the inflows of foreign investment generated by it, were stronger than the national goal of protecting the telecom economy, even though Korea has successfully launched a digital phase of the national economy, as was its goal, with the KII.

Third, in addition to these implicit and explicit external constraints, there was the government's own desire to escape technological dependency on outsiders through its R&D project for the ATM switch system. Despite the success in employing the technology to build the KII, the HAN/B-ISDN project ultimately failed to accomplish all that the government had hoped. The broken dream of independence through innovation in the high-tech industry revealed not only the myopic zeal of the technocrats, but also the overwhelming power of the foreign telecom equipment manufacturers in core technology. Despite the massive R&D expenditure—Korea ranked first in R&D expenditure among the developing countries from 1996 to 2002, allocating 2.5 percent of its GDP to R&D (World Bank, 2005)—the government has succeeded only in catching up in low- and mid-tech telecom sectors. Korea's "internal causes as the basis of change" were robust, but they were ultimately trumped by the accumulated wealth, power, and technological capital of the advanced countries, and by technological change that made ATM switches outmoded.

Between the dialectic mechanisms of global pressures and national aspirations, the Korean government functioned in several roles. With its promotion of structural adjustments, it acted as a *mediator* between the homogenizing power of liberalization and the protection of the local telecom market. By providing incentives for the private sector, such as sponsoring seed money and new telecom licenses, it acted as an *initiator* of change and innovation. Overall, it acted as a *leader*, driving the KII project forward by enticing and persuading the participation of the various stakeholders. The KII project is thus the manifestation of a unique mixture of national sovereignty and foreign influences (see Figure 3.6). Although the government was forced to accept the terms of the global hegemonic order, it laid the foundation for a "second-stage catching-up" system (Chang, 2006), following the precedent of late-industrialization under the military regimes. To put it another way, when heated to "a suitable temperature" by the dynamics of the early 1990s' external constraints and internal desires, "an egg finally changed into a chicken"—a chicken that found itself trapped in the snares of the global network of Empire.

This chapter focused on the dynamics of external–internal factors that conditioned the KII project; the next chapter examines the Korean-style "second-stage catching-up" model, which enabled the launch of the KII project through the state's symbiosis with the *Chaebols*, Korea's powerful domestic conglomerates.

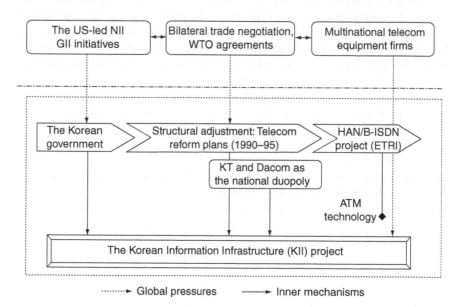

Figure 3.6 The dynamics of the global–local nexus surrounding the KII project (source: author's diagram).

4 The state–business symbiosis in Korea's broadband infrastructure plan

[S]tate power reflects the prevailing balance of forces as this is institutionally mediated through the state apparatus with its structurally inscribed strategic selectivity.

(Jessop, 2002: 40)

[T]he State really does exhibit a peculiar material framework that can by no means be reduced to mere political domination. The state apparatus—that special and hence formidable something—is not exhausted in state power. Rather political domination is itself inscribed in the institutional materiality of the State. ... [T]he basis of the material framework of power and the State has to be sought in the relations of production and social division of labor.

(Poulantzas, [1978] 2000: 14)

Outline of the chapter

In contrast to the private sector development of the national backbone network exemplified by the US information superhighway initiative in the early 1990s, the Korean government was at the forefront of directing the Korean Information Infrastructure (KII) project, which was aimed at building a nationwide broadband backbone network. This chapter surveys how the "developmental state" model—a term referring to the centralized economic development of the East Asian states—was employed in South Korea by the authoritarian state under the military regimes. It then looks at how the developmental mechanism of Korea during the period of the KII project was challenged by contextual factors, such as market liberalization, the growth of the domestic conglomerates, and the social democratization that had occurred since the mid-1980s, and which led to the transition from military to civilian governments in the early 1990s. This chapter then shows how in the KII project, the state, rather than asserting its dominance over business entities, served primarily to mediate conflicts between the private sector and the relevant public agencies. To describe the close state–capital linkages in the KII project, this study focuses on the government's financial investment system for enticing the private sector to install the infrastructure, the neatly coordinated policy networks between the public and private entities, and the policy discourses by which the government achieved a national consensus on IT-driven economic development. Theoretically, this chapter aims to critically read the developmental state theories which have failed to perceive the dark side of the symbiosis between the state and the *Chaebols*. Further, by perceiving the state as situated within class and society (the state-in-society approach), this chapter examines the evolutionary phases of the state's power from the military regimes to the civilian governments. This evolution was influenced chiefly by two factors: the emergence of Korean civil society and the *Chaebols'* growth in the market.

A final flowering of the developmental state

From the late 1980s onward, the Korean government had to rapidly transform its developmental mechanisms in response to external pressures, such as the WTO Agreements and the US–Korea bilateral trade negotiations. It also had to respond to internal ones, such as the mass protests against the authoritarian state since 1987, the growth in power of the elite *Chaebols*, and the decline of the foreign market due to Korea's export-oriented manufacturing industry. Driven by the global–local dynamics, the "strong state" model in Korea has gradually withered and been replaced by the "flexible state" or "market-driven state."

The Korean Information Infrastructure (KII) project was designed during this decline in the power of the state. Imitating the US National Information Initiative (NII), the KII's main goal was to interconnect the nation through a high-speed broadband network, and eventually to promote IT productivity in the private sector and to create a larger job market through this network. In contrast to American NII initiative, which was led by the private sector, in Korea the government took the leading role in guiding the KII, from start to finish. Through the KII project, the three major stakeholders—the state, the national telecom duopoly (KT and Dacom), and the *Chaebols*—have become deeply interpenetrated, by means of state financial support, organizational collaboration, and a hegemonic consensus manufactured by the government's IT-related rhetoric. The KII project represents a newer developmental state model, which is characterized more by the collaborative ties between the state and the private sector than the older model of the state's dominance over the private sector. Inheriting the legacy of the old developmental state, the KII project was a final example of the state's ability to launch, guide, and complete a major national IT policy initiative—final because, as will be evident by the end of this chapter, the state no longer has the power to intervene in the market in the same way it once did.

This study, therefore, regards the KII project as an example of an evolving phase of the developmental state model. To investigate the symbiotic relationship between the state and the private sector in the KII project, this chapter first explores the scholarly literature based on the developmental state theories that have described the patterns of such collaborative ties. It then focuses on the prior-investment system led by the government, the policy consultation bodies created for the project between the state and the telecom incumbents, and the government's IT policy rhetoric for creating a hegemonic consensus. This chapter then critiques the logic of inclusion/exclusion in the KII project by evaluating the degree to which the project had a transparent and consultative policy setting that included other stakeholders, such as the public and the small- and middle-sized firms. It then concludes that the denser the network of state– business alliances or linkages becomes, the more citizens are excluded from the decision-making processes.

As to methodology, this chapter uses data from in-depth interviews with gov- ernment officials from the Ministry of Information and Communication (MIC), the National Computerization Agency (NCA—now the National Information Society Agency [NIA]), and the telecom companies KT and Dacom. It also ref- erences official documents relating to the project, published by the MIC and the NCA, that contain organizational charts and describe the major stakeholders' relationships, and the changes in their policy networks, based on the shifts in specific policy goals.

The transformative phases of the developmental state in Korea

The era of economic growth through dictatorship

In modern Korea, the concept of the developmental state arose under the first military regime (1963–79), that of Cheong-hee Park, who came to power by coup d'état. Park achieved rapid economic growth by upgrading the import- substitution economies[1] of the Syngman Rhee (1948–60) and Po Sun Yun (1960–62) administrations, which were largely dependent on US aid, to export- oriented economies through the state–bank–*Chaebol* nexus. Park's regime is commonly described as *kaebal-dokjae*, which means "economic growth through dictatorship." During the Park regime, government–business relationships were formed under the "overall guidance of a pilot planning agency" (Johnson, 1987: 145), such as the Economic Planning Board (EPB), which set forth a socialist- style national plan for industrialization.

Throughout the nation, the Park regime propagated the motto, "Export is the only way to survive!" To accomplish this agenda, Park created five key govern- ment planning bodies to direct the nation's economic activity: the EPB, which reinforced its control over the economy through the management of the national budget and foreign borrowing; the President's Economic Secretariat, which exer- cised considerable influence over economic decision-making up through the Doo-hwan Chun administration (1980–88); the Ministry of Trade and Industry, which was crucial to implementing economic policy; the Ministry of Finance, which was responsible for regulating and supervising all domestic and foreign financial institutions operating in the country; and the Ministry of Construction, which developed an aggressive policy program of infrastructure expansion. In addition, to promote its export-oriented growth policy, the Park administration encouraged the private sector to launch quasi-governmental trade organizations, such as the Korea Trade Promotion Agency and the Korea Foreign Traders' Association (Hart-Landsberg, 1993).

Relying on these governmental bodies and quasi-governmental organizations, the Park administration launched the first Five-Year Economic Development Plan (1962–66), which was the first of six successive Five-Year EDPs set forth between 1962 and 1991. The basic objective of these EDPs was to industrialize the domestic economy and maximize economic growth through export.[2] According to a national economic index released by the Bank of Korea in 1991, due to Park's growth policy, heavy industry in manufacturing and exports grew rapidly until, by the late 1970s, it occupied nearly 50 percent of the Korean economic structure, and 65 percent by 1991.

The Park administration's export-oriented industrial policy promoted the emergence of the *Chaebols* in the early 1970s. To expand the heavy and chemical industries (such as steel and iron, nonferrous metal, machinery, shipbuilding, and petrochemical refineries), the government supported selected large domestic corporations such as Hyundai, Samsung, Daewoo,[3] Lucky Goldstar (LG), Ssangyong, and SunKyong. These top six corporations (listed in descending order of size) showed an average annual capital growth rate of more than 30 percent during the period from 1971 to 1983 (Koo & Kim, 2005). These firms' share in GDP reached 17.1 percent in 1978, up from 9.8 percent in 1973, and by 1978 the top 46 *Chaebols* were responsible for nearly 60 percent of the value creation in manufacturing (SaKong, 1993). The military regime's inability to control the *Chaebols'* growth led to endemic overcapacity in automobile production: Hyundai Motors' passenger car production operated at 52 percent of the market capacity in 1969 and at 61.8 percent by 1979, when Kia and Daewoo operated at 55.4 percent and 24.6 percent capacity, respectively (Kang, 2006). The government expanded the highways to boost domestic market demand as an answer to the overcapacity of *Chaebols* such as Hyundai, Kia, and Daewoo. The crony capitalism between the state and the *Chaebols* since the time of the Park administration has became typical in the rent-seeking relationships that tie the two together, a relationship in which political funds are traded for economic favors. The military junta also made it clear that since they held the banks in their hands, it was easy for them to regulate the *Chaebols*. The military authoritarianism of the Park regime became the impetus to initiate the Korean-style "developmental state" model through the so-called "state–bank–*Chaebol* nexus."

Industrial modernization, in combination with Park's economic interventionism, deeply wounded both urban and rural life in Korea. For instance, in the metropolitan areas, concrete multi-dwelling units and high-rise apartment complexes began replacing green zones, which inflated the price of housing rapidly by unleashing speculation in the market.[4] At the same time, in rural areas from 1970 onward, the *Saemaul Undong* ("new community movement") swept across farming villages in the name of modernizing and enhancing the lives of farmers. The village restructuring project, initiated by the military junta, rapidly "modernized" rural areas through village relocation and redevelopment, up into the mid-1980s. What the regime actually contributed to the movement was 800 free bags of cement in 1971 and 1972,[5] along with an indoctrination of villagers with ascetic ideals such as diligence, austerity, thrift, and mutual cooperation. As a typical side effect of industrialization, a rural exodus caused massive depopulation, leaving households behind in the villages. The *Saemaul Undong* was, in fact, accomplished by the labor of elderly villagers and by their own financial contributions, rather than by the government's investment. For this project, the farmers were responsible for 70 to 80 percent of the total amount of financial investment between 1972 and 1978 (Moon, 1991), and the average debt per farm household was approximately US$3,500 by 1988 (Lie, 2006). Every household in a rural area has been in debt since then, still paying the price for obtaining modern amenities such as electricity, telephony, and cement-roofed housing.

The *Saemaul Undong* did contribute to renovating the poor conditions of land use in such aspects as irrigation, farm feeder roads, small bridges, and farm equipment. In urban areas, high-rise apartments lowered the cost of installing electric and telephone lines, and electrical and communication infrastructure was expanded in both urban and rural areas under the Park regime. Telephone facilities were expanded from 120,000 lines in 1961 to 1.7 million nationwide in 1977 (Kim, 1993). As a result of the housing renewal project, by 1982, rural electrification and the installation of a telephone system were almost completed (Moon, 1991). Nevertheless, the modernization programs directed by the military junta destroyed the traditional and nature-friendly living environment in South Korea. Under the rubric of "sanitation," roads paved in concrete or mortar and houses roofed in slate or cement replaced the "pre-modern" country lanes and traditional grey straw-thatched roofs of farmhouses, leaving the countryside faded and desolate. As the expansion of electric and communication networks modernized the living conditions of villagers, it also created new consumer demand for home appliances such as TV sets, refrigerators, electric cookers, and electric irons, as well as an increase of telephony subscription in rural areas. The rural demand played a significant role in increasing the consumption of electric products supplied by *Chaebols* such as Samsung, Daewoo and LG, which from the early 1980s onward succeeded in launching electric home appliance businesses not only domestically but also internationally, well beyond their successes in the heavy, chemical, and shipbuilding industries during the 1970s.

Nevertheless, up into the 1980s and even the early 1990s, the Korean economy was based on a labor-intensive economy, far behind the technology-intensive economies of the advanced countries. As shown in Table 4.1, despite Park's industrial modernization project, high-tech products accounted for less than 3

Table 4.1 Export shares of technology-intensive products (%)

Country	1965	1975	1984
France	7.3	8.4	7.7
Germany	16.9	16.8	14.5
Japan	7.3	11.6	20.2
Korea	**0.0**	**0.5**	**2.9**
United States	27.5	24.5	25.2

Source: Leipziger & Petri (1993: 11).

percent of Korea's total exports in the mid-1980s. The Park administration thus became an archetype of the developmental state, and successfully accomplished industrial modernization in the shortest time. The Park regime was based on a strong repressive state, the state's dominance over the private sector, and growth-oriented interventionism involving labor exploitation and suppression.[6]

As regards of the control of labor, for instance, the Park regime established a "ghost" national labor union, the so-called Federation of Korea Trade Unions, in order to moderate local union demands, prohibit any potential labor disputes, and discipline recalcitrant workers (Han & Ling, 1998). Further, comparisons of the Gini coefficient[7] of inequality for income, between 1965 and 2010 in Figure 4.1, can be viewed with skepticism. The Gini coefficient value of over .40 signifies that income inequality is very significant nationwide, and Figure 4.1 shows that, during the period of industrial modernization under the Park regime, the Gini values reached more than .40, even though it has fallen below .40 (average of .35) since the early 1990s. Nevertheless, Figure 4.1 shows the Gini values have gradually increased under the civilian governments, from 1992 onward.

This income inequality level of the Gini coefficient around .35 is a phenomenon that prevails in most capitalist societies. Nevertheless, Korea shows Gini coefficient values in real assets (.71), including housing and gross personal wealth, are more than double that of income (.31) as of 2009 (Statistics Korea, 2011). These high indicators of inequality reveal the cumulative effects of developmentalism through a number of the national construction and urban planning projects since the Park regime.

Park was assassinated in 1979 by his intelligence chief, but the military-backed interventionism in the market under the administration of General

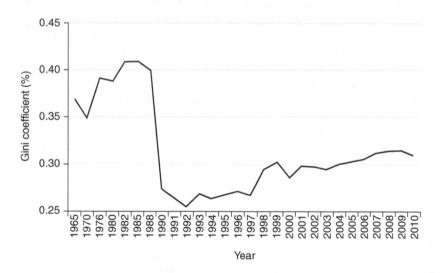

Figure 4.1 Income inequality in Korea, 1965–2010 (source: Data from Leipziger *et al.* [1992] from 1965 to 1988, and from Statistics Korea [2011] from 1990 onward).

Doo-hwan Chun, who once again came to power in a military coup, was extensive until the 1987 pro-democracy movement forced him to introduce a direct presidential voting system. After taking power, Chun appointed technocrats who had earned doctoral degrees in economics in the US and were known as followers of the neo-liberal Milton Friedman (Kim, 1999). This hardly means, however, that the Chun administration whole-heartedly embraced laissez-faire economics. Despite being somewhat influenced by the global trend of neo-liberalism, promoted from the early 1980s onwards by Reagan in the US and by Thatcher in Britain, Chun still intervened directly in the market.

Chun always saw Cheong-hee Park as his role model, and his regime was the embodiment of the strong, repressive state. For instance, under the Chun administration, "labor-management councils" were mandated for all enterprises, effectively destroying autonomous union activities (Han & Ling, 1998). Korean corporations' strategies to weaken workers' militant tempers have ranged the gamut from dirty tricks such as detention, verbal abuse, and demotion all the way to the use of the latest computerized surveillance devices. By dividing workers into spatial, gender, educational, and occupational strata, both the government and the private sector have joined to manage those "who should be trained like lambs," according to a Confucian managerial ideology (Lie, 2006). Furthermore, in the December of 1980, to silence voices critical of his regime, Chun enacted the Basic Press Act[8] and forcibly conducted the *eonron-tongpaehap*, the "compulsory reform of the media." Chun commanded KBS, the state-owned broadcaster, to absorb the TBC television network, which was owned by Samsung Corp. He also ordered the pro-government newspaper, *Kyonghyang Shinmun*, to absorb *Shin-A Ilbo*, a daily newspaper, and forced at least six local newspapers to close their business permanently. Over 700 journalists were dismissed from their jobs, and the remaining newspapers were subjected to a high degree of government control (Billet, 1990). As another example of his use of state power against the *Chaebols*, in 1985 Chun dismantled the seventh largest conglomerate in the nation, the Kookjae group, which had around 200 subsidiaries at that time, merely because it refused to donate "political funds" (protection money, in essence). This example shows that the regime had the power to punish the *Chaebols* for the slightest disobedience, and also illustrates the rent-seeking relations between the ruling junta and the business elites.

In the changing political climate brought about by the democratization movement of 1987, the public began to critique the symbiosis between the government and the *Chaebols*. The domestic conglomerates themselves began to demand a market economy free from the government's direct intervention (Ko, 2001). Due to the rapid growth of the *Chaebols* and the rising political pressure from below, the government could not wield absolute power over the private sector any more. During the presidency of Tae-Woo Noh (1988–93), Chun's designated successor, the technocrats chose a *via media* approach between direct interventionism and deregulation, one in which the *Chaebols* were granted lucrative business licenses, special loans and other financial benefits from government agencies, and contracts to build the national infrastructure to promote market efficiencies. For instance, in 1992 the Noh administration licensed SK (Sun-kyong), the sixth largest *Chaebol* in the nation, as the cellular phone provider over the other, more competitive bidders, because the son of SK's owner was married to President Noh's daughter (Ko, 2001). Although the license was ulti-mately withdrawn due to the public's growing antipathy, the case was a typical example of Korea's crony capitalism.

The era of big capital's ascendancy over the state

Throughout the period of rapid IT growth based on state-led IT policies and ini-tiatives, the civilian governments have continued, and in some ways even expanded, a crony relationship with the *Chaebols*, which have grown since the Park's regime through the state's financial sponsorship, exclusive grants of busi-ness licenses, and selection of major actors in a newly emerging economy. Under the administration of Young-Sam Kim (1993–98), the first democratically elected president, the government endorsed the Federation of Korean Industries (FKI), an organization largely representing the *Chaebols'* interests, to select the assignees for the telecom licenses during the telecom reform of 1993. In 1995 the government allowed the *Chaebols* to enter the media and IT industry by granting them profitable new licenses for cable television services (Shim, 2002). The *Chaebols* became the largest recipients of the lucrative profits stemming from the state's permission to launch new business in the telecom and media sector.

Responding to the shift of the world economy into the digital mode of pro-duction, the *Chaebols* began to abandon exports of low and medium-low techno-logy products in order to create new sources of profit from the high-tech industry, while adjusting their activities to cooperate with the government's IT policy plans. This foray by the *Chaebols* into the new IT sector represented the creation of the so-called "e-*Chaebols*" (Chang, 2003). In the broadband Internet service market (the KII-P), KT is the national incumbent, with a 50 percent market share. LG's subsidiaries, LG Dacom and LG Powercomm, together com-prise a second ranked provider, with a market share of 14 percent, as of 2007, even though several small service providers have now entered into that market (NIA, 2007). The *Chaebols* have also extended their market dominance into the new mobile telecom service business, where they are the dominant vendors of cell phones. Moreover, technological convergence in the mobile telephony market has legitimated the deregulation of the domestic mobile telecom market, in such a way as to further extend the *Chaebol*-owned mobile network operators' dominance into other broadband communications and multimedia content serv-ices, through acquiring stocks in younger companies (see Figure 4.2). SK Telecom, a subsidiary of Sunkyong, now dominates over half of the Korean mobile telecom market, while KTF, a subsidiary of KT, has a market share of 32 percent and LG Telecom of about 17 percent. The mobile telephony market is "the goose that lays the golden eggs" for the Korean government and industrial conglomerates.

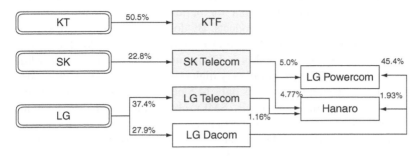

Figure 4.2 The *Chaebols'* entrance into the domestic telecom service market (Unit: Stock shares [%]) (source: Data from the companies' websites [as of December 2006]).

Note
In addition to its share possession of 4.77%, SK Telecom acquired the stock shares of 38.89% from Hanaro, and occupied its ownership in 2008.

The Korean government rapidly created a profitable new market for the *Chaebol*-owned mobile network providers. In other words, the government created the new market—or rather, they structured a new market in such a way that only the *Chaebols* could benefit from it.

Their privileged position in the domestic market enabled the *Chaebols*, especially Samsung and LG, to expand into a variety of other IT sectors, such as their global sales of mobile handsets, flat panel displays, and semiconductors. For instance, as of 2001, Korea's share of the global semiconductor market was 5.7 percent, but its market share of dynamic random access memory (DRAM) chips totaled 41.5 percent, with 27 percent going to Samsung and 14.5 percent to Hynix (formerly known as Hyundai Electronics). Samsung and Hynix were ranked first and third, respectively, among global producers of DRAM chips. As of 2000, Samsung Electronics and LG Philips LCD (a joint venture of the *Chaebol* LG and the Dutch company Philips) were ranked first and second, respectively, in the market for large-size TFT-LCD screens, with a combined market share of 32 percent (Hong *et al.*, 2004). As of February 2007, the Korean production of mobile handsets and system facilities made up almost 30 percent of the global market share and accounted for about US$17 billion of exports (among global mobile handset manufacturers, Samsung Electronics was ranked third, and LG Electronics, fifth). The export of mobile handsets alone was about ten percent of total national exports (NIA, 2007). The typically duopolistic structure of the *Chaebols* can be seen in the equipment market for broadband Internet network, where ADSL hardware and modem production is dominated by LG Electronics and Samsung (Jeon & Bae, 2007).

The state's crony relationship with the *Chaebols*, while it has produced dramatic economic growth, has also produced negative effects on many economic actors. The IT industry is capital-intensive and R&D-intensive, compared to other low and medium-low technology sectors. As with the export-oriented policies under the military regimes, the civilian government has strategically favored the large conglomerates, both for building a new economy and for enhancing the export of high-tech products. By doing so, they have put Korea's small and medium enterprises (SMEs) in IT manufacturing far behind the *Chaebols*: the employment share of SMEs in IT manufacturing is 41 percent, while their share in the non-IT sector is still very high at 77.9 percent. The value-added share of SMEs in IT manufacturing is only 14.5 percent, while it is 58.3 percent in the non-IT sector. In other words, SMEs obtain their revenues from the medium-low technology products and also have a very low level of productivity in IT manufacturing. Meanwhile, the largest five *Chaebols* contributed almost half of Korea's GDP as well as one-half of all exports in 2001 (Campbell II & Keys, 2002).

The labor situation under the civilian governments has differed little from the disciplinary control of workers under the military regime. According to a survey requested by the Joint Committee to End Surveillance of Workers (Hangil Research and Consulting, 2003), almost 90 percent out of a random sample of 207 Korean workplaces had monitored workers with a variety of surveillance devices including web log-files, email programs and computer hard drives, telephone conversation recordings, closed-circuit television (CCTV) camera systems, electronic ID cards for gate passes, and the Enterprise Resource Planning (ERP) system.[9] In this survey, Korean workers expressed increasing anxiety about the conditions of workers burdened by the installation of refined surveillance devices for labor control, and complained about such reactionary effects of surveillance as weakening the unionized actions of workers, intensifying the labor load, making job status more unstable, and increasing managers' abuse of power. As evidence of the poor labor conditions in Korea, Table 4.2 shows that, even when viewed in the context of the worldwide decline in the rate of unionization, Korea has the second lowest rate of unionization among the OECD countries from 1970 to 2008, except France, which also shows the highest bargaining power for trade unions. With regard to the bargaining power of the workers, at 14 percent Korea has the lowest rate in Table 4.2.

In the mid-1990s, the domestic *Chaebols* also expanded their scope into the global market through building subsidiaries and investing the capital. Further, the *Chaebols* borrowed low-interest foreign loans—by 1996, the average debt ratio of the 30 top conglomerates reached 450 percent—without screening by the government. The *Chaebols'* dependence on foreign financial capital accelerated the 1997 economic crisis, due to volatile foreign hedge funds, speculative capital, and international lending. Under the pressure of the WTO Agreement on Basic Telecommunications and the IMF bailout program—in which Korea obtained US$58 billion of emergency loans—the Kim Dae-Jung administration (1998–2003) privatized KT, the state-owned telecom incumbent, and fully opened the domestic banking, media, and telecom markets, among others, to foreign investors.[10]

The government's dominance over the *Chaebols* has gradually waned, while the larger *Chaebols* have accumulated even more power as the medium-sized

Table 4.2 The rate of unionization in OECD countries, 1970–2008

Country	1970	1980	1990	2000	2008	Bargaining coverage rate
Australia	44	48	40	25	19	80
Belgium	41	54	54	56	52	90
Canada	32	35	33	28	27	34
Denmark	60	79	75	74	68	69
Finland	51	69	72	76	68	95
France	22	18	10	10	8	95
Germany	32	35	31	25	19	73
Japan	35	31	25	21	18	20
S. Korea*	**13 (20)**	**15 (21)**	**17 (18.4)**	**11**	**10**	**14**
Mexico	–	–	43	18	–	n/a
Portugal	–	61	32	24	20	80+
UK	45	51	39	31	27	36
USA	27	22	15	13	12	15
OECD Average	42	47	42	34	27	60

Source: (OECD StatExtracts, 2011), OECD (2003), Visser (2003), Kong (2000: 97), and for Korea, Shin (2006, March 25), followed in parentheses by figures from the Yearbook of Labor Statistics (Ministry of Labor, 1991), which are thought to be inflated.

ones have declined or been absorbed.[11] President Moo-hyun Roh (2003–08) confessed the state was losing its power to regulate the *Chaebols* when he commented, "We have already entered into the age of big capital having the upper hand over the state" (Kim, 2005, May). The Samsung bribery scandal provides an illustration of how widespread the *Chaebols'* power may be: in January of 2008, at the insistence of civil rights groups, the Roh administration launched an investigation of Samsung centered on whether it had amassed slush funds; peddled influence by routinely bribing government officials, the media, and members of the judiciary; and engaged in shady stock deals to pass control of the group from its chairman, Kun-hee Lee, to his only son. Courageous whistleblower Yong-chul Kim, the former head of Samsung's legal affairs team, joined by members of the Catholic Priests Association for Justice, told a radio station that "the list of bribe-takers includes not just top prosecutors and ministers in the Roh administration, but also people recently nominated or mentioned as possible members of the cabinet or high-ranking staff members of the Blue House [the Korean White House]" (*Korea Times*, 2008). Lee was convicted of evading nearly US$39 million in taxes, but he received a pardon from the government (Moon, 2008; Bixler, 2010). The public, therefore, is skeptical that the "Republic of Samsung" can ever truly be brought to justice, given the extent of Samsung's power in Korean society (*Asia Sentinel*, 2008).[12] This scandal reveals that the parasitic bond between corrupt state bureaucrats and monopoly capitalists is still very much alive, even under a politically progressive administration, and that the balance of power has rapidly shifted towards the latter since the 1997 financial crisis.

Under president Myong-bak Lee's administration (2008–present), the business-friendly policies have accelerated disastrously, removing laws to limit the expansion of *Chaebols*, the maintenance of a high exchange rate to promote export, corporate tax reductions which favor only a few *Chaebols*, and paramilitary labor oppression. There have also been massive layoffs of workers and the chronic creation of precarious workers, and cutbacks in health care, public education, and core social services. While authoritarian and suppressive characteristics in the area of human rights and freedom of speech, reminiscent of the military regimes, have re-emerged, the government's neo-liberal market policies have given more economic power to the *Chaebol*s. Yong-chul Kim, the whistle-blower on Samsung in 2008, later unveiled the immoral aspects of the nation's highest ranked conglomerate in his book *Thinking Samsung* (2010), a 474-page exposé. Kim depicts the group's chair and his "vassal" executives at Samsung as bribing thieves who "lord it over" the country, the government, and the media. He also portrays the prosecutors as opportunists who are subservient to and afraid of Samsung. Even though Kim provided a list of prosecutors whom he said he had helped Samsung to bribe while he was working inside the group's headquarters, the prosecutors concluded that there was no evidence of bribery (Choe, 2010).

Most conglomerates have expanded greatly in terms of the number of subsidiaries and assets under the Lee administration. According to the Fair Trade Commission's (FTC) data as of April 2011, the number of Samsung Group's affiliates and subsidiaries has increased 32.1 percent since 2008, from 59 to 78, with its assets going up 59.9 percent to KR230.9 trillion *won* (US$213 billion), resulting mostly from the lowering of the corporate tax rate. After its inauguration, the Lee administration lowered the corporate tax rate from 25 percent to 20 percent, which is one of the lowest corporate income tax rates in the world; most of the benefits, however, went to the top ten businesses. In 2009, large businesses with profits of KR500 billion *won* (equivalent to US$400 million) or more had tax benefits of some 2.6 trillion *won* (US$2.1 billion). Meanwhile, SMEs with profits of KR500 million *won* (US$400,000) or less had only KR48 billion *won* (US$38.4 million) in tax reductions (Jung, 2011). Under the Lee administration's *Chaebol*-friendly market policies, Samsung's assets have become more than the combined assets of the second largest *Chaebol*, Hyundai Motor Group, amounting to KR126.7 trillion *won* (US$101.4 billion), and the third largest, SK Group, amounting to KR97 trillion *won* (US$77.6 billion). Samsung's asset holdings have ballooned almost 60 percent over the past three years, since President Lee took office in 2008 (Kim, 2011, April 11). In 2010, the asset values of the largest 20 *Chaebols* had increased to 83.2 percent of Korea's GDP, whereas they were half that in 2002 (Kwak, 2011). While the government sponsored fattening the pockets of the *Chaebols*, jobs, in comparison, have grown at a sluggish rate since the launch of the Lee administration, and class inequalities and social polarization have rapidly deepened. The present government's slogan of the "trickle-down effect," suggesting that the market profits of the *Chaebols* and wealthy property owners would flow down to the SMEs and low-income brackets, has turned out to be empty.

The Lee administration has launched physical infrastructure policies such as the "Four Major Rivers Restoration Project" despite the overwhelming opposition of citizens. The Lee administration has poured an astronomical amount of money into public relations for the purpose of justifying the so-called "multipurpose green growth project" and into renovating the four major rivers—the Han, the Nakdong, the Geum, and the Yeongsan—in an extremely destructive way. Despite the government's PR initiatives and its claims that the massive project will provide such benefits as water security, flood control, and ecosystem vitality, many criticize this project as simply building artificial leisure and recreation facilities, while permanently spoiling the natural riparian vegetation. The market-driven model of "renewing" previously preserved ecological areas reflects the changing mode of profitable resources in Korea-style neo-liberal capitalism—degrading the common natural heritage and landscape, and creating a new value productive chain from the privatization of the public commons.

In sum, Korea's democratic turmoil in 1987 began the momentum to weaken the absolute power the state had enjoyed since 1963, while the 1997 financial crisis under the civilian government remarkably enhanced the *Chaebols'* power through their alliance with foreign capital; once dominated by the state, it is the *Chaebols* that now dominate. In response to shifting external and internal factors, the evolving relationship between the state and the conglomerates has transformed the developmental state model from that of the strong and repressive state, through that of a limited or flexible state, to that of the market-driven state.

The state's symbiosis with the *Chaebols* signifies the retrogressive aspects of the Korean economy even in the era of the new economy. Castells (2000a: 190–205) describes the Korean *Chaebols* as far more "hierarchical, authoritarian, and patrilineal" than the Japanese *keiretsu* and the Taiwanese *guanxiqiye* networks,[13] because, in addition to being controlled by a central holding company owned by an individual and his family, the Korean *Chaebols'* rapid development was enabled by an anti-labor business climate and the denial of SMEs' entry into new markets.

The infrastructural broadband plan as a legacy of the developmental state model

The close relationship between the state and the conglomerates in Korea has often been termed *jeongkyong yuchak* ("the symbiosis of two entities"), which has a negative connotation.[14] As part of this symbiosis, the government granted moneymaking licenses to, and invested public funds in, the largest conglomerates, and in return the *Chaebols* donated large sums to political slush funds. A unique mechanism of the developmental state is to transcend simple rent-seeking links between the two dominant elites, and to transform their symbiosis into a mechanism for economic growth. Developmentalism, promoted under the slogan of national modernization, conceals such chronic problems as an unethical business culture, power elitism, cronyism, corruption, corporate suppression of labor, deep class divisions, and the public's exclusion from the decision-making process. Nevertheless, the unethical mechanisms of *jeongkyong yuchak* have been a driving force for economic growth, curbing the excessive penetration of foreign capital and enhancing the market competitiveness of domestic conglomerates.

Many scholars have explored the transformations of state–business relationships in Korea, focusing on cross-regime variations in economic development, and specifically, the shifting balance of power between the two. Analyses of Korean state–business relations include a shift "from dominance to symbiosis" (Kim, 1988); "governed interdependence" (Weiss, 1988); a "pragmatic mix of government guidance with private initiative" (Jeon, 1994); the "patron–client relation" (Nam, 1995); a shift from "the stern but stable state-directed symbiotic partnership to a more unruly and erratic partnership" (Moon, 1994); "embedded autonomy" (Evans, 1995); "public–private reciprocity" (Fields, 1997); the shift from the developmental state to the "post-developmental" or "market-driven state" (Kim, 1999; 2005); "path dependency" (Jang, 2000); the "state production of oligopolistic capitalism" (Castells, 2000b); an "eclecticism beyond orthodoxies" (Clark, 2002; Clark & Jung, 2004); a "state–*Chaebol* alliance based on a more populist social contract" (Hundt, 2005); a "transformative state in which the state acted as senior partner rather than commander-in-chief" (Cherry, 2005); and the demise of "Korea, Inc." (the state–banks–*Chaebols* complex) and the rise of "neo-liberal consensus" (the coalition of *Chaebols*, technocrats, politicians, economic experts, and NGOs) (Lim & Jang, 2006; Lee & Han, 2006).

Despite their slightly different foci and analyses, most studies note the major contextual factors weakening the state's power, such as the growing *Chaebol*-dominated economy, increasing democratization, and global pressures for liberalization. They also agree that the Korean state's *modus operandi* has changed considerably from the military regimes to the civilian governments. Some of the studies (e.g., Kim, 1999, 2005; Lim & Jang, 2006; Lee & Han, 2006) further subdivide their analyses into periods marked by such historical events as the citizens' uprising of 1987 and the IMF financial crisis of 1997. Some scholars (e.g., Jeon, 1994; Nam, 1995) describe the shifts in the state–*Chaebol* relationship as if the older relationship has been completely annulled by the new. The present study, in contrast, sees the state–business linkages as transformative and continuously evolving, while retaining embedded traces of the past.

As shown in Figure 4.3, the KII project, which extended from 1995 to 2005, was accomplished during Korea's evolution from a limited or flexible development state to a market-driven or post-development state. These phases of evolution are quite distant from the strong state model exemplified by the first two military regimes (those of Park and Chun). Initiated during the flexible state phase, the KII project involved coordinated state–business relationships, which were maintained through continuous negotiation processes carried out by a series of intermediary committees. Nevertheless, the entire project was initiated, developed, and guided by the state—a situation which would be difficult, if not impossible, to replicate in Korea's present, post-developmental state phase of

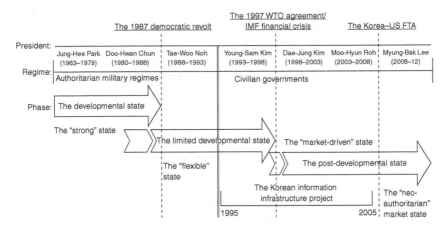

Figure 4.3 The evolving phases of the developmental state (1963–2012) and the KII
project (source: compiled by the author).

evolution. In other words, an explanation of the KII's success requires consideration of the *"Chaebol-governance* process and the political institutional arrange-
ments for the state–firm relationship based on the 'politics of reciprocal
subsidy'" (Mansell & When, 1998: 123, italics in original).

The close state–business linkages throughout the KII project

The major goal of Young-Sam Kim's administration was to shift Korea away
from its export-centered economy, which had been the major mechanism of
market productivity under the military regimes, and to search out a new source
of profits for the domestic conglomerates. Kim favored the affiliation of Korea
with the global economy and regarded the KII as a powerful engine to drive the
nation's economic structure towards the knowledge-based economy. By interconnecting government agencies and public institutions with high-speed broadband networks, he sought to upgrade the nation's infrastructure and expand its
capacities to create a new, IT-driven market. In 1994, the Kim administration
announced the broad master plan for the KII and launched the Ministry of
Information and Communication (MIC), which absorbed the major IT-related
administrative functions from other ministries. In 1995, the government also
issued the "Framework Act on Informatization Promotion" (FAIP, Act No.
4969), which included the legal provisions for conducting the KII policy plan. It
set forth the R&D goals to be met, provided the funding for the long-term IT
project, and established the top decision-making committee and its subsidiary
bodies.

The KII project has been highly praised as a successful policy experiment by
government officials, policymakers, scholars, and journalists from other countries, who focus on Korea's attainment of "broadband heaven" through vigorous

state leadership and corporate cooperation. Few, however, have examined the inner mechanisms of the KII project's success, such as the state-led funding structure, the special steering and intermediate committees, and the consensual dynamics of IT discourse. This section investigates the mechanisms that made the 11-year state-led project viable, and examines how the state–business linkages have became more flexible and less consistent since the demise of the strong, repressive state.

Taming the telecom incumbents with the carrot, not the stick

Information infrastructure projects such as the KII are typically burdensome to the private sector, and corporations are therefore usually less than enthusiastic about such plans, which involve massive, long-term investment, high risk, and uncertain returns. To involve Korean Telecom (KT) and Dacom in the KII project, the Kim administration offered a variety of enticements: preferential tax treatment, the granting of new licenses, and investment loans underwritten by the government. As one manager of KT noted, KT, the domestic telecom incumbent, "was relatively favorable to the government, which was its dominant stockholder until KT was completely privatized [in 2002]."[15] The government had also allowed Dacom to acquire licenses for international and long-distance telephony services during the national telecom restructurings of 1990 and 1994, respectively. These were initiated for the purpose of curbing the international pressure for telecom market liberalization, and Dacom had rapidly emerged as the second largest telecom company in Korea. As a result, the government was able to gain the cooperation of the two telecom incumbents without any great conflict. A deputy director of LG Dacom described the situation this way:

> The KII project was very supportive of the private partners in that the government minimized our business risk by its public investment. At that time nobody dared to invest the enormous funds for it; through the public funding, Dacom was able to leapfrog ahead by facilitating the nationwide optical networks. The contribution from public investment was highly significant.[16]

A manager of KT also agreed on the effect of the state-sponsored investment:

> It is obvious that the state-led "investment first, construction next" policy plan gave KT and Dacom the incentive to participate in the KII project without a great business risk, and also minimized the potential friction between the government and us throughout the project. In those days, KT, as the first partner in the government project, benefited from the immense state-led investment that allowed us to expand the optical networks.[17]

The "investment first, construction next" principle was the telecom companies' major incentive to join in the KII project, allowing them to minimize their investment risk and cost at the early stages of the project. KT and Dacom also regarded the huge project as a chance to upgrade their copper lines to high-speed fiber optic networks.

For the building of the backbone networks connecting the public agencies and institutions—the so-called KII-G—KT was allotted a 70 percent share and Dacom a 30 percent share. The KII-public (KII-P) was independently built as a commercial network, using the budgets of the telecom companies themselves, and the KII-testbed (KII-T), the optimal high speed R&D network, was built by a public-private partnership. For the KII-G, its most important backbone network, the government invested a total of US$6.2 billion over the three phases. At the beginning, the government, as the major stakeholder, aimed to own the backbone network directly and grant the telecom companies a 25-year lease to it. The government—specifically the MIC, as funding distributor, and the National Computerization Agency (NCA, now the National Information Society Agency), as funding manager and coordinator—also pressured the telecom operators to apply an 80 percent or 90 percent discount to the proposed online service charges for public agency subscribers in the September of 1997. As Che-Hyun Jo, the Deputy Director of Dacom and one of the key actors in the KII-G project, noted in his official interview with the NCA (2005), the discount rate requested by the government was burdensome, and the mood became very dark within the telecom companies. The sensitive issues of the KII-G network ownership and service charges triggered critical conflicts between the government and the private sector (MIC & NCA, 2006: 130). In addition, the Board of Audit and Inspection's questioning of the MIC's funding method for installing the optical lines in 1996 jeopardized the completion of the project itself (131).

This crisis at the early stages of the project (1995–97) finally caused the MIC to change the subscriber costs and ownership structure. It decided to transfer ownership of the fiber optic backbone lines to KT and Dacom, and to establish a joint public–private sector KII fund (a so-called "bilateral netting account") out of which the KII-G would be built. From this fund, the government would subsidize 40 percent of the service charge for subscribers in government agencies and public institutions. In return, the two telecom companies agreed to reimburse the joint fund a portion of their profits year by year until their government loans were paid off, and to offer a 40 percent discount rate to KII-G subscribers. As an official at the NCA, which managed the cost system between two entities, commented, the new cost mechanisms for the KII-G, enabled by the government subsidies, led to a breakthrough in the conflicts between the government and the private sector.[18] Further, since a 40 percent discount and a 40 percent government subsidy was applied to the service charges, government agencies and public institutions were able to receive broadband Internet for 20 percent of the actual cost, and institutional users grew rapidly—from 2,184 subscriber lines in 1996 to 30,137 lines in 1998 (Lee *et al.*, 2009). Once a critical mass of subscribers had been reached, the government was able to complete the KII-G phase of the project without further difficulty. The KII-G recorded the highest growth rate (795 percent) of subscribers in 1997, as compared in 1996, the first year of service, and the growth rate then stabilized to an average rate of 20 percent growth annually from 1998 to 2005. As of September 2005, 32,000 public agencies and institutions were subscribers to the KII-G (MIC & NCA, 2006).

The increase in subscribers from public institutions and agencies brought a more stable flow of profits to the telecom companies, and this, in turn, furthered the development of the KII-P, the commercial network. At this point, the government could not overtly intervene in guiding the KII-P because of external pressures brought to bear on the government. As an official of the NCA (now the NIA) described it,

> In the mid-90s, the government had no choice but to leave the KII-P's development in the hands of the private sector. Under strong global pressure to liberalize the telecom market, the government could not intervene in the market or lead the KII-P directly, but could only recommend the government's roadmap to the private sector. Otherwise, it might cause serious friction in US–Korea trade relations.[19]

Despite this, since 1997 the government has successfully stimulated private investment in the local loop and facility-based competition by introducing the so-called "cyber-building certificate program" into the KII-P. Through this certificate program, apartments and buildings were ranked according to their capacity to handle high-speed Internet. As a public official who worked for the KII project pointed out, because South Korea's population is largely located in a few large urban areas and because most residents live in large apartment buildings, the MIC's facility-based Internet promotion policy was effective in expanding the penetration of high-speed Internet service into the general public. He added that, in the early stages of this program, the certificate system also allowed construction companies to raise the mortgage price on new government-certified "Internet-ready" apartments (interview with Moon [2007, June 7]). The demand created through the indirect promotion of broadband Internet assured the telecom companies and the construction companies—the latter of which were mostly owned by the *Chaebols*—a steady stream of new customers. Further, since 2001 the Ministry of Construction and Transportation (MCT) has required that all new apartments or multi-dwelling units have broadband Internet connections (Falch, 2007; Lee & Chan-Olmsted, 2004).

Most of this study's interviewees, who were directly involved in implementing the KII project, agreed that the KII-G was the significant factor in the KII-P's development and furthered network-based economic growth. As Y. Lee, executive director of the NIA, noted,

> In the 90s, the Korean economy was competing in very few areas of the world market, such as shipbuilding and microchips; due to the KII project, it is now ranked first in the telecom service market for the first time. It would have been impossible without the construction of the KII to reach the current state where IT represents 30 percent of foreign exports. In my

personal view, the industrial repercussions of the KII go well beyond our imagination. Think about these: the world-class digital services such as Internet banking, CyWorld [a popular Korean online community site], and web portal service are all products of the KII project.[20]

A deputy director of LG Dacom described the "spillover effect" of the KII-G (the public network) to the KII-P (the commercial network) this way:

Although the two projects [KII-G and the KII-P] were separately operated, each is closely related to the other in the way in which the KII-P has been developed on the basis of the electronic network built by the KII-G. Dacom's broadband transmission lines for commercial users "technically" overlap those [of the public network], even though the two networks are "logically" separated.[21]

A manager of KT also agreed on the infrastructure effect of the state-sponsored investment:

It is obvious that a part of the backbone networks was used for the commercial network. Both overlap in some ways. In that sense, the KII-G contributed [to the development of the KII-P] to some degree.[22]

The two interviewees from the facility-based telecom service providers directly involved in constructing the KII (KT and Dacom) considered the commercial network to be underpinned by the KII-G's optical lines, which were mostly supported by the government's prior investment. Further, open access to the already-built cable and high-speed optical networks, and the competition between various forms of service within the KII-P, are influential factors that enhance the commercial networks. The broadband open access to commercial broadband networks (through a regulatory process known as "local loop unbundling," or LLU) allows any carrier to provide service over networks such as cable. For this reason new entrants into the market, such as Hanaro Telecom, Thrunet, Dreamline, Onse Telecom, and other small and middle-sized private vendors, can provide service nationwide and using multiple technologies, even if they have no physical network presence in the area (see Table 4.3). For instance, a carrier such as Hanaro has open access to KT's broadband network as well as to Thrunet's extensive cable network (ITU, 2005). The open access and competition in the broadband market in Korea has given rise to more technological choices for consumers, such as Asymmetric Digital Subscriber Line (ADSL)-based Internet service (as of 2009, used by 20 percent of total broadband subscribers), as well as cable modem service (Hybrid Fiber Coaxial [HFC] service, used by 32 percent of subscribers), apartment local area network (LAN) service (used by 34 percent), and other broadband services such as FTTH (fiber to the home), wireless LAN, satellite, and WiBro.

To summarize, the domestic telecom companies were fully supported by the state, first through the immense financial underwriting of the KII-G and the

Table 4.3 Broadband Internet service providers and their subscribers in Korea

Provider	2002	2003	2004	2005	2006	2007	2008	2009					
								Total	xDSL	HFC	LAN	FTTH	Satellite
KT	4,992,395	5,589,058	6,077,694	6,241,789	6,352,542	6,515,541	6,771,538	6,952,833	3,005,221	–	2,265,132	1,681,625	855
SK Broadband	–	–	–	–	–	–	3,543,669	3,846,597	172,058	1,616,982	1,281,058	776,499	–
LG U⁺ LG Dacom	146,336	201,704	206,197	213,272	111,905	67,793	28,589	11,907	83	2,994	8,835	–	–
LG Powercom	–	–	–	261,916	1,204,293	1,721,328	2,182,362	2,509,818	–	943,612	1,566,206	–	–
Hanaro Telecom	2,872,351	2,725,563	2,748,934	2,773,213	3,612,749	3,658,115	–	–	–	–	–	–	–
Thrunet	1,301,620	1,293,364	1,287,916	836,625	–	–	–	–	–	–	–	–	–
Dreamline	169,529	149,598	133,927	99,723	28,370	1,152	417	45	–	8	37	–	–
Value-added carrier	367,135	619,103	857,026	1,154,506	–	–	–	–	–	–	–	–	–
Non-facility based carrier	174,012	177,047	218,456	256,666	179,621	164,430	158,473	163,295	4,911	7,049	151,335	–	–
Onse Telecom	452,109	423,062	391,289	353,001	220,156	–	–	–	–	–	–	–	–
CATV system operator	–	–	–	–	2,262,403	2,507,210	2,786,276	2,810,732	36,897	2,542,811	231,024	–	–
CATV relay operator	–	–	–	–	15,251	16,008	13,132	11,199	538	5,271	5,250	140	–
Network operator	–	–	–	–	55,408	58,061	50,475	42,041	2,709	29,215	9,797	320	–
Total	10,405,486	11,178,499	11,921,439	12,190,711	14,042,698	14,709,998	15,474,931	**16,348,472**	3,222,417	5,147,942	5,518,674	2,458,584	855

Source: NIA (2007; 2010), KCC & KISA (2010).

Note
LG Powercom launched broadband service in September of 2005; due to the *Chaebols*' entrance into the telecom market, small-sized telecom vendors have all disappeared: Hanaro Telecom acquired Thrunet and Onse Telecom each in 2005 and 2007, Dreamline was liquidated in 2007, and SKT (SK Broadband) acquired Hanaro Telecom in 2008.

assurance of fixed subscribers, and then through the MCT's promotion of the KII-P through the certificate system. Underpinned by the KII-G's optical lines and by the open access to and competition within the broadband market, the KII-P has experienced rapid growth. With regard to the KII-G, rather than the state dominating the private sector by top-down command, as in an earlier period, disagreements between the two were settled by a series of bilateral nego-tiations between the state and the telecom companies. The commercial telecom market of the KII-P was managed by a combination of limited state intervention and market competition. As a principal researcher at the NIA notes, "These close public–private relationships reflect the specific political system of Korea."[23] The KII project thus is a prime example of the limited or flexible state model—of the shift in state–capital relations "from dominance to symbiosis" (Kim, 1988).

Intermediary organizations for the KII project

In the early 1990s, before the launch of the KII project, the Economic Planning Board (EPB), which then regulated the national budget office, was hesitant to allocate the immense public funds necessary for the project because its cost–benefit justification was weak. Further, the Ministry of Trade, Industry, and Energy (MOTIE) argued that most equipment for the networks fell under its jurisdiction, and thus that the MOTIE should be responsible for the KII project, whereas the MIC's focus was on the regulatory aspects of the network-based telecom market (Jeong & King, 1996). The KII project, however, was seen as the engine in a plan for national economic growth, and neither bureaucratic grid-lock nor budgetary concerns could be sustained for long in the face of such a vision.

Just after the Basic Plan for the KII project was announced in 1993, the gov-ernment organized the KII Taskforce to draw up a more concrete roadmap for the project. The taskforce was made up of officials from the MIC and the NCA (now NIA), from the telecom provider KT, and from the Electronics and Tele-communications Research Institute (ETRI), which is the government-sponsored R&D institute. Based on the taskforce's preliminary investigation into the viabil-ity of the KII project, in May 1994 the government created the KII Steering Committee (Presidential Order No. 14275), which was composed of the Prime Minister, as the chair, and twelve relevant cabinet ministers. Under the KII Steering Committee, the government appointed the KII Working Committee, chaired by the Vice-Minister of the Korea Development Institute (KDI, a semi-governmental think-tank), and including high-ranking officials of the relevant government agencies. Under this KII Working Committee, the government organized the KII Planning Board to carry out such concrete tasks as designing the master plan, gathering the public funds, and developing the technologies to be employed within the backbone network.

As shown in Figure 4.4, the IT Policy Chief at the MoC (now MIC) was the head of the Planning Board, which was made up of six divisions, each related to some aspect of the project's scope: the KII Coordination & Planning Division,

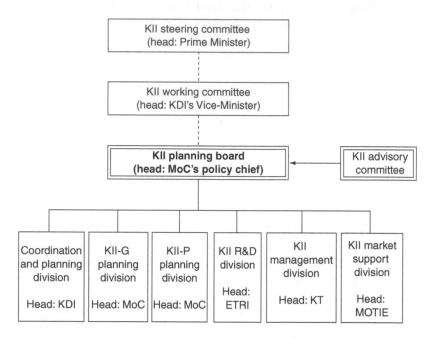

Figure 4.4 Organizational chart of the KII Planning Board (source: author and data largely from the MIC & NCA [2006: 61]).

the KII-G Planning Division, the KII-P Planning Division, the KII R&D Division, the KII Management Division, and the KII Market Support Division.

The members of these six divisions were selected from the following: the public officials of the MIC, the MOTIE, the KDI, and the Ministry of Finance and Economy; experts and researchers from the ETRI and the NCA; and officials from the telecom companies KT, Dacom, and Korean Mobile Telecom (now SK Telecom). With the help of the KII Advisory Committee, set up for the purpose of policy advice, the Planning Board directed the KII project from its inception until 1995, when its affairs were transferred to the Informatization and Planning Office at the MIC (NCA, 2006; MIC & NCA, 2006). From early in the national IT project, therefore, the government ensured the interconnection of the private sector and the relevant public agencies through this Planning Board.

The KII was developed in three phases, based on the shifting of specific policy goals. During the first phase of building a backbone network (1995–97) and the second phase of backbone network completion (1998–2000), the KII-G Steering Council and the KII-G Service Council—which succeeded the KII Planning Board in 1995—were assigned to monitor the ongoing probable issues and discuss the service cost, quality, and upgrades with the private sector representatives. These councils mediated a series of conflicts between the state and the private sector in the earlier phase of the project. In contrast to the KII-P, which was mostly left to the self-ruling mechanisms of the market, the government steadily steered the KII-G project to completion by means of these intermediary organizations. By the beginning of the second phase of the KII project, President Dae-Jung Kim was politically overburdened trying to manage the IMF financial crisis and the WTO agreements, both of which occurred in 1997. The government considered requesting the National Assembly to reduce the budget allotted to the KII project, but decided to maintain the pre-assigned quotas of the KII infrastructure investment. On the threshold of the third and final phase of the KII project (2001–05), the Kim administration began to focus on the backbone network as a significant catalyst for market development.

To comply with Kim's ambitious vision, in 2001 the government organized the Committee for the KII Advancement, which included the major private actors and public institutions involved in building the three backbone networks—the KII-G, the KII-P, and the KII-T. Figure 4.5 shows the organizational chart of the Committee for the KII Advancement. The Office of the KII Advancement—a new entity created by the NCA—coordinated the whole organization by mediating between the four subcommittees: the KII-T Advancement Subcommittee, the KII-G Advancement Subcommittee, the KII-P Advancement Subcommittee, and the R&D Subcommittee. Each Subcommittee was composed of high-ranking officials from the government agencies, the mobile and landline telecom service providers, the government-sponsored R&D research centers, the IT policy research institutes, the major *Chaebols* as the telecom equipment manufacturers, the IT-related business associations, and the universities[24] (NCA, 2003, January). By embracing new entrants into the project—such as the mobile telecom service providers, the commercial Internet service providers, and the *Chaebols* as telecom equipment manufacturers—in addition to the established participants, the government sought to maximize the economic effects of the KII project (see NCA, 2003, January, discussing the goals of the KII Advancement Committee).

The main issues discussed by the Committee were promoting the domestic telecom equipment market, nurturing the software and media content market, and creating commercial value from the KII (NCA, 2003: 10–11). The

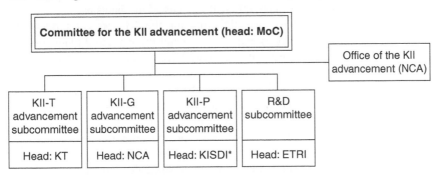

Figure 4.5 Organizational chart of the Committee for the KII Advancement (source: NCA [2003, January]).

Note
* Korea Information Society Development Institute.

Committee for the KII Advancement promoted upgrading the national information infrastructure in order to reposition it for the new economy. The telecom equipment market, however, was getting worse. After 2001, the national telecom vendors ceased to produce and install the domestically-made asynchronous transfer mode (ATM) switch, which was a critical component of the earlier high-speed information network, and they replaced many of the ATM switches with foreign IP-based router equipment. The ATM was a core technology, developed by a coalition of the state, the R&D institute (ETRI), and the *Chaebols*, by which the government had created a new domestic demand for telecom manufacturing, and thus had shielded the national telecom market from the dominant market power of the multinational telecom companies. The change in technological paradigm created by the emergence of the Internet, however, forced the government to shift its R&D support from a growth policy based on the old ATM switch to one based on the new IP-based router (see Chapter 3). Ultimately, the state–private sector attempt to develop a core IP network technology and redirect the technology's developmental path failed.

According to a principal researcher at the NIA, the government spent KR four to five billion *won* (approximately US$500 million) on operating the intermediary organizations described above. This expenditure signifies the government's bid to enhance bureaucratic efficiencies. In fact, the IT-related inter-ministerial structures such as the KII Planning Board were a legacy of old National Basic Information System (NBIS), a national computerization project launched under the Chun administration. Chun first conceived of information and technology as a new engine of economic growth, as well as a bureaucratic tool to rationalize the organizational structures of the public sector through the use of a backbone network (see Chapter 2, which discusses the NBIS in detail). The NBIS Steering Committee, an inter-ministerial agency established in 1989, served as a model for the civilian government when it came to establish the KII Steering Committee in 1994. Since the period of the military regimes, then, intermediary organizations have served as institutional bodies to minimize internal conflict, and to enhance the speed of decision-making processes through efficient consensual mechanisms.

The series of intermediary organizations for the KII project reflects the Korean government's inability to enact the national infrastructure plans through a top-down command structure over the private sector, and its anxious desire to attract them into the policy planning process. The intermediary organizations were quite efficient, at least in lessening the friction with the private sector, but at the same time they excluded the voices of civil society from the decision-making process. Figures 4.4 and 4.5, above, show graphically the lack of any conduit to transmit the citizens' concerns to the special committees. From the start of the KII project, the government simply considered the supply side for enhancing the broadband networks through a strategic partnership with the private sector, ignoring the possibility of citizen participation. The government could defend itself by arguing that the KII project served the public interest by enabling more high-speed Internet access and at lower prices. The national IT policy initiative, however, manifested such undemocratic characteristics as uncritical technocratic IT promotion, preferential treatment for a few private sector incumbents, and profit-driven strategy plans. The logic of exclusion, relying on the top-down policy-making process, enabled the government to exhibit its cause rather than to hear the real voices of the citizens.

The exhibitionist IT policy initiatives and discourses

The government heralded its desire to shift Korea's economy into one suitable for the digital mode of global economy by a series of policy plans. Table 4.4 chronicles a variety of state-led IT policy plans and reforms in the telecom market in Korea during the period of 1993–2011, which overlaps the period of the KII project. Since the mid-1990s, when the KII project was launched, the civilian governments announced and implemented a series of major IT initiatives and plans, such as Cyber Korea 21, the e-Korea Vision 2006, and the U-Korea Master Plan. The KII project is also closely related to the large-scale introduction of e-government, e-commerce, and IT economy, as well as to post-KII projects such UBcN and IP-USN as the next-generation broadband networks.

Since the early 1990s, the government's nationwide IT policy has been greatly mobilized by the technocrats' "exhibitionist" policy plans, aimed at accomplishing the goal of "globalization" (*shegyehwa*), a term that dominated the rhetoric of the Young-sam Kim administration (see Chapter 3). The KII project would not have been possible without the active propagation of IT policy plans; each successive administration has propagated a series of IT policy initiatives and their accompanying rhetoric. In 1996, to evoke the national goal of building a backbone network, the Kim administration announced the Basic Plan on Informatization Promotion (BPIP), the first IT policy initiative at the national level (MIC & NCA, 2005). The first goal of this initiative was to popularize the slogan of IT-based development throughout Korea, among government officials at the national and the provincial level, as well as in the private sector. The second goal was to develop a roadmap for the KII under government guidance, and to adapt it to the rapidly changing environment of electronic backbone networks being built in the advanced countries. The third, more concrete, goal was to enhance the transmission capacity and geographic coverage of the broadband network through the KII project. By improving the penetration rate of the high-speed Internet, the government believed that Korean society would become "a world-class strong IT country" (MIC, 1996).

The Kim administration used the BPIP as a public relations tool for promoting the KII project. Under President Dae-Jung Kim, IT policy was promoted by even more colorful rhetoric (rather than using common policy titles like "plan" or "initiative," the Kim administration decorated the name of Korea with futurist adjectives or nouns like "cyber," "e–," or "vision") expressing the dream of a flourishing, IT-driven Korean society. Kim, once a prominent political activist, was focused on alleviating the economic recession that had taken hold of Korea since the 1997 IMF crisis. The financial crisis meant that the Kim administration, which took office in the March of 1998, inherited the heavy political burden

Table 4.4 Informatization progress in Korea, 1993–2011

Year	Milestone	Contributions and accomplishments
1993	Launching Informatization	• Opened Government Administration Information System, the part of the NBIS • Introduced market competition in paging services (10 new operators) • Popular distribution of personal computer
1994	Promoting Informatization	• Established Plan for Korea Information Infrastructure (KII) • Founded the Ministry of Information and Communication • Commercialized Internet services • Began the duopoly system for mobile services.
1995	Stabilizing Informatization [KII launched]	• Established the Framework Act on Informatization Promotion • Confirmed the Blueprint for the KII: two facility-based telecom service providers (KT and Dacom), exclusively involved in building the KII-G • Invited competition in national long distance market (2nd license to Dacom) • Launched cable TV service
1996	Dawn of Internet and mobile network	• Joined the OECD • Enacted the Framework on Informatization Promotion Act • 27 new licenses granted: three for personal communication services (PCSs), six for trunked radio systems (TRSs), 11 for second-generation cordless telephones (CT-2), three for PCS, two for leased line facility rental, one more for international telephony (Onse enters international market as 3rd service provider), one for radio paging, and three wireless data transmission. • SK Telecom launched digital CDMA services (and also absorbed KMTS, the mobile telephony subsidiary of KT)
1997	Opening the Internet era	• Completion of the KII's first phase (Built 80 call zones linking 14,955 public institutions with the capacity of 45 Mbps) • Began e-commerce services and its preparation • Ten new licenses granted: one local operator (Hanaro), 1 long-distance operator (Onse Corporation), seven TRSs, and 1 paging operator
1998	Coping with Y2K Problems and the growth of Internet culture	• Shaped countermeasures on Y2K Problems nationwide • Launched public administration services through Internet • Popularization of Internet Plaza (PC Cafe/Network Game Room)

Year	Theme	Details
1999	Raid growth of the IT venture and users	• Established Cyber Korea 21 (The Second Master Plan of Informatization Promotion) • Rapid increase of IT venture businesses • Mobile phone, surpassed fixed line subscribers in numbers • Launched mobile Internet service
2000	Popularizing Internet and e-business	• Completion of the KII's second phase (Connecting all 144 call zones, including 28,686 public institutions and schools, with ATM switches with the capacity of 155 Mbps) • Established master plan to promote e-commerce • Applied e-document to all government agencies • Expanded e-business to offline businesses
2001	Activating mobile Internet infrastructure	• Organized the Committee for the KII Advancement • Stimulated mobile Internet through mobile phone, PDA • Profiled as the world's best broadband Internet infrastructure (OECD Report) • Launched Digital Terrestrial TV Broadcasting Service
2002	Maximizing digital competitiveness	• Established e-Korea Vision 2006 (The Third Master Plan of Informatization) • Laid the foundation of e-government • Initiated IMT-2000 mobile service • Launched Digital Satellite Broadcasting service
2003	Shift of informatization from a supply pull to a demand creation	• Announced Broadband IT Korea Vision 2007 (Revision of the Third Master Plan for Informatization Promotion) • The issue moved from a facility-based development of the network over to a service-based one, due to the maturation of the domestic telecom market • Established the Road Map for e-Government • Launched mobile banking service
2004	Build ng new IT growth Infrastructure	• Promoted the building of IT growth-engine infrastructure • Number of Internet users exceeded 30 million people. • Built Broadband convergence Network (BcN) implementation plan • Drew up u-Sensor Network master plan • Established IPv6 promotion master plan • Promoted IT839 Strategies • e-commerce transactions reached KRW300 trillion.

continued

Table 4.4 Continued

Year	Milestone	Contributions and accomplishments
2005	Beginning of digital convergence era [Completion of the KII]	• Completion of the KII's third phase (Linking 32,000 public institutions with ATM-MPLS high quality IP service with the capacity of 1 Gbps) • Issued the Master Plan for IT839 Strategies • Built mid- and long-term information security roadmap • Launched terrestrial and satellite DMB service • Banking via the Internet exceeded banking done by tellers
2006	Launching the ubiquitous infrastructure	• Established U-Korea Master Plan • Launched commercial services on BcN, WiBro, and High-Speed Downlink Packet Access (HSDPA) • Achieved total e-commerce volume of KRW400 trillion
2007	Striving to enter into the ubiquitous society	• Achieved terrestrial DMB terminal penetration of four million • Launched nationwide HSDPA service
2008	Popularization of broadband Internet	• Announced the National Informatization Master Plan' (2008–12) to construct cutting-edge electronic infrastructure for digital convergence • Broadband Internet subscribers exceeded 150 million • Launched commercial IPTV services • Established Korea Communications Commission (KCC)
2009	Building and upgrading of u-Infrastructure	• Launched to build the converged infrastructural networks such as UBcN and IP-USN (2009–12) • Ranked 2nd in the world on ICT-development index measured by ITU
2010	Promoting the mobile Internet subscription	• Announced the Mobile Internet Promotion Plan to enhance smart mobile phone competitiveness and develop next-generation mobile technology • More than 50.2 million registered mobile phone users in a population of 50.51 million (as of September 2010)
2011	Popular distribution of the smart phone	• As of March 2011, more than two million registered iPhone users (out of 16.2 million smart phone users) since its debut in November 2009

Source: Mostly compiled and modified from the charts from NIA (2007; 2010), NCA (2006), OECD (2000), World Bank (2006), KCC & KISA (2010).

of attempting to restructure the domestic market, so as to open it to competition from global conglomerates. While Dae-Jung Kim had advocated a democratic reform of the old authoritarian regime, under the conditions of increasing globalization his policy shifted to the radical adoption of neo-liberal economic policies, and to promoting the information and culture industries over the labor-intensive heavy industries. Because of Kim's success in enacting political reform, opposition to his administration's economic drive toward privatization and commercialization was muted (Cho, 2000: 422).

In his inaugural speech on February 25, 1998, Kim emphasized the value-added economic effects of the cultural industry and began to suggest that the development of software and media contents be prioritized over other strategies to nurture the national economy (*Yonhap News Agency*, 1998). In the March of 1999, the government announced a second IT policy initiative, CyberKorea 21 (CK21) (MIC & NCA, 2005). Since that time, both culture and IT have been widely regarded as key elements necessary for earning foreign dollars and creating a new job market. Due to the so-called "Korean wave" (or *Halryu*),[25] which refers to the growing appeal of Korean popular culture in other Asian countries (Koh *et al.*, 2005), Korea's exports in the cultural industry such as music, games, films, animation, and television programs have experienced a sharp rise—they amounted to US$4.95 billion (0.3 percent of total export) in 2000 and US$13.73 billion (0.42 percent of total export) in 2006 (MCT, 2007).

The policy goal of CK21 under the Kim administration was to create a "knowledge-based society," improving "national competitiveness" and "the quality of life to the level of the more advanced nations" (NCA, 2002: 79). CK21 highlighted policy support for IT businesses, and encouraged policy goals for advanced information and communication economies by setting forth planned guidelines for IT growth. CK21 also stressed the state-driven IT education program, the so-called Informatization Education Plan for Ten Million Citizens, and used this slogan to create 300,000 new IT-related jobs and to increase the digital literacy of citizens (MIC & NCA, 2005). During this period, the government sought to encourage the demand side of the KII, striving for the creation of a critical mass of consumers through public IT education. Impelled by Kim's call for the rapid completion of the KII in his New Year's message in 2001, the MIC announced the Basic Plan for the KII Advancement to accelerate the KII's construction. In the September of that year, the government organized the Committee for the KII Advancement, which was aimed at the market adoption of the nationwide information infrastructure, and in the April of 2002, the government announced its market-driven policy initiative, the "e-Korea Vision 2006" (eKV06).

The MIC's eKV06 stated that its goal was both to promote the "information society" at the national level and to gain "strong ties of international cooperation with the global information society" (NCA, 2003: 10). To do this, eKV06 declared that the government itself must "create a smart government structure with high transparency and productivity" (e-government), encourage private corporations "to strengthen global competitiveness by promoting the informatization of all industries" (e-business), and enable citizens "to enhance their ability to utilize information and technologies" (e-education). Through implementing these goals, the government hoped to persuade Korean society to become "a global leader e-Korea" (MIC & NCA, 2005: 100–4). Once the KII project entered its final phase, the government's IT policy agenda targeted three areas: bureaucratic efficiencies through "smart government," e-commerce through the development of media contents, and mass digital literacy through the public and private educational institutions. While the policy visions set forth in the e-government and e-business areas can be read as expanded and concretized provisions of the previous market-oriented IT policies, eKV06's addition of e-education for citizens seems to be a distinct advance on the policies of CK21 or the BPIP. It is notable as the first instance of the Korean government considering at a national policy level such public issues as the "information gap" between individuals and between regions. As is typical of the bureaucratic approach to the citizenry, the government restricted its role to inconspicuous tasks, such as supplying computers or promoting commercial Internet access, as well as the routinizing and rationalizing of electronic services for citizen requests for official documents. The focus was on a quantitative approach that emphasized outward appearance and growth, as seen in the dramatic growth of the IT industry. The government promoted the cultivation of digital technology as a necessity for increasing the efficiency of government bureaucracy, to improve national productivity, and to become an active part of global society.

President Moo-hyun Roh, who took office in the March of 2003, was even more focused on the promotion of IT-based development of Korean society.[26] In the December of the same year, his administration issued the "Broadband IT Korea Vision 2007" (BK07), which set forth IT as the real engine for national wealth in Korea that would finally raise the yearly salary in Korea to US$20,000 per capita. BK07 emphasized the geopolitical position of the Korean economy as "the electronic hub for the East Asian countries." To accomplish this, with the KII plan nearing its end, the government began to design the next generation of infrastructure plans for advancing the private sector networks. For instance, BK07 set forth the goal of building the total broadband multimedia networks of convergence; the details were set forth in the "Basic Plan for the Broadband convergence Network" (BcN) and "U-Sensor Network" (USN), issued in the February of 2004; the "Distribution and Promotion Plan of the next Internet Protocol IPv6," issued in the April of 2004; and the "Master Plan for IT839 Strategies," issued in the July of 2005[27] (NIA, 2007). In BK07, the Roh administration also emphasized that the quality of life in Korea would be improved by the rapidly increasing opportunities arising from e-commerce with the completion of the KII-P. While Roh succeeded in promoting the development of an Internet-based society in Korea, his IT initiatives overemphasized business-oriented growth policies based on values such as "efficiencies," "competitiveness," and "productivities," to the detriment of public welfare values such as "sustainability," "public commons," and "equal opportunities." For instance, BK07 described IT primarily in terms of its being a panacea for Korea's economic recession and as "the engine for new growth that would create a GDP per capita of US$20,000" (MIC & NCA, 2005: 104–10).

Similar to President Noh's IT policy direction, President Myung-bak Lee announced the "National Informatization Plan" (2008–12) as soon as he took office in 2008, with the major focus upon building the infrastructure suitable for the new digital convergence age (NIA, 2010). The Lee administration began upgrading the BcN and USN, implemented during the Noh administration, with UBcN and IP-USN. By constructing the convergent networks, the government anticipated the ability to provide subscribers more qualified service with the advanced bandwidth, even when they are mobile. Along with the renovation project aimed at building the convergent u-infrastructure, the Lee administration also desired to make its IT policy distinct from that of past administrations by using the term "green IT" (NIA, 2010). Seemingly, the policy rhetoric of "green IT" was in line with the growing market responding to global climate change and the potential energy crisis: key objectives include "'greening' IT and using it as an engine for new growth," "facilitating transition to IT-converged and smart low-carbon society," and finally "improving IT-based capacity to respond to climate change" (NIA, 2010: 12). In actuality, the Lee administration's policy rhetoric of "green IT" is contradicted by its most energetic policy plan, the environmental disruption of the natural riparian ecosystem in the country's major rivers, through the "Four Major Rivers Restoration Project." In other words, President Lee has overused the term "green" at the rhetorical level while concealing the destructive aspects of his administration's "polluted IT" policies. Interestingly, throughout his 64 radio speeches, President Lee has used the word "green" as many as 34 times overall, and thus placed that word as part of the lexicon of his decorative policy discourses, alongside "economies" (247 uses), "crisis (149 uses), and "growth" (74 uses) (Lee, 2011).

Table 4.5 shows the major IT policy initiatives implemented by each civilian government. Interestingly, each president promoted a new IT-related discourse with its own IT policy initiative, especially at the beginning of each political term. Throughout the four presidencies, the discourses are centered on Korea's active affiliation to the global society and the advancement of domestic IT economies. The goals center on the creation of a new IT job market, a large demand for broadband Internet initiated by IT education, e-governance, and e-commerce.

Through the IT policy initiatives, each government gave the private sector— specifically, the *Chaebols*—its blessing, and persuaded its citizens to be members of a Korean-style "information society." The state's promotion of IT to its citizens has boomeranged upon itself by increasing the consumption expenses per household: the rate of IT-related consumption (5.4 percent) per household in Korea is burdensome, almost double that in Japan (3.1 percent) and triple that in the US (1.6 percent). Figure 4.6 suggests that, although Koreans spend less per megabit speed than other countries do, they are overburdened with a variety of IT consumption costs (these include fees for using the online digital content, mobile phone subscriptions, and other IT service charges).

Table 4.5 Major IT policy initiatives under the civilian governments, 1993–2013

President	Young-sam Kim (1993–98)	Dae-Jung Kim (1998–2003)	Moo-hyun Roh (2003–08)	Myung-bak Lee (2008–present)
Government rhetoric	Globalization, dog-eat-dog competition	Liberalization, knowledge-based society	Global IT leader, participatory society	Advanced Knowledge Information society
IT policy initiative	**Basic Plan on Informatization Promotion (1996–2000)**	**CyberKorea 21 (1999–2002)**	**e-Korea Vision 2006 (2002–06)**	**Broadband IT Korea Vision 2007 (2003–07)**	**National Informatization Master Plan (2008–12)**
Goal	Constructing basic electronic backbone network	Creating new IT-related job market	Upgrading the IT infrastructure	E-government, East Asian hub of the IT industry	Remodeling the IT infrastructure for digital convergence
Phase [KII]	1st Phase (1995–97)	2nd Phase (1998–2000)	3rd Phase (2001–05)	BcN (2006–08)	UBcN, IP-USN (2009–13)

Source: author and NCA (2006) and NIA (2008; 2009; 2010) data.

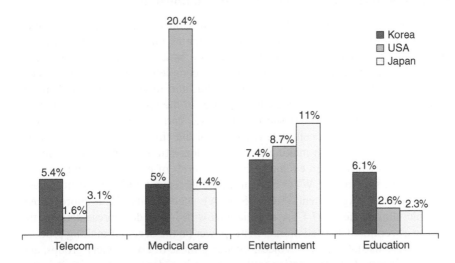

Figure 4.6 Rate of IT consumption per household in Korea, Japan, and the US (source: Bank of Korea [2006]).

Further, due to the bureaucratic desire of all civilian administrations, which hoped to bequeath a monumental policy inheritance to the citizens within their term, the completion year of the KII project was repeatedly moved forward, first to 2015, then to 2010, and finally to 2005, when it was actually completed. A principal researcher at the NIA observed,

> The reason the KII project was completed by 2005 rather than by 2015 is directly related to the presidential pledges of each administration, which aimed to accomplish its political outcomes by "exhibitionist" policy initiatives. It is obvious that the three phases of the KII project were greatly curtailed or condensed in response to the inauguration of a new president.[28]

For instance, due to the 1998 inaugural speech of Dae-Jung Kim, the MIC was forced to make a new IT policy initiative, CK21. BK07 was launched at the time of Roh's inauguration, even before the eKV06 initiative of his predecessor had been implemented (see Table 4.5). In fact, the five IT initiatives over four presidencies largely promoted Korean IT development in order to meet the exhibitionist (or public relations) political goals of each administration, rather than to fulfill the "soft" goals of improving the citizens' ability to access, use, and recreate information freely. Consequently, the rhetoric of these initiatives—such as that of surviving global competition and of regenerating the national economy—successfully played upon the citizens' anxieties to the extent that there is now one broadband Internet service per household, and allowed the state-led project to be completed with ease and even ahead of schedule.

Casualties of the state–*Chaebol* crony relationship

To sum up, in contrast to the old military regimes, the civilian governments since 1993 have articulated various mechanisms, such as intermediary organizations and the exhibitionist (or public relations) policy initiatives, in order to successfully guide the state-led infrastructure plan to completion. The Korean government's attempts to stimulate the private sector, and to create new IT demand, was extremely successful over the three phases of the KII project. Nevertheless, the process by which the KII success story was carried out raises at least one serious issue: that of the complete exclusion of the citizens, as previously mentioned, from the decision-making process of domestic telecom policies. In the same way, they have been excluded from the series of multilateral and bilateral negotiations, such as the WTO basic telecom agreement and the recent Korea–US Free Trade Agreement (KORUS FTA) negotiations. In a more recent example, during the 2007 FTA negotiations with US trade representatives, the Korean government exerted monopolistic power on the decision-making process, ignored various stakeholders' voices, including those of civil society groups, and even disseminated disinformation to the citizens in order to accomplish its political goal.[29] As the next chapter indicates, these undemocratic aspects of the government's IT policies have evoked civil society's resistance to the policymaking processes behind the closed doors. One case that highlights these tensions occurred around the KII-based system of collection and management of citizens' data, as embodied in the National Education Information System (NEIS), a holistic vision of monitoring citizens' profile information.

5 The transformation of state surveillance practices toward a grid of control

Thanks to the techniques of surveillance, the *physics* of power, the hold over the body, operate according to the laws of optics and mechanics, according to a whole play of spaces, lines, screens, beams, degrees and without recourse in principle at least, to excess, force or violence It is a power that seems all the less *corporal* in that it is more subtly *physical*.

(Foucault, [1975]1995: 177, emphasis in original)

The digital language of control is made up of codes indicating whether access to some information should be allowed or denied. We're no longer dealing with a duality of mass and individual. Individuals become *"dividuals,"* and masses become samples, data, markets, or *"banks."*

(Deleuze, [1990] 1995: 180, emphasis in original)

Today's *circuits of communication* and the databases they generate constitute a Superpanopticon, a system of surveillance without walls, windows, towers or guards. The quantitative advances in the technologies of surveillance result in a qualitative change in the microphysics of power Technological change, however, is only part of the process. The populace has been disciplined to surveillance and to participating in the process.

(Poster, 1990: 93, emphasis in original)

Outline of the chapter

While the previous two chapters investigated politico-economic aspects surrounding the birth and development of the KII project, the present chapter focuses on how the Korean Information Infrastructure (KII) functions as a virtual network to enhance the government's surveillance power over its citizens. The "National Education Information System" (NEIS), initiated in 2003, is a nationwide database system aimed at managing more than 350 pieces of personal information about each of the eight million students in South Korea, in a central server computer operated by the Ministry of Education and Human Resources (MEHR). This policy initiative, which was first a plan for the integrated management of students' profiles, but later evolved into a plan for a central database system monitoring each student, could not have been conceived without the material existence of the KII. This chapter first investigates the shift in South Korea from a *disciplinary society*, in which there is the visible and physical violence of power, to a *control society*, with its modulating and normalizing techniques of power. Under South Korea's authoritarian military regimes (1948–92), the national ID system and the National Security Law were the state's primary means of social control over its citizens. Under the civilian governments (1993–present), the government's deployment of institutional power has been based more on the logic of free-floating control and the articulation of micro-power. This chapter examines how the techniques of power were gradually transformed from a centralized and hierarchical model into a distributive and dispersed network model, based on the flow, speed, and mobility of the KII.

Theoretically, this chapter supports Gilles Deleuze's thesis that today's society has become increasingly based on digital technology, which is used for the reproduction of power systems—an idea summarized by his term "control society"—while never abolishing the conditions of disciplinary suppression by way of state power over the citizens. To observe the new techniques of social control based on the electronic backbone network, this chapter examines the policy debate over the introduction of the NEIS, a plan that ignited the anger of civil rights movement groups, as well as that of unions for lawyers, parents, teachers, and professors, who attempted to block its implementation. Although the overall scope of the NEIS was reduced due to these protests, it remains an example, as the end of this chapter shows, of the state's continuing bureaucratic desire to manage citizens' data electronically.

The desire for social control

The present chapter examines the recent asymmetric relationships between citizens and the state, especially as they are revealed in the Korean government's surveillance practices. Since the launch of the Korean Information Infrastructure (KII) project in 1995, Korea, even more than most countries, has been subject to the dual effects of the bureaucratic state and the advance of digital technologies, owing to the authoritarian and hierarchical structures of Korean politics and business, as Castells (2000b: 262–6) has observed. The East Asian development model of an information economy, specifically the South Korean development model, can be described as one characterized by a "democratic deficit" (Venturelli, 2002: 81). Due to the abatement of the Cold War, by the time the first civilian government took office in 1993, it was able to begin a shift from the anti-communist rhetoric of previous regimes[1] to a more pragmatic rhetoric of achieving prosperity through IT-based bureaucratic efficiencies. The North–South summit meeting of leaders from both Koreas, in the June of 2000 in Pyongyang, increased the momentum for ending the rigid anti-communist sentiment that inspired the South's National Security Law. Since then, South Korea's government has instead focused on promoted digital technology as the foundation of a flourishing welfare state. Due to the government's pro-IT policy, Korean society has accomplished rapid growth in networking and mobile technology, while at the same time, the nationwide backbone network, as well as the high penetration rate of mobile phones, has allowed the government elites increasing electronic access to citizens' data. The new material conditions of electronic networks have enabled the government to monitor citizens' activities through real-time surveillance practices, to integrate citizens' local data into the national database, and to sort the collected information based on the government's specific purposes in a given situation.

This chapter explores the ways in which the Korean government's desire for social control was articulated and realized under the new material conditions of digital networks, specifically, of the Korean Information Infrastructure (KII) project. First, this chapter examines the changing patterns of surveillance practices from the period of the military regimes (1948–92) to that of the civilian governments (1993–present): while the surveillance practices of the former were based on the disciplinary logic of confinement, censorship, centralization, and physical violence, the surveillance practices of the latter have increasingly been based on a digital grid of control, along with intensification of past disciplinary techniques of power. Second, this chapter looks at a series of controversial laws and policy initiatives under the civilian governments that have enabled the government elites to perform electronic network-based censorship or surveillance over Korean citizens. Third, to delineate the institutional desire for control through the electronic backbone network, this chapter focuses on the societal debate over the introduction of the "National Education Information System" (NEIS) in 2003, which led to a mass protest of the citizens, as an archetypical case of institutional surveillance. Finally, this chapter explores how the NEIS—an offspring of the KII project—stands as an example of the emerging digital surveillance techniques expressing the state's desire for social control.

As the data for its analysis, this chapter references the NEIS and other privacy-relevant laws, along with press conference reports, documents on public hearings, written reports of events, and policy analysis reports, most of which were published by the Jinbo Network and the Citizens' Action Network, organizations defending citizens' cyber-rights in Korea.

The rise in government surveillance practices

Many countries are increasing their surveillance of citizens in order to enhance societal control. The bureaucratic interests that underlie the current strategies aim to install a code of control within each technical artifact (such as the KII), and thus technological rationalization will be complete when technical design merges with social and political hierarchies. According to the *Human Rights Watch Report 2008* (HRW, 2008) and *Freedom on the Net 2011* (Freedom House, 2011), state-led censorship and surveillance of bloggers and citizens has been pervasive in authoritarian countries such as Egypt, Iran, Jordan, Pakistan, Saudi Arabia, Syria, Thailand, Tibet (under the Chinese government), Tunisia, Turkey, and Zimbabwe, in the name of preserving the social order. For instance, the Chinese government has employed new technology to tap 153 million users' cell phones, especially those of political dissidents using text-messaging services (Kurtenbach, 2004). Further, the Chinese government has been oppressing their citizens and those of subject territories (such as Tibet) by severely censoring what they can access online. Internet giants like Google and Yahoo! have helped facilitate this oppression in order to gain access to the Chinese market (Våge, 2004). In Thailand, as of 2010, dozens of Internet users had been charged under various laws for expressing their views online, particularly those critical of the role of the monarchy in Thai politics since the military coup of 2006, and the authorities have been allowed to block any website (Freedom House, 2011). In their special report *Enemies of the Internet: Countries under Surveillance*, Reporters Without Borders (2011) reported that some 3,700 sites in Turkey are blocked, partly for arbitrary and political reasons. Moreover, Turkey's Internet regulator has enforced upon Internet service providers and website hosting companies a list of 138 keywords that are henceforth to be banned from the Turkish Internet.

Surveillance practices in the developing countries differ little from those of advanced Western countries such as the UK, the US, and Australia, although the latter's surveillance techniques are more refined and complicated. For instance, the UK government has supported the so-called "Celldar project" that intends to enable locational tracking of users wherever a mobile phone receives a signal (Burke & Warren, 2002). "Celldar" conceals its aim of ubiquitous surveillance under the ideological cover of "protecting national security from terrorism," but this potentially repressive project seems to mirror Latour's (1992) description of how impulses of state control will be realized and "delegated" to technological devices. Similarly, since the September 11, 2001 terrorist attack, the US government has also gained easier access to mobile phone and email conversations (Cauley, 2006). The US federal government has increasingly gained the bureaucratic power of monitoring the citizens by shifting the security concept from national security to homeland security (Relyea, 2002).[2] For example, since September 11 there have been well-publicized, large-scale instances in the US of Internet and wireless carriers tapping citizens' communications on behalf of the federal government, without the issuing of a court order. In Australia, since 2008 the government has announced the policy plans for a layered filtering scheme, sustained by the convenient rhetoric of protecting children from pornographic and illegal material. However, the regulatory plan would police and deny access to political, as well as pornographic, content.

As shown by these examples from various different countries, the increasing patterns of surveillance and censorship can be largely characterized by the bureaucratic drive to preserve the security of society (Beniger, 1986: 11), that is, to preserve the stable reproduction of society from both internal and external attacks—at the cost of a reduction in citizens' privacy rights. The invasion of privacy, in other words, is regarded as a price worth paying for the promise of security. Advanced democratic states, while avoiding the blatant denial of Internet access frequently shown in authoritarian states, have begun to regard a regulatory control of electronic space as more strategically important in controlling citizens (see Open Net Initiative, 2011).

It should be noted, however, that private corporations have also introduced electronic monitoring devices into the workplace, such as those that record and store telephone conversations, voicemail messages, computer files, e-mail messages, and Internet connections. Corporations use high-tech surveillance technologies to monitor efficiency and to ensure behavior that is in the company's best interests; in South Korea, however, they are also used to prevent workers from organizing and to oppose union activism. In this context, technology affiliates itself with the private desire for a "panoptic" workplace. Even without the monitoring of overseers from a physical watchtower, technology functions for corporations as "a fail-safe system to increase their sense of certainty and control over both production and organizational functions" (Zuboff, 1988: 390). For private corporations, the suppressive side of technology can be activated by an aggressive desire for labor control. The government normally interacts with the private sector to produce both the economic foundation and the normative standards for surveillance (Phillips, 2003). This combinative effect of surveillance by the state and the private sector illustrates the gradually expanding "asymmetry of power between individuals or groups of individuals on the one hand and powerful governmental and commercial entities on the other" (Doty, 2001: 123).

In Korean society, systematic surveillance practices conducted both by the state and by the private sector have risen in recent times. Korea has historically experienced shifts in the practices of power concurrent with major shifts in its political life. The next two sections of this chapter investigate in detail the historical transformations of state surveillance techniques from the military regimes to the civilian governments. This investigation establishes the context in which to understand the evolution of government surveillance in Korea's recent history, as well as the newly emerging surveillance techniques that have largely been made possible by nationwide expansions of telecom infrastructures such as the KII.

Solid and disciplinary power

After being liberated from three and a half decades of Japanese military occupation (1910–45), Korea was split into two nations through civil war in 1950, and the country was left in ashes. Korea had little experience with the representative system of democracy found in advanced Western countries, and this political immaturity enabled a series of autocratic governments to wield oppressive power over the citizens during the first two civilian governments (1948–62) and the following three military regimes (1963–92). Using anti-communist opposition to North Korea as a rationale, these South Korean governments justified their repressive practices against citizens in the name of national security. From the time of General Cheong-hee Park, who seized power in 1963, up until the early 1990s, anti-communism was a powerful ideological shield to suppress political dissent and citizens' demands for human rights. Throughout the 1960s, 1970s, and 1980s, citizens were controlled by a pervasive grid of military-authoritarian practices: the national ID system identifying each Korean, the use of paramilitary violence to break worker unions, the use of closed-circuit television for policing, the widespread practice of government eavesdropping, and politically motivated investigations of activists. The military regimes employed a wide variety of means to compel most citizens to be docile subjects, imposing curfews, forcibly shearing the hair of "hippies," torturing political activists, searching citizens' possessions on the street, and silencing the voice of dissent in the public arena.

In 1979 Park was assassinated, and on December 12 of that year General Doo-hwan Chun spearheaded a coup d'état. As soon as he seized power, Chun declared nationwide martial law, which was directed at banning all political activity, crushing the labor movement, closing the universities, and arresting pro-democracy politicians and activists, including Dae-Jung Kim (Shelley, 2001). These actions sparked an uprising in Gwangju on May 18, 1980. For the five days of the uprising, the citizens of Gwangju held the city: over 200,000 people participated in demonstrations, and in the provincial capitol building (which served as the headquarters for the citizens' army) hundreds of citizens took up arms against the military regime. During this period, when Gwangju was completely blockaded by siege and cut off from contact with the outside world, a Citizens' Council was spontaneously organized to defend the city, maintain public security, distribute food and water, and prepare to offer armed resistance to the military. On May 22, 1980, however, the military regime brutally quelled the uprising, massacring as many as 2,000 people—striking workers, protesting students, and citizens—and took control of Gwangju.[3] Chun then used the demonstrations in Gwangju as a pretext for furthering his repressive policies.

The Park and Chun administrations (1963–88) typify the brutal era of repressive and disciplinary society at the institutional level. During this period, the state's regulatory control apparatus was twofold: the National Security Law and the national ID system. In the name of ferreting out spies or sympathizers of communist North Korea, and of protecting South Korea from the dangers of communist infiltration and influence, the National Security Law (NSL) had already been enacted in the December of 1948 under Syngman Rhee, the first president of the republic (1948–60). Over the next half century, military dictators used the NSL's elastic definition of "anti-state groups" to suppress all political opponents. The NSL, which is still in force and was last revised in 1996, still defines "anti-state groups" in such a way as to allow arbitrary interpretation of the term. According to Article 2 of the NSL, "anti-state groups refer to domestic or foreign organizations or groups whose intentions are to conduct or assist infiltration of the Government or to cause national disturbances" (as revised May 31, 1991). The NSL prescribes up to seven years in prison for those who praise, encourage, disseminate the materials of or cooperate with anti-state groups (Article 7), and five years' imprisonment for failure to report "anti-state" activities (Article 10). Using this law, any official who desires to punish political opponents can legally imprison or even execute them, relying on the law's ambiguous language. Although Korea's Constitution declares that "all citizens enjoy freedom of speech and the press, and of assembly and association" (adopted on 17 July 1948: Chapter 1, Article 21), the NSL has empowered the government to effectively override the Constitution.

Many countries have used identity cards in one form or another, but the national ID system in Korea is a total surveillance system, able to individually identify each Korean. Originally, a Resident Registration System was used for regulating the population's data on the basis of place of birth and residency. This system was a legacy of the Japanese imperialist occupation of Korea (1910–45). The project of regulating the entire citizenry was established under Park, who in 1968 extended the notorious registration system to the whole populace, and by 1975 the data was managed by means of computer databases. Since that time, all citizens have been required to obtain and to carry a national ID card. If the police ask to see the card, a citizen must be able to provide it. Each citizen must obtain a personal identification number assigned by the state, which must then be used for all kinds of purposes over the citizen's lifetime. Also, all citizens over the age of 17 must have all ten fingerprints on file. In all, the government collects more than 140 different pieces of profiling information on each citizen.[4] Successive Korean governments have defended the bureaucratic efficiency of the system and emphasized that it is the price to be paid for protecting citizens from crime and for identifying victims in accidents. This ID system is little different from that of a Big-Brother-type "superstate"; it regulates all citizens with a thirteen-digit personal reference number,[5] not unlike the bar code system used on commercial goods. A citizen would have severe difficulties without it, because one must submit it any time one buys certain goods, rents a house, drinks a beer in a bar, applies for loan from a bank, applies for employment at a business or a school, or even when one posts a comment on the Internet. The regulatory control of citizens is an example of a serious violation of fundamental human rights of privacy, because it is permanent in duration and vast in scope.

Using the regulatory weapons of the national ID system and the NSL, military dictators controlled Korean citizens for more than 25 years. For instance, the national ID system was the easiest way to ferret out political dissidents—students, union organizers, politicians, and other citizens critical of the military regime—during on-the-street questioning or a crackdown by the intelligence officers. General Chun, the worst of the dictators, recognized the value of the intelligence agencies in maintaining control over the citizenry. Just before he came to power via military coup in 1979, Chun took control of both the Defense Security Command (DSC), whose original mission focused on counter-communist activities and fighting military corruption, and the Korea Central Intelligence Agency (KCIA), which had been created in 1961 under the presidency of Park (renamed the National Intelligence Service (NIS) in 1999). After taking power, Chun used the KCIA and the DSC as domestic surveillance and spying agencies to collect, analyze, and, whenever useful, fabricate intelligence information about the citizenry. For instance, these agencies created imaginary underground spy rings loyal to communist North Korea and then falsely accused citizens of belonging to them, as illustrated in the 1985 case of a group Korean students studying abroad in the US (*Hankyoreh*, 2008, June 23), and the 1986 case of Hee-Chul Kang (Lawyers for a Democratic Society, 2005); in both cases, the individuals involved were convicted of espionage, and only after serving long prison sentences were they finally cleared of the charges.

The integration of the intelligence agencies, the national ID system, and the NSL enabled the development of an extreme disciplinary society to control and suppress the "abnormal" or "other"—striking workers, protesting students, progressive politicians, and, in general, any citizen critical of the government. During the dark days of these repressive military regimes, Korean citizens were eager to have more political rights, such as freedom of speech, expression, and assembly. Under the Chun government in 1987, a university student (Chong Chul Park) was killed by water torture during police interrogation. Although two policemen were charged and the Interior Minister and the national police chief were dismissed in the aftermath of the incident, demonstrations in Seoul and other cities had to be dispersed by the police with tear gas (Haberman, 1987). By June, confronted with nationwide rioting, Chun was forced to step down from the presidency and allow direct presidential elections in Korea. 1987 was a momentous year for South Korea, as it marked the beginning of the end of the repressive military regimes. In the December of that year, citizens elected a president by direct popular vote for the first time in 26 years, even though Tae-Woo Noh, a former military colleague of Chun's, won the election by fraud (Han, 1988). Nevertheless, with the Noh administration (1988–93), Korean society entered an era less brutal than that of the Park and Chun administrations. During the Noh administration, the NSL, the national ID system, and other repressive surveillance mechanisms were still in place, but their use began gradually to shift and be modified.

Liquid and normalizing power

The citizens' political victory in the second direct presidential election in the December of 1992 ushered in a more stable phase of civilian government. From this point onward, the public's focus gradually shifted from demands for political democracy to demands for freedom of expression. This shift can be viewed as extending democratic concerns into a new cultural arena. With the widespread dissemination of digital communications since the mid-1990s, Koreans have discovered the freedom afforded by electronic conduits of cultural expression. Ironically, these changes were facilitated by the Young-Sam Kim administration's policy drive to shift the Korean economy from traditional labor-intensive industries to cultural or knowledge-based economies.

The new material conditions of electronic mobility were firmly undergirded by the launch of the Korean Information Infrastructure (KII) project in 1995, which has promoted the rapid growth of commercial broadband Internet service nationwide, as well as the increase of bureaucratic efficiencies in government agencies. The eruption of socio-cultural exchange spurred by the mobility and interconnectivity of new communication technologies has also acclimated citizens to speaking out in their own voices and expressing their own values. The ecology of the citizens' autonomous culture has gradually shifted, from the street barricade struggle of resisting authoritarian regimes by throwing stones and Molotov cocktails, to resisting the dominant discourses of society through electronic forms of cultural expression such as Internet cafés, electronic forums, blogs, and text messaging with mobile phones.

Due to the civilian government's pro-IT policies, more than nine out of ten households now have high-speed Internet access. The number of mobile phone users is rapidly growing: as of September 2010, there were over 50.2 million registered users out of a population of 50.51 million (KCC, 2010)—and the high-speed data communications of mobile phones provide seamless multimedia services throughout the country (MIC, 2007; NIA 2010). According to data from the Organization for Economic Co-operation and Development (OECD, 2005), the process of digitalizing all telecommunication networks in Korea was completed in 2003. In fact, most Koreans spend their time on electronic networks (Fackler, 2007)[6]—playing online games in Internet cafés, decorating their blogs, communicating with each other using mobile devices, connecting with hobby or other interest groups through Internet portal sites, and exchanging audio-visual materials with others. This constant communication through electronic media, and the rise of a culture of free expression via these new media, led to the state's desire to control the communicative networks of Korean "netizens." This desire first took place indirectly, through suppressing online users' free speech rights by the application of more rigid copyright law: between 1957, when South Korea's Copyright Act (No. 8029) was first enacted, and 2004, it has been revised eleven times—three of them since 2000. The trajectory of the Act's revisions can be summarized in a phrase: the "reinforcement of intellectual property rights" for copyright owners and holders (Hong, 2005: 9).[7] The government frequently uses the charge of copyright infringement to arrest those who express criticism of the government on the Internet. For instance, the Myung-bak Lee administration arrested the CEOs of major online storage companies for violating copyright by illegally transmitting video files and movies; however, netizens suspect the real cause was that their websites became famous for users' live broadcasts of candlelight vigils protesting the import of US beef, part of the government's KORUS FTA negotiations (*Chosun Ilbo*, 2008).

In Korean digital society, few constitutional provisions exist to protect citizens' privacy rights against the government's systematic surveillance practices. Such practices are still widespread under a civilian government because state agencies have continued to hire officials who served under the military regimes, and government hiring has continued to be dominated by Korea's traditional "clan culture," in which affiliation by region, educational institution, and birthplace are paramount. Yet because the disciplinary mechanisms of the military regimes conflict with the gradual development of citizens' socio-cultural freedom, the power system since the advent of the civilian governments has tended to reconfigure itself using "soft" mechanisms, such as creating integrated electronic databases or hiding identifiable tracking codes within the technological artifacts themselves. For instance, the electronic ID card and e-passport, containing a chip with fingerprints and other personal information, can be used to identify and monitor any citizen at any time or place. New urban geographies dominated by electronically "hyperpanoptic" devices (Poster, 1990) reflect the new phase of Korea's policing of its citizens through diverse surveillance techniques.

Table 5.1 gives a timeline of the regulatory control of electronic communications, showing privacy-related scandals and legislation under the civilian governments. The various legislative acts found in the timeline of events in Table 5.1 are intended to regulate the new spheres of citizens' communication activities, including the Internet and cell phones. The main direction of government surveillance, as evidenced in the timeline from 1997 to the present, can be summarized as follows: First, the government has desired to update the traditional disciplinary tools, such as the national ID system and the closed circuit TV (CCTV) system, by digitizing and interlinking them over the Net. Second, the government has continuously legitimized the control of electronic space by means of legal enactments (e.g., the Framework Act for Establishment of the Public Order in Telecommunications of 2000, the Act on the Use and Protection of Location Data of 2004, and the 2005 revision of the Act on the Promotion of Information and Telecommunication Network Use). Third, the government has introduced "positive technologies of power" (Foucault, [1999] 2003: 48),[8] such as e-ID cards and e-passports, for the purpose of invisible social control in wired space. Fourth, locally dispersed data on citizens has been integrated into a central server, as will be seen in the NEIS case below. Finally, the scandals in Korea's large corporations are representative of the country's unethical business culture, which has few qualms about leaking customers' data to third parties, whether intentionally or accidentally.

Under the Young-Sam Kim administration (1993–98), electronic surveillance of citizens was undeveloped; it was marked mainly by the government's desire to collect citizens' data through the introduction of the e-ID card in the last year of Kim's presidency. Although the Kim administration had begun to introduce the new pro-IT policies and initiatives, including the KII project, from 1995 onward, network-based surveillance practices were still embryonic and had yet to be applied nationwide. The state's electronic surveillance practices increased rapidly under Dae-Jung Kim's administration (1999–2003), during which the nationwide electronic backbone network was almost completed and the distribution of mobile telephony dramatically expanded. Even under the civilian governments, control mechanisms of the military regimes, such as the national ID system and the National Security Law, have been used as the major mechanisms to manage citizens. With the new information and telecommunications policies promoted by the civilian governments, however, especially under the administrations of Dae-Jung Kim and of Moo-hyun Roh (2003–08), the rigid and visible techniques of power have become more integrated with and veiled by the digital networks—that is, the techniques of control have shifted to more refined and invisible ones.

The invention of positive technologies for free-floating control is the most significant of all of these, because it can hide beneath an ethical patina the real intention

Table 5.1 Regulatory control of the electronic networks under Korea's civilian governments, 1993–2011

Dates	Events
(1993–98)	**The Young-Sam Kim administration**
November 1997	• Submitted revision of the "Resident Registration Act" (including introduction of the electronic ID card), but this was defeated by citizens' opposition
(1998–2003)	**The Dae-Jung Kim administration**
1999	• Instead of e-ID card, introduced the plastic resident registration card
July 2000	• Proposed to enact the so-called "Framework Act for Establishment of the Public Order in Telecommunications"
November 2001	• Introduced the "Rating System of Internet Contents," led by the Information Communication Ethics Committee
March 2003	• Introduced the "National Education Information System" (NEIS) to manage more than 200 items of personal information about eight million students in a main computer server
June 2003	• Installed 340 CCTV (Closed-Circuit TV) systems (360 degree rotation/22× zoom) in Kangnam-Ku district in Seoul, sparking social protests
October 2003	• Allowed investigators to access cell phones' short text messages without a warrant
November 2003	• Proposed the "Protection from Terrorism Act," which aimed to increase the investigative power of the National Intelligence Service
(2003–08)	**The Moo-hyun Roh administration**
September 2004	• Proposed an "Act on the Use and Protection of Location Data" that offered little protection to the citizen from illegal mobile tracking by a third party
December 2004	• Organized a task force for the "National Total Management Information System of Crime and Justice" (NTMIS) to integrate citizens' legal data on a central server
February 2005	• The Samsung SDI mobile tracking scandal: Samsung secretly tracked union workers by using cloned cell phones, but the Public Prosecutor terminated the investigation because of extreme difficulty in locating perpetrators
June 2005	• Proposed revision of the "Protection Act of Telecommunications Secrets," making it easier for prosecutors to eavesdrop on phone calls
October 2005	• New ID cards planned for 2007 to protect against ID forgery
October 2005	• Installed CCTV systems (270× zoom/1 km visibility range) in the Cheonggyecheon public park in Seoul, and gathered images of over three million citizens
December 2005	• Proposed revision of the "Act on Promotion of Information and Telecommunication Network Use" to enact the "Enforced Real-Name System" (ERNS), mainly led by the Ministry of Information and Communication (MIC), for the purpose of forcing users to put their real names and resident ID numbers whenever posting any message on the Internet

continued

Table 5.1 Continued

Dates	Events
April 2007	• Revision of the "Protection of Communications Secrets Act" enacted in 2004
June 2007	• 37 major Internet sites (portals & government sites) forced to adopt the ERNS identity verification system
(2008–)	**The Myung-bak Lee administration**
March 2008	• Provincial government officials discovered using Voice over Internet Protocol (VoIP) to eavesdrop on subordinates in Kyonggi-Do province
April 2008	• Ministry of Foreign Affairs and Trade required new e-passports to conform with the US Visa Waiver Program (VWP), which requires that passports have a chip containing fingerprints and other personal information
April 2008	• Lax privacy policies of the ISPs and telecom companies revealed: 22 former and current executives and managers of Hanaro Telecom charged with leaking private information of its customers to telemarketers
	• Auction, an Internet shopping mall and subsidiary of eBay, facing two massive lawsuits after hackers stole IDs, passwords, phone numbers, and shopping logs of 10.81 million customers in February of 2008
	• LG Dacom facing a class action suit for leaving customer records open on the Internet between 2005 and March of 2008, during which time eight million subscribers' data was stolen
May 2008	• Wiretapped and blacklisted about 800 Internet users who were critical of the government
	• Korea Communications Standards Commission (KCSC) began to censor and delete online messages without a warrant, in the name of obscenity, defamation, and national security infringement (KCSC demanded censoring of a total of 41,103 online postings — an average of 113 per day — in 2010 alone)
	• Prosecuted public criticism against the president, the government, the ruling party, or major newspapers (using the Cyber Election Crime Act)
November 2008	• The number of the ERNS sites increased to 153 (the websites having more than 100,000 visits per day)
April 2009	• "Minerva," a blogger critical of the government policies, imprisoned for 18 months, on charges of "spreading false information online"
	• YouTube refused to adopt the ERNS system and banned users whose "country content preference" is set to S-Korea from posting any content
	• Passed the new anti-file sharing provision, the so-called "three-strikes" rule, suggested by the ruling Grand National Party (GNP)
September 2009	• Shared and sorted the profile info of online users critical of the government among the 42 governmental bodies by installing the "Cyber Data Search/Collection System" initiated by the Korean National Police Agency

Table 5.1 Continued

Dates	Events
March 2010	• Announced plans to introduce the e-ID card with a smart chip in 2013 • Investigating authorities' requests for citizens' data rapidly increased, as revealed by the 2010 Parliamentary Inspection
July 2010	• Launched the database system aimed at gathering the DNA information from suspects, juvenile offenders, and convicts who are related to any of 11 different crimes
April 2011	• Prosecutors tried to collect DNA from workers on strike and were confronted by citizens' opposition • Passed a revision of "the Youth Protection Act" that bans those under the age of 16 from playing online games from midnight through 6 a.m.
May 2011	• JinboNet requested the UN Human Rights Council's attention to the situation of human rights and ICT in South Korea in regard to freedom of expression on the Internet
September 2011	• The National Intelligence Service (NIS) has gathered citizens' online activities by using a surveillance technique known as "deep packet inspection" to spy on their emails sent and received using Gmail and Google accounts.

Source: compiled by the author.

of control directed at establishing the new digital rule of cybersociety. For instance, the enforcement of the "real name system" prevents anonymity of expression, which can be considered as a form of pre-censorship (i.e., it exerts a "chilling effect" on free speech). Moreover, the new technique of control embeds the old disciplinary technique of the national ID system within it, because it uses the national ID database to verify real names on the Internet. Introduced under Dae-jung Kim's administration, the "rating system of Internet contents" has in reality been used to stifle minority voices on the Internet, such as those of political radicals, gays and lesbians, high school drop outs, and feminists. In contrast with the "real name system," the rating system on Internet contents is a form of post-censorship, which intends to regulate "aberrant" websites that deviate from the ruling norms of power.

In addition to this pre- and post-censorship of the Internet, the government and the private sector have shown an increased desire for real-time surveillance in the wireless sphere. For instance, the use of mobile phones for labor control in the Samsung SDI case[9] confirms once again the undemocratic tendencies of the Korean business culture of surveillance, as well as the government's acquiescence in longstanding practices of the *Chaebols,* such as the blacklisting of militant workers. A political dispute was also ignited by the eavesdropping of the National Intelligence Service (NIS) on the cell phone conversations of a news reporter working for a daily newspaper (Joo, 2004). On further investigation, it was revealed that government agencies, including the National Police Agency and the NIS, tracked mobile phone users in 12,184 cases in 2002, in 20,773 cases in 2003, and in 16,497 cases in just the first half of 2004. Cell phone users tracked included 12 politicians and five journalists (*Media Today*, 2005). Significantly, the intelligence agencies' eavesdropping was made possible by the voluntary cooperation of SK Telecom, one of the largest mobile telephony carriers, which gave access to its customers' records without any consideration of privacy. These surveillance scandals and practices in Korean society reveal the confluence of unethical business interests, randomly collecting citizens' personal information, and an underdeveloped political system which trivializes citizens' privacy rights.

As shown in Table 5.1, while the previous civilian governments had major tendencies toward free-floating control, the administration of Myung-bak Lee (2008–present) has dramatically intensified the surveillant techniques aimed at controlling each citizen. For instance, the investigative authorities have asked for targeted citizens' location data, as well as personal calling data, without a warrant: the number of requests for tracking citizens' cell phone and Internet data has steadily increased, from 244,976 cases and 41,158 cases in 2005 to 358,375 cases and 561,467 cases in 2009, respectively (Joint Korean NGOs, 2010). As in previous years, the eavesdropping of these public agencies was made possible by the voluntary cooperation of the big telecom operators, which freely exposed its customers' records. Since its inauguration in 2008, the Lee administration has introduced technology-related censorship and surveillant techniques, such as censoring online messages, widely through the Korea Communications Standards Commission. The government has indicted or imprisoned online users and bloggers critical of government policies, extended the "Enforced Real Name System" (ERNS) onto more websites and online forums, collected and sorted the DNA samples from militant workers on strike, banned young adults from playing online games at night, and other heavy-handed measures.

While the military regimes used physical oppression (such as imprisonment, abduction, torture, and police violence) and disciplinary control through collecting data about citizens (such as the residential ID system, wiretapping, surveillance, and on-the-spot inspections), the civilian governments have rapidly built the Internet backbone and wireless networks, not only to adapt to the global trend of digital capitalism, but also to conceal the state's surveillance and control techniques within technological artifacts. During both periods, a common goal has been the "war of speed" aimed at both control and growth. This local dynamic of building major national infrastructures was not decided by a simple affiliation into the global market so much as by complex processes of domestic control and economic development, through the mass mobilization of the citizens toward informatization. In Korea, the major drive towards informatization has been not only the state's desire to support the domestic conglomerates, as discussed in previous chapters, but also its desire to regulate citizens with the normalizing control of network technology. In the process of Korea's informatization, the legacies of control constructed by the military regimes have become the material basis of the electronic backbone networks, which are currently advancing the technocratic desire for centrally amassing and managing data on every citizen.

A case study: the "National Education Information System" (NEIS)

The civilian governments not only enforced the collection of network-based data on the citizens, but also centralized local databases as part of their aim to become more of a control society. The nationwide networks for special purposes such as the "National Education Information System" (NEIS), inaugurated in 2003, the "National Total Management Information System of Crime and Justice" (NTMIS), inaugurated in 2004, and the "Cyber Data Search/Collection System," in 2009, are instances of the central government's modulation and assembly of locally dispersed micro-powers (see Table 5.1).

The NTMIS, for example, aims to integrate citizens' criminal and legal data in one central database system operated by the Ministry of Justice, whereas previously such data had been managed separately by the police, prosecutors, courts, and other special criminal investigation agencies. Similarly, the NEIS is designed to integrate the information from over 10,000 schools and education agencies in a central server, operated by the Ministry of Education and Human Resources (MEHR). The records of eight million students—more than 350 items of personal information about each student, including academic, health, activity, and family records—which had previously been managed in each school or district, have now been integrated into the Ministry's central database. In a climate of weak legal and technological privacy protections, the government pushed forward with the NEIS, despite the protests of civil rights groups in Korea, based on the bureaucratic elites' utilitarian rationale that centralizing the management of all citizens' data would be efficient for managing organizational society (in the case of the NEIS, the national school system).

The introduction of these database systems to manage each citizen's personal information would be inconceivable without a national electronic backbone network, the KII, which enables the integration of local data with the central database. The following sub-sections investigate the historical origin of and controversy over the NEIS, the counteraction of the citizens against the NEIS, and its implications in relation to the KII.

Prehistory of the NEIS

The NEIS was originally derived from the earlier National Basic Information System (NBIS), a national computerization project launched under the Chun administration. From 1987 to 1996, the NBIS was a nationwide computerization project made up of five major information networks,[10] one of which was the Education and Research Information System (ERIS), the predecessor of the NEIS. The NBIS, under the military regime, was the first state-led IT network building plan to computerize the administrative affairs of government agencies and public institutions, and by building the ERIS the government expected to create a new labor market through IT education. In the December of 1988, the ERIS was again split into two separate project units—the Education Information

System and the Research Information System—because the government aimed to develop each project separately. Implemented under the guidance of the MEHR, the goal of the Education Information System was quite simple: by 1996, the government aimed to create one PC training room per school, each equipped with 20 computers (to be shared by two students apiece) and a PC with a printer for the teacher (MIC & NCA: 2005). This PC-supply policy contributed to shifting the schools' documentation activities from hand-written documents to a computerized system—a "stand-alone" (S/A) computing system, since the concept of the networked PC system had barely been conceived at the time (the late 1980s). In 1998, the MEHR introduced the "client-server" (C/S) system, which enabled the schools to largely interconnect themselves through an Intranet. This C/S system was managed directly by school principals on a separate school server within each school. To construct the C/S system, which was installed in 8,651 (86 percent) out of a total of 10,061 primary and secondary schools, the government had invested around US$150 million up to 2001 (Joint Struggle Committee for Human Rights in Information Society and Against the NEIS [hereafter JSC], 2003a).

Since 1998, the information backbone network (KII) has gradually expanded throughout the nation's major metropolitan areas, and the demand for high-speed broadband Internet has rapidly increased as well. To create a critical mass of subscribers for the KII, the government offered a steeply discounted institutional rate on service charges; in general, government agencies and educational institutions received a 40 percent discount on broadband service charges from the service providers and a 40 percent government subsidy, so that they paid only 20 percent of the actual cost (see Chapter 4).[11] The government further discounted the rate to subscribers from elementary, middle, and high schools by charging them only 13 percent of the actual cost, and even offered them free access to the Internet at 256 Kbps (MIC & NCA, 2006). To accomplish this massive discount of service charges, the MEHR had already requested the government to benchmark the "E-Rate" offered by the US government, which is a 20 percent to 90 percent subsidy for schools and libraries, drawn from the Universal Service Fund (US Department of Education, 1997). Following this US standard, the steep discount rate for educational institutions in Korea became decisive in creating the momentum to expand the broadband service to isolated schools in remote areas.

In 2001, the KII project was entering its third phase—the optical backbone network for interlinking the government agencies and public institutions (KII-G)—and the government began to focus on the quality of the network service and the development of commercial media contents, since the physical backbone network had been completed. Due to the government's sponsorship of subscriptions, the broadband Internet services of educational institutions, through the physical conduit of the KII-G, had grown enough to cover the entire school system. To exploit the new material conditions brought about by the KII (the increase of broadband interconnectivity and the national coverage of the optical networks), President Dae-Jung Kim announced eleven e-government initiatives. The goal of e-governance was to digitize key administrative and civil information and construct a seamless web of data through the national backbone network. The government planned to develop such IT policy programs as the Internet-based Civil Service, the e-Procurement System, and the National Finance Information System, as well as the National Education Information System (NIA, 2007). Through these programs, the government wanted to create integrated online government services, such as "a service enabling any citizen to report, file, or pay taxes over the Internet" (NIA, 2007: 29).

The government introduced the NEIS as part of the e-government initiative to connect the nation's 10,870 primary and secondary schools to 16 provincial education boards, in order to handle educational affairs electronically. Since the NEIS was designed as a state-led e-government initiative, the government designed it as a centrally integrated database system, interlinking educational institutions under a bureaucratic vision. The locally managed C/S system was abruptly dismantled even before it was fully installed. While it was discarding the enormous investment in the old C/S system, the government spent an additional US$52 million to install the NEIS and more than US$500 million to upgrade the schools' PC systems with new models. Between March and September, 2002, the MEHR undertook a system design and deployment for the NEIS with the technical support of Samsung SDS, and then from the September of 2002 to the February of 2003, it conducted a pilot test at 267 schools in order to determine the feasibility of the NEIS. In the February of 2003, as the Presidential Transition Committee was preparing for the Moo-hyun Roh administration to take office, the Korean Teachers and Educational Workers Union (KTU), or *Jeongyojo*, a left-wing labor union, along with civil society groups, requested that the new Roh administration cancel the implementation of the NEIS. They argued that it threatened the civil rights of students and teachers and would create problems such as infringing on the privacy of students and parents, bureaucratically controlling teachers, and overburdening staff with computer work, since teachers would be required to register every detail of school management and of students' academic performance, health, and enrollment records (Alliance of Seventeen Human Rights Groups, 2003). However, on March 1, 2003, the inauguration day of the new administration, the MEHR launched the NEIS, heedless of the request from civil rights groups.

Bureaucratic efficiencies vs. an Orwellian vision

The NEIS is a typical example of a policy program directed by the central government. The proponents of expanding the NEIS to the entire nation—the government, the MEHR, and the system developer—have defended the "openness" of the system, in contrast to the "closedness" of the locally operated C/S system (Presidential Commission on Policy Planning [PCPP], 2008), emphasizing the efficient management of an "integrated" system of students' records on a central server. Meanwhile, opponents of the NEIS—the KTU, the coalition of parents, and the civil rights groups—have criticised the scope of data collection and the security weaknesses of a central server controlled by the MEHR.

The strongest criticism of the NEIS has been directed against the amount and the sensitivity of the personal information it collects on each student (Jung, 2003). The NEIS collects 358 personal records per student, as previously mentioned, which are broken down into the following three categories: student academic and enrollment records, school management information, and health records. "Student academic and enrollment records" consists of 45 records for each student, such as resident ID number, passport picture, attendance, lateness, sick leave, accidents, special talents, behavior patterns, and written evaluations. "School management information" consists of 170 items related to each student's socio-economic status and much more, including whether the student is a beneficiary of a social security program, receives special education, is the head of a family, or has been subject to disciplinary action at school. In addition, the birth dates and educational backgrounds of students and parents, and records of counseling, delinquency, deviancy, and imprisonment all fall under the "school management information" category. "Health records" include 143 records about a student's health, such as preventive inoculation, physical condition (obesity, eyesight, color blindness, hearing difficulties, nose trouble, malnutrition, mental disorders, and allergies), the results of pathology tests, and disease history. Besides these detailed records, the NEIS also incorporates 24 other sections, including data such as a school's budget, salaries, equipment, facilities, accounting, and personnel records, including 27 items of personal information on each teacher, such as the state of their health, their property (including real estate), records of political activities, and criminal records (Kim & Kim, 2004; JSC, 2003a). The database also links each student's personal information with that of his or her parents, including their birthdates, residential ID numbers, and educational backgrounds. The NEIS therefore enables the state to control vast amounts of specific personal information about students, parents, and teachers. This so-called "open" system integrates these privacy-sensitive data into the central server of the MEHR, and that database is once again integrated and re-sorted into the national ID number database, and other databases containing even more personal information about individuals: the scope is thus truly Orwellian.

This integration of databases signifies a new stage of integration and articulation between micro-power in the local and macro-power in the central government. One issue raised by this is that if these integrated data points in the central server are vulnerable to security breaches, the damage could be unlimited in scope. Already in early 2003, Korea was substantially affected by a virus attack that crippled the domestic Internet system.[12] The so-called "1–24 Computer Disaster" was caused by a security flaw in Microsoft's web-server software, and since then many Koreans have begun to believe that any networked computer is vulnerable to a malicious virus or hacking. Other doubts were created by the sudden shift of government policy from the C/S system to the NEIS. The government had already invested massively in the C/S system, and, up until the April of 2001, the MEHR had announced no other plan than to expand the installation of the C/S system into every school. Interestingly, according to a monograph released by the JSC (2003a), just after the MEHR's briefing about the

C/S system in the Blue House (the Korean White House), the Special Committee for E-government—a special joint taskforce for implementing eleven e-government policy goals under the Dae-Jung Kim administration—caused the MEHR to change their policy plan from the C/S to the NEIS. This report adds that the government urged the MEHR to cooperate with Samsung SDS, a network system developer and subsidiary of Samsung Corporation, to shift school networking from the C/S system to the NEIS. After that, according to a recent policy report from the Presidential Commission on Policy Planning (2008), a total of 88 people—12 public officials from the MEHR and 76 persons from Samsung SDS—began to launch to analyze, design, and build the NEIS, with no participation from the general citizenry, more broadly selected expert groups, or the relevant civil society groups. In fact, these two reports confirm that the government and Samsung SDS exclusively arranged a secret deal to replace the C/S system with the NEIS. By doing so, the traditional citizen–state relations in regard to privacy were abolished and the state as mediator was replaced by the private vendor. The government's collusion with the *Chaebols'* IT-related affiliates in constructing a privacy-related IT system was a scheme that would be repeated often in the development of the next-generation Internet control techniques (see Deibert & Rohozinski, 2010).

These opaque decision-making processes and controversies over the government's IT-driven educational policy finally evoked the mass protest of citizens against the NEIS, as discussed in the next section.

The battle over the NEIS

From early 2003 onward, the KTU and other civil society groups were already developing a civil disobedience movement against the implementation of the NEIS (JSC, 2003a), which they claimed would allow the government to keep and control an unconstitutional database system threatening the civil rights of students, teachers, and parents. On February 18, the KTU filed a petition with the National Human Rights Commission (NHRC),[13] claiming the NEIS violated human rights by its systematic surveillance of students' records. On March 3, the KTU also launched a sit-in protest against the NEIS, and on March 17, the parents' group also announced their opposition to the NEIS' implementation. Nevertheless, the government continued to implement the database system despite these protests.

The NHRC (2003) issued policy recommendations siding with the civil rights group, judging that the three categories of students' records (school management information, student academic and enrollment records, and health records) infringed upon basic human rights under international law as well as under the national constitution's protection of privacy.[14] The NHRC recommended that each school continue to use the C/S system to store such private information, while enhancing the security level of the system. The NHRC also called for the government to remove the three privacy-sensitive categories containing students' information and teachers' personnel records from the NEIS (Privacy

International, 2007). As its scope is limited to issuing policy recommendations, the NHRC has no power to enforce its rulings, but the NHRC's recommendations in this case had sufficient impact throughout Korean society that the government was forced to scale back its implementation of the NEIS. The Ministry of Education and Human Resources (MEHR) officially announced that it "would consider the NHRC's recommendations with respect" (*Hankyoreh*, 2003, May). On May 26, the MEHR, in its negotiations with the KTU, finally seemed to accept the NHRC's policy recommendations to drop the three contested categories of students' data and to revise the whole process of implementation. Table 5.2 shows the number of items that the government agreed to remove from the NEIS database and what items remain.

Although the government agreed to drop 60 percent of the personal information from the original database, a total of 122 privacy-sensitive records were still problematic. Despite the civil rights groups' concessions during negotiation, the MEHR later betrayed them by announcing that it would allow each school to choose its own database management system, raising the suspicion that schools would be pressured to adopt the original version of the NEIS (JSC, 2003b). Reacting to this announcement from the MEHR and under persuasion from the Provincial Offices of Education, which are subdivisions of the MEHR, some primary and secondary school principals began to voluntarily introduce the NEIS into their computer system, although the principals' decisions were taken without any agreement from the teachers (*Yonhap News Agency*, 2003).

The MEHR's betrayal aroused public outrage. On June 18, human rights activists launched a hunger strike struggle against the NEIS (People's Solidarity for Participatory Democracy, 2003, June). On June 20, the KTU visited the MEHR building to protest the government's adherence to the NEIS and to launch a nationwide rally with large demonstrations to halt its implementation, chanting the slogan, "The MEHR must stop the NEIS policy of an ostrich sticking its head in the sand!" (*Hankyoreh*, 2003, June 21). Facing such a strong backlash, the government realized that the MEHR had lost the credibility to lead the NEIS policy program, and instead created a Committee for Educational

Table 5.2 The three contested categories of NEIS data

Categories	Original plan	Removed	Retained	Percentage removed
School management information	170	56 (37)	114 (133)	33 (22%)
Student academic and enrollment records	45	45	0	100*
Health records	143	135	8	95
Total	358	236 (217)	122 (141)	66 (61)

Source: JSC (2003a: 7).

Notes
* 100% is to be removed after a student's graduation.
Numbers in parentheses refer to the figures for special schools for the disabled.

Informatization (CEI) headed by the Prime Minister. Ostensibly, the CEI was to listen to the various stakeholders' voices in redesigning the NEIS plan. The KTU argued that, in reality, the government arbitrarily appointed CEI members behind closed doors and entirely excluded the anti-NEIS civil rights groups. The KTU claimed that "the government should never have included on the Committee persons who opposed the NHRC's policy recommendations" (*Hankyoreh*, 2003, June 24). On June 25, a large number of civil society groups, human rights organizations, and unions—including the People's Solidarity for the Participatory Democracy, the Lawyers Association for a Democratic Society, the KTU, and the Democratic Labor Party—jointly held a press conference demanding that the CEI be reformulated on the basis of transparency and democracy. On July 8, the 43 civil rights groups opposing the NEIS established a Joint Struggle Committee to Protect Human Rights in Information Society and Against the NEIS (JSC). The JSC announced to the media that it would "organize a pan-national movement against NEIS, to conduct national campaigns for abolishing the e-government project [the NEIS], which infringes on human rights, and more broadly, to discuss the citizens' human rights in an information society" (JSC, 2003, July). The JSC also declared that it would reinforce solidarity with the international organizations fighting for human rights such as the United Nations Human Rights Council, Privacy International, Education International, and the International Labor Organization. In the September of 2003, the JSC began to stage a massive candlelight vigil protesting against the NEIS in several major cities and a one-person picket protest[15] in relays in front of the entrances to schools.

To end the long-lasting conflict surrounding the NEIS, in the September of 2004, the government again entered into negotiations with the KTU, and came to the conclusion that in the September of 2005 the NEIS would be tested in a revised form and installed in the following year. Both parties agreed on some controversial points: First, the plan to have a central server of the NEIS managed by the MEHR would be nullified. Instead, each individual school could choose the S/A, the C/S, or the NEIS system. If choosing to introduce the NEIS system, a high school must install an individual Intranet server unable to connect to outside servers, and an elementary or middle school must construct a group server system capable of linking no more than 15 schools internally. Second, once the NEIS was operated by the server of an individual school or a group of schools, the three privacy-sensitive categories for students' records (school management information, student academic and enrollment records, and health records) could be kept, on the condition of deleting some highly sensitive records (Kim, 2004, September). Third, to save the costs of building the distributive networks, Linux was adopted as its major operating system. In the March of 2006, the revised NEIS was officially launched; by 2007, Linux, an open source operation system, was installed on 2,335 NEIS servers (Kim, 2007, July).

Although the civil rights groups failed to abolish the NEIS, they did accomplish the goal of blocking the government's desire to manage students' personal information through a central sever system. In this case, public protest achieved its goals, or at least some of them. Through a dramatic bargaining process, the

NEIS scandal came to an end; privacy issues in the education system, however, have not. For instance, despite the March 2005 passage in the National Assembly of a revised Basic Education Act with a new provision to protect students' personal information, illegal activities such as the leaking of students' data to private educational service companies are increasing (Park, 2007, August). The Ministry of Education, Science, and Technology—created under the new president, Myung-bak Lee, by a reshuffling of the MEHR and the Ministry of Science and Technology—has installed CCTVs in 70 percent of school buildings in the name of monitoring gang activities in schools (Noh, 2008). The state's desire to collect students' personal data seemed to backfire and was almost foiled in the NEIS case, but the government's interventionist plans to install CCTV in most schools or, most recently, to introduce heavy-handed regulation such as a night-time curfew on playing online computer games for those 16 and under (see Table 5.1; *The Economist,* 2011), signify that the state is incessantly seeking to monitor students. At the same time, the increasing leaks of student data to private companies (*Hankyoreh,* 2005) indicate that the private sector is on the prowl for whatever it can obtain from these expanding stores of government data.

The KII was the government's chosen instrument for improving the global competitiveness of the national economy, providing citizens with more efficient public services, and promising them a better quality of life. The government considered the KII, and within it, the NEIS, as the first step to creating a rosy digital future by interconnecting the public educational institutions at the national level. The case of the NEIS, however, made the public aware that anti-democratic and retrogressive aspects of Korean political culture have been deeply embedded within the design of such technical codes.

Lessons about surveillance, privacy, and protest in the broadband Internet era

Even among Asian countries, South Korea is known as a country highly passionate about education, where parents are wholly devoted to improving the social status of their children through their investment in higher education. From elementary through high school, Korean students strive fiercely to enter the exclusive universities in and around the Seoul metropolitan area. The government and the public and private educational institutions have also justified promoting stronger competition among students and wielding disciplinary control over them. The NEIS case represents a worst-case scenario resulting from the technocratic education policies by which the state has regulated students' academic affairs and their personal information. The NEIS also became a locus of confrontation between privacy groups and proponents of IT efficiencies, in which neither party was able to accomplish its ultimate goals. To install the integrated database system, the government used the plea of the "efficiencies" of systematic management to justify bureaucratic control of citizens. The opponents resisted the NEIS's lack of privacy safeguards (Park, 2007) and warned of the potential dangers of a state-controlled database system.

The NEIS controversy in Korea offers several lessons about surveillance, privacy, and protest in the age of nationwide networks like the KII: First, surveillance cases similar to that of the NEIS are arising with increasing frequency in the digital age, all aimed at bolstering the bureaucratic capacity for social control. It is obvious that national networks like the KII not only promote the national economy but also stimulate and refine government surveillance practices such as the "free-floating" control of digital databases (Deleuze, [1990] 1995; see Chapter 1). Second, with the conjoining of digital technologies and bureaucratic control, citizens' privacy rights evaporate more easily, and their losses are more difficult to perceive, than in the disciplinary society under the military regimes. Third, the confluence of an underdeveloped political system, vulnerable citizens under assault by bureaucratic and business interests, cronyism between the *Chaebols* (e.g., Samsung SDI and LG CNS) and the government in creating national database systems such as the e-ID card and the NEIS, and the lack of legal privacy protections continuously reinforce the pervasive use of public power in Korea. Fourth, despite these constraints, in the new era of civilian government, Koreans' political engagement—as can be seen in the robust alliance of civil society groups against the government's NEIS policy—has become mature enough to counteract the new network-based surveillance techniques. In this lies the hope for Korea's IT future.

6 Conclusion

Beyond a developmental state model

> The essentially social character of technology lies not in the logic of its inner workings, but in the relation of that logic to a social context.
>
> (Feenberg, 1991: 82)

> Analysis of objective conditions take us this far but no further. [...] The *kairos*— the opportune moment that ruptures the monotony and repetitiveness of chronological time—has to be grasped by a political subject.
>
> (Hardt & Negri, 2009: 165)

The real conditions behind Korean-specific developmentalism

This book's origins were in questioning the popular belief among policymakers that the Korean Information Infrastructure (KII) project has improved the quality of Korean society and culture and further upgraded the country's IT status in the global community. It is obvious that policy rhetoric, which ignores the real conditions behind the successful KII policy plan, creates a barrier to an accurate evaluation of the KII project by telecom policymakers, politicians, and communication scholars. In fact, Korea's developmentalism—its continuing efforts to catch up to the economic power of the advanced nations—has been founded on close linkages between the state and powerful corporate interests, a partnership which has neglected the participation of the citizenry. Each chapter of this book has noted the opaque decision-making processes surrounding the KII, such as allotting the KII business licenses for specific vendors, KT and LG Dacom (Chapters 2 and 3); redesigning the KII as a regulatory means to control the citizens, as in the case of the National Education Information System (NEIS), though this attempt was largely thwarted by public reaction, as detailed in Chapter 5; and excluding the citizens' voices from the intermediary organizations built to facilitate the KII, as discussed in Chapter 4. The underdeveloped political culture of Korea led the KII project to become a policy that is only half-ripe: it serves as the material foundation which has made Korea an IT powerhouse but also, as a policy, it represents already entrenched corporate interests and reinforces bureaucratic efficiencies for social control. This book has confirmed that Korea's past legacies of authoritarian interventionism and developmentalism under the military regimes still haunt such projects as the KII. Although planned and implemented under civilian governments, the KII could not escape the authoritarian and undemocratic character of the politico-social structure inherited from the military regimes.

This book has examined in detail the major contextual factors conditioning the KII project: the global constraints conditioning its telecom policies (using globalization theory), the dense state–capital linkages (using developmental state theories), and the bureaucratic desire for control (using critical geographies). As the background for investigating the major driving forces that conditioned the birth of the KII project in the early 1990s, Chapter 2 surveyed how, from the period of Japanese colonialism, throughout the military regimes, and up to the current civilian government, different regimes have changed space and spatialization in Korea by building national transportation and information infrastructures. Specifically, this chapter examined how the state-led infrastructure plans in each of these eras have been closely related to the economic goals of the various regimes. Under colonialist rule, the infrastructure across the peninsula was built to serve the Japanese imperialist desire to access the Manchurian market. The later military regimes had a strong sense that they must industrialize the national economy, which lagged far behind the advanced nations. This industrial modernization project rapidly developed the economy. In the early 1990s, however, Korea experienced an economic recession as a result of losing its privileged export status, based on low-wage labor in textiles and heavy industry. The civilian government's main goal, therefore, was to shift the national economy towards a knowledge-based system, and they chose the KII as an infrastructure to revive Korea's economic growth in the new digital economy. This chapter, thus, situated the KII project not only within the succession of past administrations' infrastructure plans, but also within the response of the Korean government and business to the new digital mode of capitalism.

In terms of global constraints, Chapter 3 examined how Korea's state-sponsored project to create the most developed broadband network in the world was catalyzed by the context of market liberalization, a process led by the US and other developed countries, and including the WTO regulations and the US Trade Representative's designation of Korea as a Priority Foreign Country. This chapter investigated the methods Korea used to confront the pressures of economic globalization, which had two contradictory aspects: the voluntary affiliation of Korea into the unified global economy and the local adjustment to survive within the hierarchical system. While the government's series of IT-driven policy plans aimed at positioning Korea's IT infrastructure in the forefront of universal global capitalism in the digital age, this chapter showed that tensions have arisen between the strong wave of economic liberalization and the desire to protect and promote national sovereignty. The de-nationalizing processes of globalization, rather than being a simple integration of local economies into the global, have also fed nationalizing dynamics at the same time (Sassen,

2006). The development of the ATM switching technology, an essential part of the KII, illustrated how the Korean government wanted not only to enlist the local economy as part of the global network of capitalism, but also to promote priming-the-pump policy plans in order to create new profitable resources for the local market. The state leadership in the KII project was an active expression of the national IT strategy, though in the case of the ATM switching technology it ended with a "broken dream" when the ATM technology became outmoded by the IP-based router. Further, within the process, this chapter showed how the state assumed a collaborative role as an agent of local capital and as a mediator controlling the inflow of global capital. This analysis once again confirms the assessment that the globalizing process is "partly inhabiting and even getting constituted inside the national" (Sassen, 2007: 2). Theoretically, this chapter exemplified the East Asian textures of localization in response to the irresistible force of economic globalization. The economic sphere of globalization can be seen as the underdevelopment or closure of local economies overwhelmed by the globalizing flows of capital, finance, and commodity, while the socio-cultural spheres of globalization have been more flexible and autonomous in their response to the universal principle of globalism. Even within the economic sphere, however, this chapter noted the strong tendencies of the local manifested under the structural hierarchy of economic globalization.

With regard to the dense state–capital linkages, typical in the developmental state model in Korea, Chapter 4 first surveyed the legacy of the developmental state model under the military regimes (1963–92) which created centralized, authoritarian national plans for industrialization. Intergovernmental organizations mediated close linkages between the state and the *Chaebols*; this model showed some continuities, but also some discontinuities with the KII policy plan under the civilian governments. Continuity was seen in the *Chaebol*-biased policy plans of the government and its intermediary organizations in both eras. For instance, like the Economic Planning Board (EPB) established under the military regime of Cheong-hee Park, the KII Planning Board was distinctively effective in implementing the IT project through its intermediary role, in which it managed the various interests of the different government agencies and the *Chaebols*. Discontinuity could be seen in the shift in the role of the state. While the developmental state under the military regime acted as a commander, directing the *Chaebols* in the execution of its plans and policies, the post-developmental state under the civilian government became a coordinator, guiding policy projects in a manner favorable to the *Chaebols*. Under the military regimes, the state and the *Chaebols* had a direct crony relationship, in which the government granted business licenses and in return, the *Chaebols* donated political slush funds. In contrast, this chapter described how the KII project's success was facilitated by indirect government subsidies to the *Chaebols* such as public investment loans, a joint public–private sector KII fund, and the promotion of Internet subscribers through the cyber-building certificate system.

Chapter 4 confirmed that even in today's Korea, "those with a connection to a few leading political figures have precedence over others who might be better qualified" to participate in policymaking (Hyun & Lent, 1999). The backward political conditions in Korea (which can be seen in the pervasive practice of ignoring the procedural consensus mechanisms of policymaking, and relying instead on personal ties or favoritism to specific *Chaebols*), combined with the dominant trends of contemporary global capitalism, have made the economy more vulnerable to crises such as the IMF financial crisis of 1997, and impeded new entrants into the market. Chapter 4 assessed the KII project as a prototypical IT policy that reflected an evolving phase of the developmental state model (the "flexible" state), an IT policy which was enacted in the midst of the shift from the "strong" state to the present "market-driven" state. The KII project has created the material conditions enabling the *Chaebols* to become "*e-Chaebols*," incumbents in the new IT sector, as well as in the traditional manufacturing sector. Theoretically, Chapter 4 contributed to a critical reading of the developmental state theories through the disclosure of the negative effects caused by the symbiosis between the state and the *Chaebols* during the KII project, and by relating the evolutionary phases of state power to the emergence of Korean civil society and to the *Chaebols*' growth.

Chapter 5 examined how the KII has also facilitated the state's control of its citizens, and how the civilian government's surveillance techniques, based on the digital networks, differs from the disciplinary surveillance techniques of the military regimes. The KII has provided the citizens more efficient public services through the e-government system, but at the same time it has enabled the government to intensify its surveillance of citizens with an invisible, mobile, and flow-based mode of social control more pervasive than a visible, disciplinary, oppressive, and place-based one. To illustrate the KII-based control conducted by the government, Chapter 5 examined the case of the NEIS, which aimed to manage the profile data of students, parents, and teachers through the central server of a government agency (MEHR). The NEIS was a unique Big-Brother-type proposal, one which could hardly be imagined without the nationwide high-speed backbone networks. It represented the conjoining of bureaucratic efficiencies and digital technologies under the conditions of an immature political culture, which gave no consideration to the citizens' privacy rights. The chapter concluded that the ensuing confrontation, between the proponents of IT efficiencies and the civil society groups that united against the NEIS, epitomized the citizens' hopeful possibilities for increased democracy in Korean public life. Theoretically, Chapter 5 confirmed Gilles Deleuze's thesis (see Chapter 1) that today's society is increasingly based on the power mechanism for social control, going beyond the use of disciplinary suppression to a digital grid of control over the citizens. In regard to the NEIS case, this chapter confirmed that, in this Deleuzean world, there is a new tendency of surveillance techniques to articulate locally dispersed micro-power (localized data) into the centralized macro power (a central server system).

In sum, it is unquestionable that the KII project, sustained by government subsidies, has enhanced the national IT indicators and elevated Korean society into the first tier of global IT development (a shift of the Korean economy from the export-oriented industrial system to knowledge-based one). Nevertheless, the legacy of developmentalism practiced by the military juntas has also left its mark on the KII project (which was carried out under the "flexible state," a mixture of the strong state and the market-driven state). Just as under the military regimes, so today the *Chaebols* such as KT, LG Dacom, SK, and Samsung have been great beneficiaries of the KII, and have become the dominant actors of the IT economy (the creation of *e-Chaebols*). Moreover, without strong protections for citizens' privacy rights, the KII can easily become (as the NEIS case shows) a further extension of the state's surveillance of its citizens, and in this way the KII signifies a shift in Korea from a disciplinary society to a network-based control society (see Table 6.1).

Further, the KII embodies a decision-making process that is confined to technocrats and business interests and has excluded the general citizenry, more broadly selected expert groups, and the relevant civil society groups. The lack of democratic decision-making processes in building the KII can be seen in such policies as the careless introduction of the NEIS, the ill-judged choice of the ATM as a core technology, and the exclusive membership of the intermediary organizations that guided the KII's design. It is thus all the more necessary to construct a democratic forum at the national policy level, which is sustained from below to work on behalf of the public welfare, against the proprietary interests of the *Chaebols*.

Towards a sustainable development model

South Korea has accomplished rapid economic growth within a brief period: under the Park regime, the "developmental dictatorship" succeeded in accomplishing industrial modernization. At the same time, it caused a "tendency toward deformation" of economic growth under conditions of extreme state intervention, a deformation that includes such phenomena as the increase of inequalities between the classes, environmental destruction, harsh labor control, and crony capitalism. At the present time, although economic policy is no longer implemented by an autocracy, the close relationships between the government and the *Chaebols* are still influential in designing the national economic plans, and civil society's ability to be involved in or monitor the policymaking

Table 6.1 The role of the KII as a catalyst

	The KII as a catalyst of the following evolving phases:
Major infrastructure	*From a physical infrastructure to a virtual infrastructure*
Catching-up economy	*From an export-oriented industrial economy to a knowledge- or digital-based economy (from Chaebols to e-Chaebols)*
Form of the state	*The flexible state (a transition from the strong state to the market-driven neoliberal state)*
Social control	*From a disciplinary society to a network-based control of society*

processes is limited. The state rhetoric of a "catching-up" economy has easily overruled voices from below, regarding them as unnecessary noise.

Policy change in Korea should lead toward reformulating telecom policies along much more socially interventionist and redistributive lines, and toward decentralizing or democratically controlling the overwhelming power of the *Chaebols*. What is needed is a democratic force from below that can exert itself against such interests, and assert instead the public's interest. Understanding the history of the KII project provides insights into how to formulate future telecom policies along much more democratically participatory lines, while restraining the overwhelming power of the telecom oligopolies and *Chaebols* and soliciting the input of citizens and citizens' groups. The results of this study suggest that the attempt of the state to intervene in a protectionist way to oppose global capitalism will only serve to further expand the power of the *Chaebols*, which will, over the course of time, simply expand into transnational oligopolies. What options are open to those who would avoid furthering the same type of collusion between the state and the *Chaebols*?

First, to end the crony linkages between the state and the *Chaebols* in Korea, civil society needs to force both the government and the *Chaebols* to guarantee small and medium enterprises (SMEs) a fair share in granting IT-related business licenses. For instance, in composing a consortium for a specific IT project such as metropolitan-area network, the central and city governments could legally require the allocation of one-half of the business rights to SMEs, along with restrictions on the share allotted to each *Chaebol*. Korean SMEs have existed in a "master–slave" relationship with the *Chaebols*, in which they have been forced into serving as the *Chaebols'* subcontracted sweatshops. The best way to revive IT venture capital in Korea is to shift away from such practices and allow SMEs equal access to the market as independent actors. None of the SMEs in Korea were able to grow large enough to challenge the established *Chaebols*; due to the favoritism shown by the state to the *Chaebols*, the rise of new *Chaebol*-sized corporations is rare, indeed, almost impossible in the current Korean market. The irrational slogan that only the *Chaebols* can nurture the national economy and compete with other countries' multinationals in the global market has prevailed; this logic of scale should instead be replaced with an IT growth thesis focusing on the SMEs' innovative and creative roles in the age of Web 2.0. The government should set out fair rules that allow SMEs to survive and compete in the market, rather than serving as "midwives" to the *Chaebols*.

Second, while the privatization and commercialization of the Internet are significant factors endangering a free culture in Korea, as they are throughout the developed world, the most urgent issue surrounding media and the Internet in South Korea is the government's continuing pre- and post-censorship, such as the Internet content rating system, the real name system that prohibits anonymous postings on discussion groups, and the accusation and imprisonment of system operators and users in order to restrict free speech. Under the contemporary undemocratic and underdeveloped political culture, the political elites can easily pollute the IT infrastructure by restricting the citizens' public lives. While

Korea has, as mentioned in Chapter 5, a National Human Rights Commission (NHRC), currently its rulings are only advisory; what is needed is for the NHRC both to restore its independence from the "neo-authoritarian" government and to be given the legal power to enforce its rulings against acts of censorship carried out by the government or its agents, by corporations, or by others.

On a broader societal level, in order to resist such invisible and concealed bureaucratic power of social control, as in the NEIS case and other ongoing privacy-related issues, citizens' privacy and human rights should be cultivated by the tactics of counter-surveillance, or a so-called "synopticon" (Mathiesen, 1997) that enables the public not only to monitor power's surveilling eyes but also to resist the surveillance networks of political power. Whereas, in its original conception, the panopticon was a disciplinary model for supervising prisoners from an all-seeing high tower, the counter-surveillance or "synopticon" designates a reversal in which the many (the citizens) watch the few (the powerful). For instance, following the example of environmental impact assessments which measure the potential results of such development projects as a dam, motorway, airport, or factory even before their launch, one of the tactics of the synopticon could be the creation of technology impact assessments (TIA) which ensure citizens' ability to monitor and participate in an IT policy from its design to its implementation. In control societies, place has been transformed into "flows." The greater the role communication networks play in the production and reinforcement of power, the more the citizens are enabled to re-appropriate the dominant system residing in the flows. It is likely that the same conditions that reinforce abilities of power can also empower the citizens. Even under seemingly rigid control, political tension exists between the codification of power and its rearrangement by the intervention of human agents.

Third, the KII was a project designed by self-assured technocrats, without considering minority voices or feedback from civil society. It has been the pattern of Korean IT policies to ignore the importance of social inclusion, and of the civic participation of marginalized community groups and user groups that should lie at the heart of IT development. What is needed is a democratic force from below that can exert itself against such interests, and assert instead the public's interest. For instance, in his history of South Africa's transitional period of 1990 to 1994, Horwitz (2003) notes the policy setting of a "culture of democratic consultation and transparency." He describes various stakeholders' "forums" in South Africa as providing a space, in a more "concerted" rather than a "corporatist" setting, for the effective intervention of civil society groups in national telecommunications policymaking processes. A well-ordered society creates the optimal conditions for citizens to participate in the policymaking processes, and within it to cultivate, for their own benefit, the virtue of cultural diversity. In contrast to the unfair conditions in the market, supported by the state's developmentalism and favoritism in Korea, this book suggests a democratic "forum" at the national policy level could be sustained from below, to work on behalf of the public welfare, against the proprietary biases of economic oligopolies that have manipulated Korean social reality up until now. Speaking of the undemocratic situation in the US telecom market, McChesney (2004, 2007) mentions the concept of "critical junctures" at which there is the momentum for media and telecom reform; at the present time, civil rights activists, such as media watchdog groups and grassroots movements in Korea, should exert pressure on the "neo-authoritarian" and *Chaebol*-friendly government to rearrange the technological and cultural resources, wealth, and power now controlled by the interests of big business and by neo-liberal deregulatory policy.

Finally, at the rhetorical level, Korean civil society needs to take a leading role in transforming the current social climate, which is dominated by the central and local governments' logic of economic development through the IT industry, and competition in the global economy. In a Korea desiring to accomplish, in a compressed timeframe, the creation of a modernity resembling that of wealthier Western societies, the spontaneous elements springing from local demands are always viewed from a business perspective of "development" and "competition." The Korean government has a strong tendency to "see the information society still in industrial terms, bent and shaped to fit the old economy of mass produced electronic hardware commodities" (Venturelli, 2002: 83). Public rhetoric in Korea needs to be enriched by adding some adjectives to these nouns: we need "sustainable" development and "fair" competition to enhance the living conditions of citizens. Civil society in Korea should encourage the government to situate IT development within the concerns of "sustainable" development, which aims to promote democratic values in the information society, such as a diversity of IT opportunities to the underserved and underprivileged, respect for privacy and human rights, and the relative independence of IT policy from the industrial approach.

These four suggestions for Korean society are in accord with the recommendations set forth in the joint Civil Society Declaration ("The Seoul Declaration"), which was endorsed by a variety of online civil rights and civil society groups around the world (such as the Electronic Privacy Information Center, the Electronic Frontier Foundation, the European Digital Rights Initiative, IT4Change, Public Knowledge, the Associations for Progressive Communications, Consumers Korea, and the Jinbo Network). The declaration was submitted to the 2008 OECD Ministerial Meeting on the "Future of the Internet Economy," held in Seoul on June 17–18. At this meeting, the world's civil society groups urged the developed countries to promote the following issues in the age of "the Internet economy": freedom of expression, the protection of privacy and transparency, consumer protection, support for pluralistic media, an inclusive digital society, cultural diversity, and other human rights issues. Going beyond the aspects of Korean IT focused on in this book, the agenda set forth in this declaration expresses essential information rights and principles that need to be taken into account in national decision-making processes related to IT polices, in order to guarantee the basic human rights of citizens around the globe.

For further research

As a macroscopic inquiry into the structural contexts surrounding the KII project and the post-KII phases, this book has limitations that need to be addressed by future research: First, with regard to the research scope, due to its emphasis on the KII's structural aspects (such as its global constraints, the close state–business linkages, social control, and the shift toward a new economy), this book intentionally minimized the autonomous role of actors who were isolated from or went against larger forces in the system. The relation between structural determination and human agency is a central concern of political economy, the theoretical base of this book, and the conceptualization of this relationship is at the core of the theory and method of the political economic approach. Nevertheless, this book excluded the role of agency in the analysis; the justification for this lies in the fact that voices from below were entirely excluded from the policymaking process throughout the KII project. For the state-led KII policy, the dialectic tension between agency and structure appears to be inactive, except in the case of the NEIS, in which it can be seen "how it comes about that structures are constituted through action, and reciprocally how action is constituted structurally" (Giddens, 1976: 161). In Korea, it is at the socio-cultural level of IT development, rather than at the policymaking level, that the louder grassroots voices have been heard, and it is at this level that one can see structural changes being brought about through human agency. For instance, the IT-related scandals and their framings in Korean society, shown in Table 5.2, illustrate the structural processes constituted by the agents' actions. Meanwhile, NGOs and citizens are rarely seen monitoring or intervening in the elites' decision-making processes for IT policies. Rather than searching Korean history for nonexistent empirical cases of policy interventions from below, future studies should expand the research scope to examine how to develop policy alternatives in the process of decision-making, and how to build a more open forum that would enable agents to be actively involved in an impetus for societal change. In other words, the dominant pattern of elitist structure in IT policy in Korea needs to be overcome by developing realistic policy alternatives, to democratize the design, use, and impact of information and communication technologies.

Second, this book has limitations in explicating the power structure among the major stakeholders, especially the political entities surrounding the KII project. This could be overcome through a network analysis detailing the policymaking processes in each of the different administrations and agencies involved. Since a political entity is composed of a class of politicians, their shared interest groups, and various government agencies, this book's approach, which presents the state as a unified entity seeking to attain a goal, is a simplification that may have lost the rich textures of the conflict involved in policy decision-making processes. Further research can fill in this blind spot by doing policy network analyses that stress the performative character of relations among policymakers and relevant interest groups, so as to understand patterns of linkage in terms of political motives and the synergistic effect of the policy activities constituted in those relations.

Finally, many researchers (see Chapter 2) from the academic field of Asian Studies have compared and analyzed the East Asian countries' economic growth and its relationship to state interventionism; however, a comparative study which aims to examine the "catching-up economy" model among these countries, in the new digital age, has yet to be performed. The present study has restricted itself to one country; future research could extend the scope to perform a comparative study with other East and South Asian countries such as China, Taiwan, Singapore, Malaysia, and Japan. All of these countries have shared political experiences analogous to those of Korea in their IT development, specifically, in having IT infrastructure plans led by the state.

Notes

Introduction: South Korea as broadband heaven?

1 Korea's *Chaebols* are family-owned business groups with large subsidiaries occupying an oligopolistic position, despite a relatively low concentration of ownership and the absence of pure holding companies.
2 This book uses "social control" in the context of the government's database of information on individual citizens based on digital technology and electronic networks, rather than in the context of violence or the threat of violence against citizens using repressive powers of the state such as the police, national guard, or military forces.
3 The collaborative links between the state and capital in Korea are well summarized in Weiss (1998: 57), Weiss and Hobson (1995: 170), and Evans (1995).

1 The political economy of networked mobility: a theoretical overview

1 This book investigates mainly the worldwide electronic network as a conduit of capital. The other significant momentum of capital accumulation in the digital age—the privatizing mechanisms of "immaterial" or intellectual labor on a global scale—is beyond the scope of this study. It is now clear, however, that the expropriation and privatization of the common cultural assets of humankind have become the ultimate goals of contemporary capitalism, and accompany the construction of a new virtual geography of electronic connectivity and mobility. Hardt and Negri (2004), for example, describe the expropriation of value in the age of digital capitalism as "the capture of value" which is produced by cooperative labor and which must be protected by powerful intellectual property laws.
2 Similar to the pan-Spanish "telenovela" culture, which is relatively independent from the monolithic cultural dominance of the Hollywood production system, Korea's cultural products—notably, its blockbuster movies, television programs, fashion, and popular music—have become favorites among Asians and even among Latin Americans. The so-called *Halryu* (韓流: "Korean wave") refers to the growing appeal of Korean popular culture in other Asian countries, and is often theoretically explained by "cultural proximity," a phenomenon first identified by empirical studies of the TV-watching patterns of Latin Americans.
3 A view of the state as an "epiphenomenon" of the system of property relations, which is merely a mirror of class rule, represents the vulgar Marxist tradition of economistic reductionism.
4 From a Gerschenkronian perspective of catching-up, Shin and Chang (2003) consider South Korea to be an "extremely backward" country. They characterize the Korean system as a late-twentieth-century example of a late industrializer, based on the "close relationship between the state, the national banks and the *Chaebols*" (25).

5 Wade (1990b: 234) summarized the autonomous features of the state's selective industrial policies that control the market: (1) government initiatives as to what technologies should be adopted; (2) public influence over private resources to carry out these initiatives; (3) a larger before-the-fact plan or strategy.

6 Weiss and Hobson (1995: 9–10) designated a new emerging group of theorists focusing on state–business links "neo-statists."

7 Mann (1988: 9) introduces one of the logistical techniques which have aided state "infrastructural" power: "rapidity of communication of messages and of transport of people and resources through improved roads, ships, telegraphy, etc." This point is significant for investigating Korea's developmental strategies in establishing the public infrastructural broadband networks.

8 Weiss (1998: 61) noted the increased autonomy of *Chaebols* such as Samsung, Hyundai, and LG group in their relative independence of finance from the interventionist state, and in the internationalized scope of their business operations. Her observation was closely related to the financial liberalization of the early 1990s, a liberalization that weakened the government's control over investment decisions and increased *Chaebol*-owned non-bank financial institutions' channeling of funding to group subsidiaries (e.g., Hahm, 2003: 12).

9 In a rent-seeking state, politicians and bureaucrats maximize their personal or political fortunes by extending rents—which in Korea were associated mostly with the privatization of vested properties, an overvalued exchange rate, high rates of protection, government procurement, and preferential credit—to the private sector (Lim, Haggard & Kim, 2003: 10–12).

10 For instance, Kang (2002: 116–21) explains the limits on the corruption of the state by using the term "mutual hostages."

11 Evans (1995: 84–5) admitted that, in the East Asian model, workers were excluded from the public–private networks, despite their key role in industrial transformation. His approach, however, was based on the "corporatist" vision of state–business–workers linkages promoting transformative growth. Evans was rarely able to free himself from the developmental project of growth, even though he considered the working class to be a missing part of the linkages.

12 This "state-in-society" view is not new among Marxists: in his discussion of the origin of the state, Engels ([1884] 1990) described how the state becomes autonomous over society, despite its origin from within society:

> The state is ... by no means a power forced on society from without.... Rather, it is a product of society at a certain stage of development ... [Eventually,] it became necessary to have a power seemingly standing above which would alleviate the conflict and keep it within the bounds of "order"; and this power, having arisen out of society but placing itself above it, and alienating itself more and more from it, is the state.
>
> (269)

2 From a physical infrastructure to a virtual infrastructure in modern Korea

1 At the end of the nineteenth century, East Asia responded to the inflow of Western power equipped with modern science and technology with the philosophy of *Dondosoegi* (東道西器, a Korean version of a Chinese term). This ideology, popular among intellectuals, held that East Asians should embrace Western technology but temper it with East Asia's superior spirituality (Oh, 2004).

2 According to the IEEE Region 10 report (2006), the first telecommunication in Korea was recorded as being on March 20 of 1902, but Kim (2002) refutes the date with the archival evidence of the *Baekbum Diary* ([1947] 2002), a well-known manuscript

written by Gu Kim, who was first Minister of State while the provisional government of Korea was in exile in Shanghai, China, during the period of Japanese imperial rule. The diary states that on August 26, 1896, the telephone line linking Seoul and Incheon was used by the last emperor of the Joseon Dynasty. The KADO report (2007) agrees with Kim as to the date.

3 During 1953–1960, financial assistance amounted to US$120 million provided by the UN Korea Reconstruction Agency and about US$1.7 billion provided by the US government (Kim & Roemer, 1979).

4 Park was a Japanese-trained major general when, on May 16, 1961, he overthrew the administration of President Po Sun Yun and Prime Minister Chang Myon (the cabinet system having been introduced for the first and last time in Korean history during the years 1960–62) and seized power, although Park did not formally assume the presidency until 1963 (Kristof, 1995).

5 The Kyong-Bu Highway was a riskier enterprise, at least from the perspective of the late 1960s. This project to connect the capital, Seoul (on the northwest coast) with Busan (in the southeast) was an attempt to drive economic activity rather than a response to demand. The project also encouraged the involvement of *Chaebols* in the construction industry (Mody, 1997).

6 The Basic Plan for Administrative Computerization was created in 1978 and revised in 1979 by the Ministry of Government Administration (MOGA) for the purpose of introducing computer hardware and the electronic database of public documents in government agencies. In the February of 1998, the MOGA merged with the Ministry of Home Affairs to become the Ministry of Government Administration and Home Affairs (MOGAHA).

7 In Korea, the legislation governing the communication services until the early 1980s was the Telecommunications Act of 1961. In 1983, to separate the two functions of policy formulation and business operations, the Act was divided into the Telecommunications Basic Act and the Telecommunications Business Act. In 1986, the two Acts were integrated into the Act on Promotion of Computer Network Expansion and Usage, in order to facilitate the NBIS project (Jeong & King, 1996).

8 The network linking Asian and Pacific regions was called AsiaNet, and included Australia (ACSNET), Indonesia, Japan (JUNET), Korea (SDN), and Singapore (Hauben *et al.*, 2007).

9 See the following site describing South Korea's high-speed railway: www.railway-technology.com/projects/koreatgv/.

10 Chapter IV, Articles 26–32 of the FAIP, entitled "Advanced Infrastructure of Information and Communications," for the first time suggests the concrete vision of the Korean Information Infrastructure.

11 Chapter III, Articles 18–25 of the FAIP, entitled "Laying Foundation for Information and Communications Industry."

12 Chapter V, Articles 33–35 of the FAIP, entitled "Public Funding of Informatization Promotion."

13 Established in 1976, the ETRI is a non-profit, government-funded research organization that has been at the forefront of developing global technological standards. The ETRI has successfully developed information technologies such as TDX-Exchange, High Density Semiconductor Microchips, Mini-Super Computer (TiCOM), ATM switching technology, and Digital Mobile Telecommunication System (CDMA).

14 Chapter IV, Article 27 of the FAIP, entitled "Designation of Exclusive Institution," requires establishing anew the board responsible for KII tasks.

15 The Informatization and Planning Office no longer exists; its functions were divided among several divisions in the MIC.

16 Hur, interview, May 28, 2007, the NIA, Seoul.

17 Kim, M., interview, June 26, 2007, the MIC, Seoul.

18 The NIS program in Korea is very similar to the Federal Technology Service (FTS),

which is a division of the US General Services Administration (GSA). The FTS provides a digital fiber optic network with voice, video, e-mail, and high-speed data communications for the US government through a contract with the major telecom equipment providers such as AT&T, Sprint, and Worldcom, and sets a standard fee for these services.

19 The four facility-based telecom service providers—KT, Dacom, Hanaro Telecom, and SK Networks—jointly operate the eGTN system, and all of the service providers except KT are involved in the NIS system (NIA, 2006, December).

20 In the January of 2004, the government passed the Act on Internet Address Resources in order to provide essential infrastructure for the implementation of the BcN, and to resolve the issue of insufficient Internet addresses.

21 QoS refers to the ability to provide better service to certain flows. This works either by raising the priority of a flow or by limiting the priority of another flow. QoS is important if network capacity is limited, especially for real-time streaming multimedia applications such as Frame Relay, ATM, Ethernet, 802.1 networks, SONET, and IP-routed networks such as Voice over Internet Protocol (VoIP) and IPTV.

22 IPv6 is the "next generation" protocol designed by the Internet Engineering Task Force of the Internet Society (ISOC) to replace the current version of Internet Protocol, IPv4. Currently, there is a growing shortage of IPv4 addresses, which are needed by all new machines added to the Internet. IPv6 fixes a number of problems in IPv4, such as the limited number of available IPv4 addresses (NIA & MIC, 2006).

3 Local telecommunications policy within the digital mode of global capitalism

1 For instance, time series analyses of US data over thirty years found a positive relation between investment in telecommunications infrastructure and economic growth (Cronin *et al.*, 1991).

2 The US Federal Communications Commission (FCC) defined broadband as an Internet connection capable of traffic capacity of 200 Kbps, as of 2005; the FCC redefined "basic broadband" as the range from 200 Kbps to 6 Mbps, as of April 2011 (see http://transition.fcc.gov/cgb/consumerfacts/highspeedinternet.html). Most Korean subscribers (more than 70 percent of households) already had broadband service of 20 Mbps in 2005 and of 50–100 Mbps in 2010 (NCA, 2005; 2010).

3 In contrast to "last mile" issues in building broadband networks, Strover (2000) suggests that from the subscriber's perspective, "first mile" issues are of equal concern. Broadband connectivity, she argues, should have capabilities that extend users into the networked nation, rather than being merely a stretch of wire originating from vendor-related concerns. In Korea, the government's approach to broadband has focused on both a "war of speed" (the expansion of traffic capacity) and "last mile" issues, rather than the "first mile" issues delineated by Strover. This is because speed and "last mile" issues can be easily quantified in order to exhibit, nationally and internationally, the success of the bandwidth increase and of overcoming the "digital divide" in providing access to the Internet.

4 Since 1992, the KAIT (Korea Association of Information and Telecommunication) has supported the MIC's IT policy from the private sector's perspective.

5 For example, the artificial duopoly system imitated the UK's deregulation plan, the classification of the carriers by facility-based ownership came from Japan's policy model, and the idea of competition and various measures to protect the market from anticompetitive behavior were derived from US policy (Kim & Ro, 1993).

6 Based on this backbone infrastructure, since 2001 Japan has developed the "e-Japan Strategy" and "u-Japan Promotion Program" for integrating wired/wireless, mobile, and multimedia communications over the Internet Protocol (IP) based architecture, similar to Korea's BcN project launched in 2004.

7 In 2006, the Singaporean government's "IT2000 Vision" evolved into "Singapore One Network for Everyone," which was directed to promote the network-based economy and join in the OECD membership (Low, 2003).

8 Interview with Lee, T. (2007, June 11), at the KT Building, Seoul.

9 Interview with Hur (2007, June 7), at the NIA, Seoul.

10 Interview with Lee, S. (2007, May 28), at the NIA, Seoul.

11 The USTR emerged as part of an informal "Washington Consensus," which also included the US State Department, the US Treasury, the World Bank, the IMF, the OECD, and the WTO. All of these institutions favor the ideas of liberalization, deregulation, and privatization (Amsden, 2007: 128).

12 Dacom was created by public-private investment in 1982. By acquiring the licenses of international and long-distance telephony services during the national telecom reform programs from 1990 to 1995, and also by becoming the selective operator of the KII project, Dacom rapidly emerged as the second largest facility-based telecom service provider in Korea, after KT.

13 The 1990 reform package divided the traditional common carrier model into three service classes—two kinds of NSPs (GSPs and SSPs), and VSPs—based on the ownership of telecom network facilities. Network Service Providers (NSPs) are telecommunication service providers who own their own network facilities. NSPs are divided into two classes, General Service Providers (GSPs), which supply nationwide wireline services, and Specific Service Providers (SSPs), which supply telecom services in geographically limited areas or provide selected types of services such as wireless services. Value-added Service Providers (VSPs) offer database and data processing services through NSPs. The government partially opened the SSP market, which allowed foreign ownership up to 33 percent, or up to ten percent in the case of government-owned corporations, and opened up the VSP market to full-blown competition (Cho *et al.*, 1996). The second telecom reform plan of 1994 integrated the subdivision of GSPs and SSPs into one division, NSPs. The third reform of 1995 divided the national telecom service classification into NSPs, VSPs, and Special Telecommunications Service Providers (STPs), who provide services such as voice resale, Internet phone, international call-back, and so on.

14 The Reference Paper of the WTO pact sets forth the basic regulatory rules for so-called fair competition in local telecom policies. The Paper includes issues of interconnection, requiring the incumbent to provide competitors or new entrants non-discriminatory equitable network access to public networks, the prevention of anticompetitive practices in telecom such as cross-subsidization and the withholding of technical specifications on network access, universal service obligations, and the independence or impartiality of signatories' regulatory bodies (see Blouin, 2000; Fredebeul-Krein & Freytag, 1999; 1997).

15 Up to the mid-1990s, Korean society in general, as well as the government, was quite negative and even fearful about the entry of foreign investors into the domestic market. For instance, one Korean economist described the situation thusly: "[D]ominance of the Korean financial market by foreign institutions was abhorred, as it would diminish authority over various instruments of monetary control, weaken many customary, informal practices associated with industrial policy, and might also alter the public-good nature of the financial system" (Lee, 1993: 7).

16 These predictions have come to pass: for instance, Hanaro Telecom, the second-largest broadband Internet and local call service provider, handed over its management control to a group of foreign investors led by the American International Group (AIG) and Newbridge Capital (Kim, 2003, July). As of December 2007, Hanaro's largest stakeholders, the AIG-led consortium, have made a backdoor deal with SK Telecom, the largest wireless service provider, to sell out all Hanaro stock in 2008. The rise of foreign ownership in the national incumbents has indeed made it difficult for the government to persuade the telecom sector to cooperate in state-led IT

projects; for example, Hanaro relinquished its participation in "WiBro," part of a government-driven IT initiative, "IT839" (for this IT policy initiative, see the next chapter).

17 Korea divides the infrastructure industry into three categories: hardware, software, and network service. Hardware is divided into two subcategories: terminal equipment (e.g., cell phones, PDAs, and laptops) and network equipment. Network equipment includes exchange/switch technology (infrastructural, private), pair cable transmission systems (xDSL), coaxial cable transmission systems (e.g., cable modem termination systems [CMTS]), optical transmission systems, signal converters, multiplexers, wire and optical fiber optic cables, LAN equipment (e.g., NICs, routers, switches, hubs), home network equipment (e.g., subscriber modems, cable modems, and xDSL modems), and wireless LAN equipment. "Network service" includes the Internet backbone service, subscriber connection service, facility leases, and operation out-sourcing, and so on (NCA, 2005).

18 Since the US forced KT to open their equipment procurement market, however, the TDX system has gradually weakened in competition with AT&T's SESS in the large-capacity switching system market. AT&T, the only foreign firm invited, succeeded in open bidding in gaining a 38 percent share of KT's digital switching systems in 1994 (Ro & Kim, 1996).

19 According to a principal researcher at the ETRI, the HAN/B-ISDN project planned to "develop network integration technologies such as a commercial ATM switching system, 10 and 100 Gbps optical transmission systems, a broadband network termina-tion system, and terminal adapters to support the nationwide information infrastruc-ture." In this R&D project, the government's main concern was "the development of the ATM switch" (Interview with Song, H., [2007, July 17] at the IT Exhibition Building, MIC, Seoul).

20 "ATM is a cell-switching and multiplexing technology that combines the benefits of circuit switching (stable capacity and constant transmission delay) with those of packet switching (flexibility and efficiency for intermittent traffic). It provides scala-ble bandwidth from a few Mbps to many Gbps. Because of its asynchronous nature, ATM is more efficient than synchronous technologies, such as time-division multi-plexing" (Cisco, 2006).

21 Interview with Jang (2007, June 07), at the NIA, Seoul.

22 Interview with Jang (2007, June 07).

23 Interview with Lee, Y. (2007, June 7), at the NIA, Seoul.

24 Interview with Oh (2007, June 11), at the PACST, Seoul.

25 Interview with Na (2007, June 7), at the NIA, Seoul.

26 Interview with Lee, T. (2007, June 7), at the KT Building, Seoul.

27 One of the interviewees (Song, D. [2007, May 29], at the LG Dacom Building, Seoul) assessed the ATM as technologically competitive in the aspects of security and QoS, despite its minor impact on economic growth. He said that many government agen-cies have still favored the ATM technology over any other equipment.

4 The state–business symbiosis in Korea's broadband infrastructure plan

1 Under Rhee's administration, the state granted the monopoly of the "three white industries"—the processing of cotton, flour, and sugar from the US—to the burgeon-ing domestic businesses that later grew to be the family-owned *Chaebols* such as Samsung and Hyundai.

2 At that time, the objectives of Korean and Japanese industrial policy were different in that Japan desired to catch up the advanced countries' economies, while Korea hoped to surpass North Korea's lead in industrialization (Harvie & Lee, 2003).

3 In the midst of the 1997 financial crisis, the US automaker General Motors absorbed

the Daewoo Group. Since then it has been named GM Daewoo and, from 2011 onward, GM Korea.

4 The construction market in Korea was, and is, dominated by five main construction and engineering firms which are subsidiaries of *Chaebols* (Samsung, Daewoo, Posco, Hyundai, and Kumho) and which also dominate the private participation in infrastructure (PPI) projects (Noumba UM & Dinghem, 2004).

5 The *Saemaul Undong* was initiated by the so-called "Cement Project" spearheaded by the military regime, which provided all 33,267 villages with 335 cement bags during the winter of 1970–71 and an additional 500 bags in 1972 (Moon, 1991).

6 As an example of how Korea's political-bureaucratic elites maintained their dominant power over the interests of big business, Johnson (1987: 157) describes the establishment of the Korean Central Intelligence Agency (KCIA, now the National Intelligence Service), which was founded as an independent government agency, originally built around a 3,000-man cadre from the existing Army Counter-Intelligence Corps, which had expanded to some 370,000 employees by 1964. The KCIA's original mission focused on counter-communist activities and fighting military corruption. Under the military regimes, the KCIA was used as a domestic surveillance and spying agency to collect, analyze, and monitor intelligence data on businesses and the citizenry. The intelligence agency enabled the development of a "Big Brother"-type disciplinary society, which monitored not only any citizen critical of the government but also overall business activities.

7 The Gini coefficient is a measure of income inequality, with a higher value indicating greater inequality The Gini coefficient ranges from 0.0 (perfect equality) to 1.0 (perfect inequality, that is, all income accrues to one household) (Leipziger *et al.*, [1992]).

8 The Basic Press Act of 1980, the legal cornerstone of General Chun's media censorship and control, was the successor to the Standards for Implementation of the Press Policy of 1962, a decree formulated and enforced by Park's Military Revolutionary Council. The Basic Press Act, like its predecessor, prescribes standards for publication facilities, and in effect functions as a regulatory force, limiting the growth of existing newspapers as well as the entry of new papers without a solid financial basis (Youm, 1986). The Act was repealed in November 1987 and replaced by the Act on Registration of Periodicals and the Broadcast Act (Youm & Salwen, 1990).

9 The enterprise resource planning (ERP) system has been rapidly introduced to control activities in many institutions, such as hospitals, in Korea. The ERP system refers to managing and integrating logistics, accounting, and human resources by means of concentrated database system software. Head (2003) describes the ERP system as a digital control mode of the new ruthless economy, similar to the industrial assembly line in that it allows managers to manage workers' activities in as much detail as they want.

10 In the aftermath of 1997, a discourse about *oeja yuchi* ("the enticement of foreign capital") has dominated Korean society as it seeks to recover from the recession (Lim & Jang, 2006). This discourse was used to legitimize the full-fledged opening of the domestic market to foreign investors.

11 Since the 1997 financial crisis, the concentration of power in the hands of the larger *Chaebols* was accelerated by such events as the collapse of the Daewoo Group, the divestiture of the Hyundai Group, the change of the LG Group into a holding company, and foreign investors' takeover attempts of SK and KT&G (Lee, 2006).

12 In the financial crisis of 1997, when the IMF forced the Korean market to follow its structural adjustment program, many Korean mega-conglomerates collapsed in the restructuring of the domestic economy that ensued, but Samsung seized its opportunity and jumped into first place in the domestic market. The different divisions of Samsung are now a set of huge monopolies, and the corporation as a whole ranks as number one among Korea's ruling conglomerates, accounting for one-fifth of the country's

exports. In South Korea, Samsung encompasses almost every profitable industry under its logo: Samsung Electronics, Samsung SDI, and Renault Samsung Motors, as well as Samsung Securities, Life Insurance, Credit Card, Heavy Industries, Engineering, Everland Theme Park, Advertising, Petrochemicals, Shopping, Cable Channels, and so on. The Samsung group is now ranked number 21 among the world's top brands, and number one in Korea (Lee, 2008). Samsung's rapid capital accumulation has been made possible by its omnipresent power in the Korean economy and society—described by such common terms as "Samsung's way" and "the Republic of Samsung"—and by its collaboration with the state in controlling the labor market. While Samsung contributes significantly to promoting Korea's national economy in the global market, its dominant market power, with a total of 62 subsidiaries, 160,000 employees across the globe (85,000 in Korea alone), and a sales record of US$173 billion (as of 2009), makes it a pervasive and overwhelming force in both the Korean economy and Korean society (Samsung, 2010).

13 In other Asian countries, business groups guided by a single entrepreneur have been dominant, similar to the Korean *Chaebols*, which historically were inspired by the Japanese *zaibatsu* (ざいばつ), large family-controlled monopolies which were dismantled in the late 1940s); in contemporary Japan, the *keiretsu* (系列) is a business group vertically integrated through majority and minority holdings, while the *kigyoshudan* (企業集団) is a business group horizontally aligned through reciprocal shareholdings (Scott, 1991; Castells, 2000a: 190). The *kigyoshudan* resembles the Chinese *guanxiqiye* (關係業, "related enterprises") found in Singapore and Taiwan (Guillén, 2000).

14 In addition to *jeongkyong yuchak*, under Park's junta, the term *gwanchi gyeongjae*, or "state-controlled economy," was commonly used to denounce the military elites' intervention in the market.

15 Interview with Kang (2007, June 5), at the KT Building, Seoul.

16 Interview with Song, D. (2007, May 29), at the LG Dacom Building, Seoul.

17 Interview with Kim, Y. J. (2007, June 1), at the KT Building, Seoul.

18 Interview with Na (2007, May 28), at the NIA, Seoul.

19 Interview with Jeong (2007, June 5), at the NIA, Seoul.

20 Interview with Lee, Y. (2007, June 7), at the NIA, Seoul.

21 Interview with Song, D. (2007, May 29).

22 Interview with Kim, Y. J. (2007, June 1).

23 Interview with Jeong (2007, June 5).

24 The participation of the universities in the KII Advancement Committee indicates the personal involvement of some professors as IT policy advisers, rather than the systematic involvement of the university research centers.

25 Korean television programs and cinema have gained a "pan-Asianist" value (Dator & Seo, 2004; Kim, 2007), and the scope of their cultural influence in the global market has become similar to the pan-Iberian/Latin American telenovela culture, which is relatively independent from the monolithic cultural dominance of the Hollywood empire.

26 President Roh has been described as "the world's first president to be elected with the broad support of the online generation" (Watts, 2003: 16). His image at the time of his inauguration was one of being technically flexible and open to the Internet. Midway in his term of office, Roh held an unprecedented "Internet conversation with the nation" on March 23, 2006, which had the largest audience in the history of online broadcasting in Korea. Moreover, the President himself uploaded five letters per month onto the presidential website, named the Office of the President Briefing, in order to promote direct communication with the nation without the intervention of the press. His nickname, "the Night-Owl President," is derived from his staying at the keyboard until late at night for decision-making and electronic approval of e-documents, through the electronic record management system that he, himself, invented (Lee & Lee, 2009).

27 IT "839" had three pillars (services, infrastructure, new growth engines); eight telecom services (WiBro, DMB, home networking, telematics, RFID, W-CDMA, Terrestrial D-TV, and Internet telephony); three infrastructures (broadband convergence network, U-sensor network, and IPv6); and nine new growth engines (mobile telephony, digital televisions and broadcast devices, home network equipment, system-on-chip products, next-generation personal computer, embedded software, digital content and solutions, vehicle-based information equipment, and intelligent robot products) (Shin, 2007).

28 Interview with Jeong (2007, June 5).

29 During the negotiations over the Korea–US FTA, the Korean government frequently concealed the details of its agreements with the US, despite the requests of civil rights groups that such information be made public; further, the government even disseminated disinformation, claiming that the bilateral trade negotiation would be wholly beneficial to Korea's citizens and its national economy, even though the risks involved could threaten local sustainability. Anger against the government's propaganda finally brought tens of thousands of demonstrators to the streets in protest against the Lee administration, which aimed to reopen the Korean beef market, once the third-largest importer of American beef, due to Koreans' fear of eating meat tainted with potentially-fatal mad cow disease. The citizens placed no faith in the Lee administration's reiterated assurances that the beef would be thoroughly inspected and safe (e.g., Hansen, 2008).

5 The transformation of state surveillance practices toward a grid of control

1 As late as 1997, however, "communist sympathizer" was still an accusation hurled at Dae-Jung Kim by those who hoped to undermine his presidential campaign.

2 According to Relyea's (2002) analysis, security concepts function as ideological and political signs that aim to promote public security and safety at the price of the civil right of privacy. These ideological concepts are easily institutionalized under threats and anxieties such as the Cold War or terrorist attacks. Since the events of September 11, 2001, existing security concepts are being reconfigured as the security threat has changed from communism to terrorism. The evolution of security concepts from national and internal security to homeland security, according to Relyea, depicts the expansive processes of consensus and persuasion by policymakers.

3 The role of the US in crushing the Gwangju uprising has never been officially clarified. Since the US government had final authority over the US–Korean Allied Forces Command, and thus the Korean government would have had to obtain official permission from the US in order to move infantry divisions, airborne units, and special task forces into Gwangju, most Koreans believe the US government was indirectly involved in the Gwangju massacre.

4 In addition to such basic data as name, sex, date of birth, and national identification number, Korea's ID system includes detailed personal data such as permanent address, current address, military record, criminal records, records of each change of residence, the issuing agency and issuance date of the ID card, photographs, family relations, and all ten fingerprints.

5 In the Korean ID system, each identifier (e.g., 681207–1xxxxxx) consists of a combination of the date of birth (the first group of six digits; in this case, the date of birth is December 7, 1968), sex (this is the first number of the second seven digits: 1 was assigned to a man and 2 to a woman, but, since 2002, these numbers have been changed into 3 or 4), and a randomly given six-digit number.

6 As one of the negative symptoms of compulsive Internet use in Korea, the *New York Times* (Fackler, 2007) reported that "a growing number of students have skipped school to stay online, shockingly self-destructive behavior in this intensely

competitive society. [...] Up to 30 percent of South Koreans under 18, or about 2.4 million people, are at risk of Internet addiction."

7 In October 2004, without any public discussion on this sensitive issue, some conservative members of the Korean National Assembly pushed through a twelfth revision of the Copyright Act that dramatically increased copyright owners' rights. The revision gave copyright owners an absolute monopoly over digital content, and extended authors' copyrights to the span of their lifetimes plus 45 years. On January 17, 2005, the revised Copyright Act, which included controversial provisions that rigidly applied proprietary rights to immaterial labor, took effect. Under the revised copyright law, copyright owners gained the rights of transmission of artistic products over the Internet and all mobile communication devices; anyone who enjoys the new culture of sharing can be prosecuted for copyright infringement. This has led to the policing of images uploaded for decorating websites, background sounds for blog sites, lyrics from commercial music, and essays copied from online newspapers or magazines. Even if such sharing is for individual, noncommercial purposes, the use of copyrighted works without their owners' permission, such as uploading and linking others' creative works, is illegal.

8 This term of Foucault's stems from the effect of digitalization on social control. By automating and systematizing control electronically, power is able to hide its real intention of social control.

9 In July 2004, 12 former and current workers of Samsung SDI, a subsidiary of the Samsung group, filed a lawsuit claiming that the company had secretly tracked their activities outside of the workplace to stop them from establishing a labor union. Samsung SDI used hacked and duplicated mobile phones to monitor militant employees and laid-off workers who were attempting to organize a trade union (Joint Committee for Fact-Finding and Management Accountability Regarding Surveillance of Samsung Workers, 2005, February 16). This scandal evoked public protests over the violation of workers' human rights. Even though there was serious infringement of the workers' rights, however, in the February of 2005 the Public Prosecutor terminated the investigation after six months, because of the extreme difficulty in locating perpetrators, and thus no one at Samsung has been held legally responsible for a systematic, intentional violation of human rights. Further, at the behest of conservative politicians of both major parties, the issue of Samsung workers' human rights was dropped from the official agenda of the parliamentary investigation. In 2010, Yong-chul Kim, the former head of Samsung's legal affairs team, publicly reaffirmed the widespread mobile tracking of Samsung workers in his book, *Thinking Samsung* (2010).

10 The National Administrative Information System, the Financial Information System, the National Defense Information System, the National Security Information System, and the Education and Research Information System.

11 Moreover, the major daily newspapers participated actively in advocating the government's goal of IT education, by means of their own IT campaigns aimed at students, such as the IIE (Internet in Education) by the *Chung-Ang Ilbo*, the KidNet movement by the *Chosun Ilbo*, the School Informatization and Internet Youth Camps by the *Dong-A Ilbo*, and GreenNet by the *Hankook Ilbo* (MIC & NCA, 2006). These campaigns, led by major newspaper companies, worked synergistically with the government's IT promotion at the national level.

12 The vulnerability of Microsoft's software provoked harsh criticism, and since then the government has begun to consider alternatives to it. At that time, despite the availability of patches, Microsoft made it difficult to keep track of its security alerts, so that some alerts did not get through. Software users were furious with Microsoft's self-contained, monopolistic software technology, and an influential Korean civil rights group, People's Solidarity for Participatory Democracy, launched a lawsuit for damages related to the Slammer virus. Named in the suit are Internet

service providers such as KT and Hanaro Telecom, the Ministry of Information and Communication (MIC), and Microsoft itself. The civil suit was brought on behalf of some 1600 Internet users and companies, but their claims were ultimately denied (the Civil Suit Bureau 24, Seoul Central District Court, 2005, December 23).

13 The NHRC is a government commission "established in 2001 as a national advocacy institution for human rights protection. It is committed to the fulfillment of human rights in a broader sense, including dignity, value and freedom of every human being, as signified in international human rights conventions and treaties to which Korea is a signatory" (NHRC, 2007). Under the Lee administration, however, the NHRC has been losing its basic function of protecting human rights, and instead has kept silent on significant human rights issues in the country. The UN and Amnesty International have urged the NHRC to maintain its independence and credibility.

14 The NHRC cited the Universal Declaration on Human Rights (Article 12), the International Covenant on Civil and Political Rights (Article 17), the Convention of the Rights of the Child (Article 16), the OECD's Guidelines Governing the Protection of Privacy and Trans-border Flow of Personal Data, and the UN's Guidelines for the regulation of computerized personal data files, as well as Article 10 (the Right to Pursue Happiness) and Article 17 (the Right to Protect Private Life) of Korea's Constitution (JSC, 2003b).

15 In Korea, a one-person picket protest in relays is a popular way to express one's anger against the authorities: one person stands or sits in front of the building where the targeted authority resides, while holding a picket or a banner, until relieved by the next protester.

References

Agger, B. (2004). *Speeding Up Fast Capitalism: Cultures, Jobs, Families, Schools, Bodies.* Boulder, CO: Paradigm.

Ahn, H.-J., & Mah, J. S. (2007). Development of technology-intensive industries in Korea. *Journal of Contemporary Asia, 37*(3): 364–79.

Alexander, A. (2003). *Korea's capital investment: Returns at the level of the economy, industry, and firm.* Washington, DC: Korea Economic Institute.

Alliance of Seventeen Human Rights Groups. (2003, February 12). *A Policy Suggestion about Human Rights to the New Government (in Korean).* Seoul, Korea.

Amin, S. (1974). *Accumulation on a World Scale: A Critique of the Theory of Underdevelopment.* New York: Monthly Review Press.

Amsden, A. H. (1989). *Asia's Next Giant: South Korea and Late Industrialization.* Oxford, UK: Oxford University Press.

Amsden, A. H. (2001). *The Rise of "the Rest:" Challenges to the West from Late-industrializing Economies.* Oxford, UK: Oxford University Press.

Amsden, A. H. (2007). *Escape from empire: The developing world's journey through heaven and hell.* Cambridge, MA: The MIT Press.

Ang, I. (1996). *Living Rooms Wars: Rethinking Media Audiences for a Postmodern World.* London and New York: Routledge.

Appadurai, A. (1990). Disjuncture and Difference in the Global Cultural Economy. In M. Featherstone (Ed.), *Global Culture: Nationalism, Globalization and Modernity* (pp. 295–310). London, UK: Sage.

Asia Sentinel. (2008, March 2). How Deep Will Korea's Samsung Scandal Go? Retrieved May 22, 2011, from www.asiasentinel.com/index.php?Itemid=32&id=1078&option=com_content&task=view.

Bank of Chosen (Ed.). (1920). *Economic History of Chosen.* Seoul, Korea: Bank of Chosen.

Baran, P. A. ([1957] 1968). *The Political Economy of Growth.* New York: Modern Reader Paperbacks.

Bartnik, R. (2007). Korean Technological Competencies: Institutional Framework and Patterns of Industrial Competition. In *Innovation and Technology in Korea.* In J. Mahlich, & W. Pascha (Eds.), *Innovation and Technology in Korea* (pp. 147–53). Berlin/Heidelberg: Physica-Verlag.

Bauman, Z. (2000). *Liquid Modernity.* Cambridge, UK: Polity Press.

BBC. (2010). *The Virtual Revolution: How 20 Years of the Web Has Reshaped Our Lives* [Television program]: BBC.

Bearn, M. (2004, May 31). Americans get a raw deal. *New Statesman*, xxii.

Belson, K., & Richtel, M. (2003, May 3). America's Broadband Dream Is Alive in Korea. *New York Times*.

Beniger, J. (1986). *The Control Revolution: Technological and Economic Origins of the Information Society*. Cambridge, MA: Harvard University Press.

Billet, B. L. (1990). South Korea at the Crossroads: An Evolving Democracy or Authoritarianism Revisited? *Asian Survey, 30*(3): 300–11.

Bixler, L. (2010). Korea's Electronics Scandal. *Ms Magazine*, Fall, 20–1.

Blouin, C. (2000). The WTO Agreement on Basic Telecommunications: a reevaluation. *Telecommunications Policy, 24*(2): 135–42.

Body-Gendrot, S. (2000). *The Social Control of Cities? A Comparative Perspective*. Oxford: Blackwell.

Bourdieu, P. (2003). *Firing Back: Against the Tyranny of the Market 2*. New York: Verso.

Bourdieu, P. (1998). *Acts of Resistance: Against the Tyranny of the Market*. New York: The New Press.

Burke, J., & Warren, P. (2002, October 13). How Mobile Phones Let Spies See Our Every Move. *Observer*.

Burkett, P., & Hart-Landsberg, M. (1998). East Asia and the crisis of development theory. *Journal of Contemporary Asia, 28*: 435–56.

C/net News.com. (2008, March 19). FCC approves new method for tracking broadband's reach. Retrieved March 31, 2011, from http://news.cnet.com/8301–10784_3–9898118–7.html.

Campbell, II, T. L., & Keys, P. Y. (2002). Corporate governance in South Korea: the *Chaebol* experience. *Journal of Corporate Finance, 8*(4): 373–91.

Cardoso, F. H. (1973). *Associated Dependent Development: Theoretical and Practical Implications*, 142–76 in A. Stepan (Ed.) *Authoritarian Brazil*. Princeton, NJ: Princeton University Press.

Castells, M. (1985). High Technology, Economic Restructuring, and the Urban-Regional Process in the United States In M. Castells (Ed.), *High Technology, Space, and Society* (pp. 11–40). London, UK: Sage.

Castells, M. (1996). *The Rise of the Network Society*. Oxford: Blackwell.

Castells, M. (2000a). *The Rise of the Network Society* (2nd ed.). Oxford: Blackwell.

Castells, M. (2000b). *End of Millennium* (2nd ed.). Oxford: Blackwell.

Cauley, L. (2006, May 11). NSA has massive database of Americans' phone calls. *USA Today*.

Central Intelligency Agency (CIA). (2008, July 24). The World Factbook. Retrieved March 24, 2011, from https://www.cia.gov/library/publications/the-world-factbook/geos/ks.html.

Chang, H.-J. (2006). *The East Asian development experience: the miracle, the crisis and the future*. New York: Zed.

Chang, S.-J. (2003). The Internet Economy of Korea. In B. Kogut (Ed.), *The global internet economy* (pp. 263–89). Cambridge, MA: MIT Press.

Cherry, J. (2005). "Big Deal" or big disappointment? The continuing evolution of the South Korean developmental state. *Pacific Review, 18*(3): 327–54.

Cho, H.-Y., & Kim, E. M. (1998). State Autonomy and Its Social Conditions for Economic Development in South Korea and Taiwan. In E. M. Kim (Ed.), *The Four Asian Tigers: Economic Development and the Global Political Economy* (125–58). San Diego, CA: Academic Press.

Cho, H.-Y. (2000). The structure of the South Korean developmental regime and its transformation: Statist mobilization and authoritarian integration in the anticommunist regimentation *Inter-Asia Cultural Studies*, *1*(3): 408–26.

Cho, S., Choi, B.-i., & Choi, S.-K. (1996). Restructuring the Korean telecommunications market: Evolution and challenges ahead. *Telecommunications Policy, 20*(5), 357–73.

Chosun Ilbo. (2008, June 17). Nowcom argues, "the CEO imprisoned, due to a political reason" (in Korean). Retrieved August 20, 2011, from http://news.chosun.com/site/data/html_dir/2008/06/17/2008061700568.html

Choe, S.-H., (2010, April 25). Book on Samsung divides Korea. *New York Times.*

Choe, S., & Pattnaik, C. (2007). The transformation of Korean business groups after the Asian crisis. *Journal of Contemporary Asia, 37*(2): 232–255.

Chon, G.-N., Park, H.-J., Kang, K.-R., & Lee, Y.-E. (2007). A brief history of the Internet in Korea. *The Amateur Computerist Newsletter, 15*(2): 26–36.

Choo, C. W. (1997). IT 2000: Singapore's vision of an Intelligent Island. In P. Droege (Ed.), *Intelligent Environments* (pp. 49–66). Amsterdam; New York: Elsevier.

Chung, C.-M. (2003). Governing Internet in Korea: NEIS and Domain Names. In *Electronic Government* (Vol. 2739, pp. 480–3). Berlin/Heidelberg: Springer.

Cisco. (2006). Internetworking Technology Handbook. Retrieved March 10, 2011, from www.cisco.com/univercd/cc/td/doc/cisintwk/ito_doc/index.htm.

Civil Society – TUAC. (2008). *The Seoul Declaration: To the OECD ministerial conference on the future of the Internet economy*. Seoul, Korea.

Clark, C. (2002). Political Development, Administrative Capacity, and the Challenge to the Developmental State Model Posed by the 1997–1998 Financial Crisis in East and Southeast Asia. In K. T. Liou (Ed.), *Managing Economic Development in Asia: From Economic Miracle to Financial Crisis* (pp. 1–38). Westport, CT: Praeger.

Clark, C., & Jung, C. (2004). The Resurrection of East Asian Dynamism: A Call to Look Beyond the Orthodoxies in Development Studies. *Asian Affairs: An American Review, 31*(3), 131–51.

Clinton, B. (1992, April 16). Remarks of Governor Bill Clinton in the Wharton School of Business, the University of Pennsylvania Retrieved February 3, 2011, from http://w2.eff.org/Infrastructure/Govt_docs/.

Cowhey, P., & Klimenko, M. (2000). Telecommunications reform in developing countries After the WTO Agreement on Basic Telecommunications Services. *Journal of International Development, 12*: 265–81.

Crandall, J. (2010). The Geospatialization of Calculative Operations: Tracking, Sensing and Megacities. *Theory, Culture & Society, 27*(6): 68–90.

Cronin, F. J., Parker, E. B., Colleran, E. K., & Gold, M. A. (1991). Telecommunications infrastructure and economic growth: An analysis of causality. *Telecommunications Policy, 15*(6): 529–35.

Dator, J., & Seo, Y.-S. (2004). Korea as the wave of a future: The emerging dream society of icons and aesthetic experience. *Journal of Future Studies, 9*(1): 31–44.

Davis, M. (1990). *City of Quartz: Excavating the Future in Los Angeles*. London: Verso.

Deibert, R. J., & Rohozinski, R. (2010). Beyond Denial: Introducing Next Generation Information Access Controls (pp. 3–13). Ronald J. Deibert, John G. Palfrey, Rafal Rohozinski, and Jonathan Zittrain (Eds.), *Access Controlled: The Shaping of Power, Rights, and Rule in Cyberspace*. MA. The MIT Press.

Deleuze, G. ([1990] 1995). *Negotiations (1972–1990)*. New York, NY: Columbia University Press.

Dodge, M., & Kitchin, R. (2001). *Mapping Cyberspace*. London, UK: Routledge.

Doty, P. (2001). Digital privacy: Towards a new politics and discursive practice. In M. E.

Williams (Ed.), *Annual review of information science and technology 36* (pp. 115–245). Medford, NJ: Information Today.

Drake, W. J., & Noam, E. M. (1997). The WTO deal on basic telecommunications: Big bang or little whimper? *Telecommunications Policy, 21*(9–10): 799–818.

Economist, The (2011, April 16). Game over; Censorship in South Korea. Retrieved September 1, 2011, from http://www.economist.com/node/18561127

Economist Intelligence Unit (2011). Full Speed Ahead: The Government Broadband Report Q2. Retrieved August 10, 2011, from http://www.eiu.com/public/topical_report. aspx?campaignid=broadbandMay2011

Elliott, A., & Urry, J. (2010). *Mobile Lives.* London: Routledge.

Embassy of the Republic of Korea in the USA. (2005, November 14). Korea's role in APEC. Retrieved May 19, 2011, from www.dynamic-korea.com/print.php?tbl=Culture &uid=200500025227.

Engels, F. ([1884] 1990). *The Origin of the Family, Private Property and the State.* NY: Penguin.

Evans, P. (1979). *Dependent Development.* Princeton, NJ: Princeton University Press.

Evans, P. B. (1995). *Embedded Autonomy: States and Industrial Transformation.* Princeton, NJ: Princeton University Press.

Fabijancic, T. (1995). 'The Dialectics of Modernity: Reification, Space, and Vision', *Rethinking Marxism, 8*(3): 90–108.

Fackler, M. (2007, November 18). In Korea, a Boot Camp Cure for Web Obsession. *New York Times.* Retrieved May 21, 2011, www.nytimes.com/2007/11/18/technology/18 rehab.html?_r=1&oref=slogin.

Falch, M. (2007). Penetration of broadband services – The role of policies. *Telematics and Informatics, 24*(4): 246–58.

Feenberg, A. (1991). *Critical Theory of Technology.* NY: Oxford University Press.

Fields, K. (1997). Strong states and business organization in Korea and Taiwan. In S. Maxfield & B. R. Schneider (Eds.), *Business and the State in Developing Countries* (pp. 122–51). Ithaca and London: Cornell University Press.

Foucault, M. (1980). *Power/Knowledge: Selected Interviews and Other Writings 1972–1977.* New York, NY: Pantheon.

Foucault, M. ([1975] 1995). *Discipline and Punish: The Birth of the Prison* (2nd ed.). New York, NY Vintage Books.

Foucault, M. ([1976] 1990). *The History of Sexuality: An Introduction* New York, NY: Vintage Books.

Foucault, M. ([1979] 1991). Governmentality. In G. Burchell, C. Gordon & P. Miller (Eds.), *The Foucault Effect: Studies in Governmentality – With Two Lectures by and an Interview with Michel Foucault* (pp. 87–104). Chicago, IL: University of Chicago Press.

Foucault, M. ([1999] 2003). *Abnormal: Lectures at the Collège de France 1974–1975.* New York: Picador.

Frank, A. G. (1969). *Capitalism and Underdevelopment in Latin America: Historical Studies of Chile and Brazil.* Revised ed. New York: Monthly Review Press.

Frank, R. (2007). Korea's Telecommunications Industry. In J. Mahlich & W. Pascha (Eds.), *Innovation and Technology in Korea* (pp. 233–53). Berlin/Heidelberg: Physica-Verlag.

Fredebeul-Krein, M., & Freytag, A. (1997). Telecommunications and WTO discipline. An assessment of the WTO agreement on telecommunication services. *Telecommunications Policy, 21*(6): 477–91.

Fredebeul-Krein, M., & Freytag, A. (1999). The case for a more binding WTO agreement on regulatory principles in telecommunication markets. *Telecommunications Policy*, *23*(9): 625–44.

Freedom House (2011). *Freedom on the Net 2011*. Retrieved May 20, 2011, from www.freedomhouse.org/template.cfm?page=664.

Frieden, R. (2005). Lessons from broadband development in Canada, Japan, Korea and the United States. *Telecommunications Policy*, *29*(8): 595–613.

Friedman, T. L. (2006). *The World is Flat: A Brief History of the Twenty-First Century*. New York: Farrar, Straus, Giroux.

Fukuyama, F. (1992). *The End of History and the Last Man*. New York: Free Press.

G-7 Chair. (1995). Chair's Conclusions. Retrieved January 28, 2011, from http://w2.eff.org/Infrastructure/Govt_docs/g7_chair_conclusions.report.

Gandy, Jr., O. H. (1993). 'Toward a Political Economy of Personal Information', *Critical Studies in Mass Communication*, *10*(1): 70–97.

Galloway, A. (2001). Protocol, or, how control exists after decentralization. *Rethinking Marxism*, *13*(3/4):81–8.

García Canclini, N. (1997). 'Hybrid Cultures and Communicative Strategies', *Media Development*, *54*(1): 22–9.

Gatlin, J. (1999). *Bill Gates: The Path to the Future*. Avon Books.

Gerschenkron, A. (1962). *Economic Backwardness in Historical Perspective: A Book of Essays*. Cambridge, MA: The Berkin Press of Harvard University Press.

Giddens, A. (1976). *New Rules of Sociological Method: A Positive Critique of Interpretative Sociologies*. London: Hutchinson.

Golding, P. (1996). World Wide Wedge: Division and Contradiction in the Global Information Infrastructure. *Monthly Review*, *48*(3): 70–85.

Gramsci, A. (1971). *Selections from the Prison Notebooks*, London: Lawrence and Wishart.

Grupp, H., & Schnoring, T. (1992). Research and development in telecommunications: National systems under pressure. *Telecommunications Policy*, *16*(1): 46–66.

Guback, T. (1984) *International Circulation of US Theatrical Films and Television Programming*, 153–63 in G. Gerbner and M. Siefert (Eds.), *World Communications: A Handbook*. New York: Longman.

Guillén, M. F. (2000). Business Groups in Emerging Economies: A Resource-Based View *The Academy of Management Journal*, *43*(3): 362–80.

Haberman, C. (1987, April 5). Decision time in Seoul, and 'clock is running'. *New York Times*.

Haggard, S. (1990). *Pathways from the Periphery: The Politics of Growth in the Newly Industrializing Countries*. Ithaca and London: Cornell University Press.

Haggard, S., Cooper, R. N., & Collins, S. (1994). Understanding Korea's Macroeconomic Policy. In S. Haggard, R. N. Cooper, S. Collins, C. Kim, & S.-T. Ro (Eds.), *Macroeconomic Policy and Adjustment in Korea, 1970–1990* (3–19). Cambridge, MA: Harvard University Press.

Haggerty, K. D., & Ericson, R. V., (2000). The Surveillant Assemblage. *British Journal of Sociology*, *51*(4): 605–22.

Hahm, J.-H. (2003). The Government, *Chaebol* and Financial Institutions in Pre-crisis Korea. In S. Haggard, Lim, W.-h., & Kim, E. (Eds.), *Economic Crisis and Corporate Restructuring in Korea* (pp. 79–101). Cambridge: Cambridge University Press.

Hall, S. (1991). 'The Local and the Global: Globalization and Ethnicity', 19–40 in A. D. King (Ed.) *Culture, Globalization and the World-system: Contemporary Conditions for the Representation of Identity*. London: Macmillan Press.

Hamelink, C. (1984) *Transnational Data Flows in the Information Age*. Lund: Gleerup.

Han, G.-j. (2003). Broadband Adoption in the United States and Korea: Business Driven Rational Model Versus Culture Sensitive Policy Model. *Trends in Communication*, *11*(1): 3.

Han, J., & Ling, L. H. M. (1998). Authoritarianism in the Hypermasculinized State: Hybridity, Patriarchy, and Capitalism in Korea. *International Studies Quarterly*, *42*(1), 53–78.

Han, S.-J. (1988). South Korea in 1987: The Politics of Democratization. *Asian Survey*, *28*(1): 52–61.

Hangil Research and Consulting. (2003). A Survey on Worker Surveillance (in Korean). Retrieved May 28, 2011, from www.jinbo.net.

Hankyoreh. (2003, June 21). The 4,289 KTU-affiliated teachers entered into the protest (in Korean). Retrieved June 24, 2011, from www.hani.co.kr/section-005000000/2003/06/005000000200306211816391.html.

Hankyoreh. (2003, June 24). The KTU asserts, "the Committee should be built under objectivity" (in Korean). Retrieved May 1, 2011, from www.hani.co.kr/section-005100006/2003/06/005100006200306241008315.html.

Hankyoreh. (2003, May 5). This week would be a big hurdle in the NEIS negotiations (in Korean). Retrieved May 24, 2011, from www.hani.co.kr/section-005100006/2003/05/005100006200305052230119.html.

Hankyoreh. (2005, April 21). The school officers and brokers arrested by leaking of studnet data (in Korean). Retrieved May 25, 2011, from www.hani.co.kr/section-005000000/2005/04/005000000200504201736092.html.

Hankyoreh. (2008, June 23). "I could never dream about this day," Kang cleaned his suspicion. Retrieved June 1, 2011, from www.hani.co.kr/arti/society/society_general/294864.html.

Hansen, M. (2008, June 20). Stop the madness. *New York Times*.

Hardt, M., & Negri, A. (2000). *Empire*. Cambridge, MA: Harvard University Press.

Hardt, M., & Negri, A. (2004). *Multitude: War and Democracy in the Age of Empire*. New York: The Penguin Press.

Hardt, M., & Negri, A. (2009). *Commonwealth*. Cambridge, MA: Harvard University Press.

Hart-Landsberg, M. (1993). *The Rush to Development: Economic Change and Political Struggle in South Korea*. New York, NY: Monthly Review Press.

Harvey, D. (1989). *The Condition of Postmodernity: An Enquiry into the Origins of Cultural Change*. Oxford: Basil Blackwell.

Harvey, D. (1996). *Justice, Nature and the Geography of Difference*. Oxford: Basil Blackwell.

Harvey, D. (2001). *Spaces of Capital: Towards a Critical Geography*. London: Routledge.

Harvey, D. (2003). *The New Imperialism*. Oxford, Oxford University Press.

Harvey, D. (2005). *A Brief History of Neoliberalism*. Oxford: Oxford University Press.

Harvey, D. (2006). *Spaces of Global Capitalism: A Theory of Uneven Geographical Development*. New York: Verso.

Harvie, C., & Lee, H.-H. (2003). *Korea's economic miracle: Fading or reviving?* New York: Palgrave Macmillan.

Hauben, R., Hauben, J., Zorn, W., Chon, G.-N., & Ekeland, A. (2007). The origin and early development of the Internet and of the netizen: Their impact on science and society, In W. Shrum, K. R. Benson, W. E. Bijker, & K. Brunnnstein (Eds.), *Past, Present and Future of Research in the Information Society* (pp. 47–62). NY: Springer.

Head, S. (2003). The New Ruthless Economy: Work and Power in the Digital Age. Oxford University Press.

Hemmert, M. (2007). The Korean Innovation System: From Industrial Catch-Up to Technological Leadership? In J. Mahlich & W. Pascha (Eds.), *Innovation and Technology in Korea* (pp. 11–32). Berlin/Heidelberg: Physica-Verlag.

Hepworth, M. & Robins, K. (1988). 'Whose Information Society? A View from the Periphery', *Media, Culture and Society, 10*(3): 323–44.

Herman, E. S., & McChesney, R. W. (1997). *The Global Media: The New Missionaries of Corporate Capitalism*. London: Cassell.

Herz, J. C. (2002, August). The Bandwidth Capital of the World: In Seoul, the broadband age is in full swing *Wired, 10*.

Hills, J. (2007). *The Struggle for Control of Global Communication: The Formative Century*. Urbana and Chicago: University of Illinois Press.

Hong, D.-p. (2005). *Development of ICT Sector in Korea*. Paper presented at the Workshop on Technology Innovation and Economic Growth.

Hong, D.-p., Choi, G.-I., & Kim, Y. (2004). A New economy for Korea. In C. Harvie, H.-H. Lee & J. Oh (Eds.), *The Korean Economy: Post-crisis policies, issues, and prospects* (pp. 165–90). Cheltenham, UK: Edward Elgar.

Hong, S. G. (1998). The political economy of the Korean telecommunications reform. *Telecommunications Policy, 22*(8): 697–711.

Horwitz, R. B. (1989). *The Irony of Regulatory Reform: The Deregulation of American Telecommunications*. Oxford, Oxford University Press.

Horwitz, R. B. (2003). *Communication and Democratic Reform in Soth Africa*. Cambridge: Cambridge University Press.

Human Rights Watch (HRW). (2008). *World Report 2008*. Washington, DC.

Hundt, D. (2005). A Legitimate Paradox: Neo-liberal Reform and the Return of the State in Korea. *Journal of Development Studies, 41*(2): 242–60.

Hyun, D., & Lent, A. J. (1999). Korean telecom policy in global competition: implications for developing countries. *Telecommunications Policy, 23*(5): 389–401.

IEEE (Institute of Electrical and Electronics Engineers) Region 10. (2006). History of IEEE Development in Korea. Retrieved May 25, 2011, from www.ewh.ieee.org/reg/10/history/06-Korea-History-of-Korea-Section.pdf.

Igarashi, M. (1994, June 13). *Creating Japan's InfoCommunications society for the 21th century* Paper presented at the Japan and the United States: Revving up for the information superhighway, International Conference Hall of the United Nations University, Tokyo, Japan.

Information Infrastructure Task Force (IITF). (1993). *The National Information Infrastructure: Agenda for action*. Washington, DC.

Ingelbrecht, N. (1995). Asia—The supplier's dilemma. In J. Ure (Ed.), *Telecommunications in Asia: Policy, planning and development*. Hong Kong: Hong Kong University Press.

International Telecommunication Union (ITU). (2003). *Broadband Korea: Internet case study*: ITU.

International Telecommunication Union (ITU). (2005). *World telecommunication/ICT indicators database on CD-ROM* (9th ed.). Geneva, Switzerland: ITU.

Jang, S.-C. (2000). *Path dependency in the state-Chaebol relationships: The financial crisis and the economic reforms*. Paper presented at the National Sociology Conference, Seoul (in Korean).

Jeon, H., & Bae, S. (2007). The world's highest broadband penetration with ADSL:

Korea. In J. K. Lee, B. G. K. Siew, & V. Sethi (Eds.), *Premier e-business cases from Asia: problem, solution, challenge, impact approach* (pp. 283–315). Singapore & New York: Pearson Prentice Hall.

Jeon, J.-G. (1994). The Comparative Politics of Economic Development in East Asia: A Conceptual Mapping. *Pacific Focus 9*(1): 65-94.

Jeong, B.-H. (2004). *South Korean universal service and Korean reunification: A policy analysis.* University of Texas at Austin, Austin.

Jeong, K.-H., & King, J. L. (1996). National information infrastructure initiatives in Korea. *Information Infrastructure & Policy, 5*(2): 119–34.

Jessop, B. (1982). *The Capitalist State: Marxist Theories and Methods.* Oxford, UK: Martin Robertson.

Jessop, B. (1985). *Nicos Poulantzas: Marxist Theory and Political Strategy.* London, UK: Macmillan.

Jessop, B. (1990). *State Theory: Putting the Capitalist State in Its Place*, Cambridge: Polity.

Jessop, B. (2002). *The Future of the Capitalist State.* Cambridge: Polity Press.

Jin, D.-Y. (2005). The Telecom Crisis and Beyond: Restructuring of the Global Telecommunications System. *International Communication Gazette, 67*(3): 289–304.

Jin, D.-Y. (2006). Political and economic processes in the privatization of the Korea telecommunications industry: A case study of Korea Telecom, 1987–2003. *Telecommunications Policy, 30*(1): 3–13.

Johnson, C. (1982). *MITI and the Japanese Miracle: The Growth of Industrial Policy, 1925–1975.* Stanford, CA: Stanford University Press.

Johnson, C. (1987). Political Institutions and Economic Performance: The Government-Business Relationship in Japan, South Korea and Taiwan. In F. C. Deyo (Ed.), *The political Economy of the New Asian Industrialism* (pp. 136–64). Ithaca and London: Cornell University Press.

Joint Committees for Fact-Finding and Management Accountability Regarding Surveillance of Samsung Workers. (2005, February 16). Press Conference Report. Retrieved March 15, 2011, from www.jinbo.net.

Joint Korean NGOs. (2010). *NGO Report on the Situation of Freedom of Opinion and Expression in the Republic of Korea since 2008*, submitted for the official visit of the Special Rapporteur, Retrieved April 20, 2011, from http://act.jinbo.net/drupal/sites/default/files/KoreaJointNGOreportonFoE.pdf.

Joint Struggle Committee for Human Rights in Information Society and Against the NEIS (JSC). (2003, July 8). *Press Conference at the Launch of the JSC (in Korean).* Neetinamu cafe', Seoul.

Joint Struggle Committee for Human Rights in Information Society and Against the NEIS (JSC). (2003a). *Problems with and alternatives to the NEIS (in Korean).* Seoul, Korea Jinbo Network.

Joint Struggle Committee for Human Rights in Information Society and Against the NEIS (JSC). (2003b). Executive Summary: the NEIS. Retrieved May 5, 2011, from http://noneis.jinbo.net/english.html.

Joo, S.-M. (2004, January 31). NIS Checks Reporter's Phone, Sparks Furor. *The Korea Herald.*

Jung, H.-J. (2003, April 1). What is missing in the NEIS. *Shin-Donga*, 263.

Jung, S.-K. (2011, March 28). *Chaebol* fend off "extended profit sharing," *Korea Times.*

Kang, D. (2006). Cut from the same cloth: Bureaucracies and rulers in South Korea, 1948–1979. In Y.-S. Chang, & S. H. Lee (Eds.), *Transformations in Twentieth Century Korea* (pp. 186–218). London and New York: Routledge.

Kang, D. C. (2002). *Crony Capitalism: Corruption and Development in South Korea and the Philippines*. Cambridge: Cambridge University Press.

Kang, M.-K. (2000). Discourse politics toward neoliberal globalization. *Inter-Asia Cultural Studies, 1*(3), 443–56.

Kellner, D. (2002). "Theorising Globalization," *Sociological Theory, 20*(3): 285–305.

Kim. (2003, June). *Nara Gyeung-Jae (in Korean)*.

Kim, B. (2006). *Infrastructure Development for the Economic Development in Developing Countries: Lessons from Korea and Japan*. Kobe, Japan: Kobe University.

Kim, B.-J. (2002). *The Basic research for a telecommunication history, data collection, and exhibition*. Seoul, Korea: Association of Korean Telecom History.

Kim, D.-H. (2003, July 3). Change in telecom policy expected. *Korea Times*.

Kim, D.-J. (1998, February 25). Opening New Age. at the inaugural speech.

Kim, D.-W. (2003). Interlocking Ownership in the Korean *Chaebol*. *Corporate Governance: An International Review, 11*(2): 132–142.

Kim, E.-J. (1993). Telecommunications development in the Republic of Korea: An alternative model? *Telecommunications Policy, 17*(2): 118–38.

Kim, E. M. (1988). From dominance to symbiosis: State and *Chaebol* in Korea. *Pacific Focus, 3*(2): 105–21.

Kim, E. S. (2003). International high performance network infrastructure of Korea, *The Public Forum on KII-Testbed*. Busan, Korea: APII Cooperation Center, KISDI.

Kim Gu. ([1947] 2002). *Baekbum Diary*. Seoul: Dolbaegae.

Kim, H. J., Pan, G., & Pan, S. L. (2007). Managing IT-enabled transformation in the public sector: A case study on e-government in South Korea. *Government Information Quarterly, 24*(2): 338–52.

Kim, J.-C., & Ro, T.-S. (1993). Current policy issues in the Korean telecommunications industry. *Telecommunications Policy, 17*(7): 481–92.

Kim, J.-H. (2007). *A New Approach for Community Development: The Case of Saemaul Undong in Korea*. Paper presented at the Improving Community Driven Development (CDD) Strategy: The Case of New Village Movement in Korea. Retrieved May 14, 2011, from http://info.worldbank.org/etools/library/latestversion.asp?240816.

Kim, K.-R. (2011, April 11). *Chaebol* asset holdings swell under Lee administration. *The Hankyoreh*. Retrieved September 1, 2011, from http://www.hani.co.kr/arti/ENGISSUE/74/472384.html

Kim, K. S. (2005). The implementation of the export-oriented Industrialization policy in the 1960s (in Korean). In L.-J. Cho, & C. Eckert (Eds.), *Modernization of the Republic of Korea, a miraculous achievement*. Seoul, Korea: Monthly Chosun.

Kim, K. S., & Roemer, M. (1979). *Growth and structural transformation*. Cambridge: Harvard University Press.

Kim, S., & Kim, S. (2004). The conflict over the use of information technology in South Korean schools *Innovation: The European Journal of Social Sciences, 17*(4), 363–75.

Kim, S.-J. (2004, September 24). NEIS launched in the March of 2006 (in Korean). *Kookmin Ilbo*, p. 7.

Kim, T.-G. (2007, July 16). Post Offices Lead Migration to Open-Source Software. *Korea Times*.

Kim, Y.-C. (2010). *Thinking Samsung* (in Korean). Seoul: Sahoe-pyongron.

Kim, Y.-K. (2005, May 16). Roh said, "The power was already handed over to market" (in Korean). *Hankyoreh Newspaper*.

Kim, Y.-N. (2007). The rising East Asian "wave" In D. K. Thussu (Ed.), *Media on the move: Global flow and contra-flow* (pp. 135–52). London: Routledge.

Kim, Y. T. (1999). Neoliberalism and the Decline of the Developmental State. *Journal of Contemporary Asia, 29*(4): 441–61.

Kim, Y. T. (2005). DJnomics and the Transformation of the Developmental State. *Journal of Contemporary Asia, 35*(4): 471–84.

Ko, K.-M. (2001). *The Political Economy of Telecom Liberalization in Korea (in Korean)*. Seoul: Communication Books.

Koh, J.-M., Lee, A.-J., & Kang, S.-K. (2005). *A plan for the sustainable "Korean wave" (in Korean)*. Seoul: Samsung Economic Research Institute.

Kong, T. Y. (1995). From Relative Autonomy to Consensual Development: the Case of South Korea. *Political Studies, 43*(4): 630–44.

Kong, T. Y. (2000). *The Politics of economic reform in South Korea: A fragile miracle*. London & New York: Routledge.

Koo, H. (1993). Introduction: Beyond State-Market Relations. In H. Koo (Ed.), *State and Society in Contemporary Korea* (1–11). Ithaca and London: Cornell University Press.

Koo, B.-H., & Kim, E. M. (2005). The role of business for the economic development (in Korean). In L.-J. Cho, & C. Eckert (Eds.), *Modernization of the Republic of Korea, a miraculous achievement*. Seoul, Korea: Monthly Chosun.

Korea Agency for Digital Opportunity & Promotion (KADO). (2007). *The Past and Present of Information and Telecommunications (in Korean)*. Seoul, Korea: KADO.

Korea Association of Information and Telecommunication. (2007). *Monthly ICT Industry*. Seoul: KAIT.

Korea Association of Information and Telecommunication (KAIT). (1995). *A Commentary for the KII Master Plan*. Seoul: KAIT.

Korea Association of Information and Telecommunication (KAIT). (2004). *Monthly report*. Seoul: KAIT.

Korea Communications Commission (KCC) & Korea Internet and Security Agency (KISA). (2010) 2010 Korea Internet White Paper. Seoul: KCC & KISA.

Korea Culture and Information Service (KCIS) (2010). *Facts about Korea*. Seoul: KCIS.

Korea Post. (2006). Information on Korean Stamps: History. Retrieved May 25, 2011, from www.koreastamp.go.kr/sp/eg/speg0303.jsp.

Korea Times. (2008, January 10). Prosecutors Launch Probe Into Samsung Bribery Scandal. *Korea Times*.

Kristof, N. D. (1995, November 24). Ruthless Ex-Dictator Getting Credit for South Korea's Rise. *New York Times*.

Kurtenbach, E. (2004 July 2). China Steps Up Surveillance, Targeting Mobile Phone Messaging. *The Associated Press*.

Kwak, J. S. (2011, May 9). Only *Chaebols* making profits from the '*Chaebol*-freiendly' policies. *Hankyoreh 21*, Retrieved May 20, 2011, from www.hani.co.kr/popups/print.hani?kswn=477005.

Langdale, J. V. (1997). International competitiveness in East Asia. Broadband telecommunications and interactive multimedia. *Telecommunications Policy, 21*(3), 235–49.

Lash, S. M., & Urry, J. (1994). *Economies of Signs and Space*. London: Sage.

Latour, B. (1992). Where are the Missing Masses? the Sociology of a Few Mundane Artifacts. In W. Bijker, & J. Law (Eds.), *Shaping Technology/Building Society: Studies in Sociotechnical Change* (pp. 225–58). Cambridge, MA: MIT Press.

Lau, T. Y., Kim, S. W., & Atkin, D. (2005). An examination of factors contributing to South Korea's global leadership in broadband adoption. *Telematics and Informatics, 22*(4), 349–59.

Lawyers for a Democratic Society. (2005, March). The spying group case of the Korean students in the US (in Korean). Retrieved May 23, 2011, from http://minbyun.jinbo. net/minbyun/zbxe/?document_srl=5697.

Lee, B. C. (2006). Political Economy of Korean Development after Liberation: A Critical Reflection. *Korea Journal, 46*(3): 49–79.

Lee, C., & Chan-Olmsted, S. M. (2004). Competitive advantage of broadband Internet: a comparative study between South Korea and the United States. *Telecommunications Policy, 28*(9–10): 649–77.

Lee, C.-P. (1993). Preconditions for a Successful Financial Liberalization and a Feedback Process of Managing Progressive Liberalization. *U.S.–Korea Academic Studies, 3*: 1–13.

Lee, H., O'Keefe, R. M., & Yun, K. (2003). The Growth of Broadband and Electronic Commerce in South Korea: Contributing Factors. *The Information Society, 19*(1): 81–93.

Lee, J. H. (2011, May 11). For the low-come class in word, but, for *Chaebols* in his heart. Hankyoreh 21. Retrieved May 20, 2011, from http://h21.hani.co.kr/popups/print_h21. hani?ksn=29594.

Lee, K. R., & Lee, K.-S. (2009). The Korean Government's Electronic Record Management Reform: The Promise and Perils of Digital Democratization. *Government Information Quarterly, 26*(3): 525–35.

Lee, S., & Jung, J.-I. (1998, November). Telecommunications markets, industry, and infrastructure in Korea. *IEEE Communications Magazine*, 59–64.

Lee, S.-J., & Han, T. (2006). The demise of "Korea, Inc.:" paradigm shift in Korea's developmental state. *Journal of Contemporary Asia, 36*(3): 305–24.

Lee, Y. (2006). Teachers Working for Change: Gender equity and the politics of teacher activism in South Korea. *Asia Pacific Journal of Education, 26*(2): 143–53.

Lee, Y.-R., Kim, B.-C., Na, S.-W., & Hur, J.-H. (2009). Analytic Study on Korea's IT Infrastructure Development Policies. NIA Research paper. NIA.

Leipziger, D. M., Dollar, D., Shorrocks, A. F., & Song, S.Y. (1992). *The Distribution of Income and Wealth in Korea.* EDI Development Studies, Washington, DC: World Bank.

Leipziger, D. M., & Petri, P. A. (1993). *Korean Industrial Policy: Legacies of the Past and Directions for the Future* Washington, DC: World Bank.

Lenin, V. I. ([1916] 1969). *Imperialism, the Highest Stage of Capitalism: A Popular Outline.* New York: International Publishers.

Lewis, P. (2004, September 20). Broadband Wonderland: Nearly everyone in South Korea has Internet access that puts Americans to shame. *The Fortune, 150*: 191–8.

Lie, J. (2006). What makes us great: *Chaebol* development, labor practices, and managerial ideology. In Y.-S. Chang, & S. H. Lee (Eds.), *Transformations in Twentieth Century Korea* (pp. 138–52). London and New York: Routledge.

Lim, W., Haggard, S., & Kim, E. (2003). Introduction: The political economy of corporate restructuring in Korea. In W. Lim, S. Haggard, & E. Kim, (Eds.), *Economic Crisis and Corporate Restructuring in Korea: Reforming the Chaebol* (pp. 1–31). Cambridge, UK: Cambridge University Press.

Lim, H.-C., & Jang, J.-H. (2006). Neo-Liberalism in post-crisis South Korea: social conditions and outcomes *Journal of Contemporary Asia, 36*(4): 442–63.

Low, L. (2003). Singapore One: The Hard Techno-Infrastructural and Soft Socioeconomic Issues. *Trends in Communication, 11*(1): 27.

Luxemburg, R. ([1913] 2003). *The Accumulation of Capital.* London: Routledge.

Magdoff, H. (2003). *Imperialism without Colonies.* New York: Monthly Review Press.

Mahlich, J., & Pascha, W. (2007). Introduction: Korea as a Newly Advanced Economy and the Role of Technology and Innovation. In J. Mahlich, & W. Pascha (Eds.), *Innovation and Technology in Korea* (pp. 1–9). Berlin/Heidelberg: Physica-Verlag.

Mallaby, S. (1995). Quick, quick, quick. *The Economist, 335*(7917): 3–5.

Mani, S. (2007). Keeping Pace with Globalisation: Innovation Capability in Korea's Telecommunications Equipment Industry. In J. Mahlich, & W. Pascha (Eds.), *Innovation and Technology in Korea* (pp. 255–86). Berlin/Heidelberg: Physica-Verlag.

Mann, M. (1988). *States, War and Capitalism: Studies in Political Sociology*. Oxford, UK: Basil Blackwell.

Mansell, R., & Wehn, U. (Eds.). (1998). *Knowledge societies: Information technology for sustainable development*. Oxford: Oxford University Press.

Mao, T.-T. ([1937] 2007). *On practice and contradiction* London: Verso.

Marx, K. and F. Engels ([1848] 1998). *The Communist Manifesto: A Modern Edition*. London: Verso.

Marx, K. ([1939]1993). *Grundrisse*. New York: Penguin Books.

Mason, E. S., Kim, M. J., Perkins, D. H., Kim, K. S., & Cole, D. C. (Eds.). (1980). *The Economic and Social Modernization of the Republic of Korea*. Cambridge: Harvard University Press.

Mathiesen, T. (1997). The Viewer Society: Michel Foucault's "Panopticon" Revisited. *Theoretical Criminology, 1*(2): 215–34.

McChesney, R. W. (1999). The New Global Media: It's a Small World of Big Conglomerates. *The Nation*. 29 November.

McChesney, R. W. (2004). *The Problem of the Media: U.S. Communication Politics in the 21st Century*. New York, NY: Monthly Review Press.

McChesney, R. W. (2007). *Communication Revolution: Critical junctures and the future of the media*. New York: The New Press.

Media Today. (2005, September 27). Confiscating the eavesdropping tapes used in the Kim DJ administration (in Korean). Retrieved May 24, 2011, from www.mediatoday.co.kr/news/articleView.html?idxno=40441.

Michael, M. G., & Michael, K. (2010). Toward a state of überveillance. *IEEE Technology and Society Magazine, 29*(2): 9–16.

Migdal, J. S. (1988). *Strong Societies and Weak States: State-Society Relations and State Capabilities in the Third World*. Princeton, NJ: Princeton University Press.

Migdal, J. S. (1994). The State-in-society: An Approach to Struggles for Domination. In J. S. Migdal, A. Kohli, & V. Shue (Eds.), *State Power and Social Forces: Domination and Transformation in the Third World* (7–34). Cambridge, UK: Cambridge University Press.

Migdal, J. S. (2001). *State in Society: Studying How States and Societies Transform and Constitute One Another*. Cambridge, UK: Cambridge University Press.

Migdal, J. S., Kohli, A., & Shue, V. (1994). Introduction: Developing a State-in-society Perspective. In J. S. Migdal, A. Kohli, & V. Shue (Eds.), *State Power and Social Forces: Domination and Transformation in the Third World* (pp. 1–4). Cambridge, UK: Cambridge University Press.

Mills, E. S., & Song, B.-N. (1979). *Urbanization and urban problems* Cambridge: Harvard University Press.

Ministry of Communication (MoC). (1993, August 21). *Basic Plan for the Korean Information Infrastructure (No. 93100–452)*. Seoul.

Ministry of Communications (MoC). (1993, July 2). *Five-year Plan for a New Economy (No. 93100–380)*. Seoul.

Ministry of Communications (MoC). (1994, March). *21C Master Plan for the Korean Information Infrastructure.* Seoul.

Ministry of Culture and Tourism (MCT). (2007). *C-Korea 2010* (in Korean), Ministry of Culture and Tourism, Seoul.

Ministry of Information and Communication (MIC). (1996). *The First Basic Plan for Informatization Promotion (in Korean).* Seoul: MIC.

Ministry of Information and Communication (MIC). (2007, July). *Subscribers of Wired/ Wireless Communication Services.* Seoul: MIC.

Ministry of Information and Communication (MIC), & National Computerization Agency (NCA). (2005). *Past and present of Korea's IT policy (in Korean).* Seoul: NCA.

Ministry of Information and Communication (MIC), & National Computerization Agency (NCA). (2006). *Past and Present of Korea's High-speed Backbone Network (in Korean).* Seoul: NCA.

Mobile Phone News. (1992, September 12). South Korean cellular licensing debacle to be continued next year. Retrieved May 21, 2011, from http://findarticles.com/p/articles/ mi_m3457/is_n18_v10/ai_12622635.

Mody, A. (1997). *Infrastructure strategies in East Asia: The untold story.* Washington, D.C.: Economic Development Institute of the World Bank.

Morley, D., & Robins, K. (1995). *Spaces of Identity: Global Media, Electronic Landscapes and Cultural Boundaries.* London: Routledge.

Moon, C.-i. (1994). Changing Patterns of Business-Government Relations in South Korea. In A. MacIntyre (Ed.), *Business and Government in Industrialising Asia* (pp. 222–46). Ithaca, New York: Cornell University Press.

Moon, I.-W. (2008). "Samsung under siege," *BusinessWeek*, April 17.

Moon, P. Y. (1991). The Saemaul (New Community) Movement, 1971. In L.-J. Cho, & Y. H. Kim (Eds.), *Economic development in the Republic of Korea: A policy prospective* (pp. 405–27). Honolulu, Hawaii: University of Hawaii Press.

Mosco, V. (1996). *The Political Economy of Communication: Rethinking and Renewal.* London: Sage.

Mosco, V. (1999). New York.Com: A Political Economy of the "Informational" City *The Journal of Media Economics, 12*(2), 103–16.

Mosco, V. (2004). *The Digital Sublime: Myth, Power, and Cyberspace.* Cambridge, MA: The MIT Press.

Myrdal, G. (1968). *Asian Drama: An Inquiry into the Poverty of Nations* (Vol. II). New York, NY: Pantheon.

Mumford, L. (1970). *The Myth of the Machine: The Pentagon of Power* (Vol. 2). New York: Harcourt Brace Jovanovich, Inc.

Nam, C.-H. (1995). South Korea's big business clientelism in democratic reform, *Asian Survey, 35*(4), 357–66.

National Assembly of the Republic of the Korea (National Assembly). (2006). Korea History: Failure to establish Daehan Empire. Retrieved May 15, 2011, from http:// korea.assembly.go.kr/history_html/history_07/mod_11.jsp.

National Computerization Agency (NCA). (2002). *Informatization white paper 2002 (in Korean).* Seoul: NCA.

National Computerization Agency (NCA). (2003). *Informatization white paper 2003 (in Korean).* Seoul: NCA.

National Computerization Agency (NCA). (2003, January). *Report: The Korea Information Infrastructure (KII) Advancement Committee and Working Committee (in Korean).* Seoul: NCA.

National Computerization Agency (NCA). (2005). *Past and present of Korea's IT policy (in Korean)*. Seoul: NCA.

National Computerization Agency (NCA). (2005). *White paper Internet Korea 2005*. Seoul: NCA.

National Human Rights Commission (NHRC). (2003, May 12). *The NHRC Decision: Policy Recommendations*. Seoul: NHRC.

National Human Rights Commission (NHRC). (2007). About the Commission. Retrieved May 12, 2011, from www.humanrights.go.kr/english/about_nhrck/introduction_01.jsp.

National Information Society Agency (NIA). (2007). *Informatization white paper 2007* (in Korean). Seoul: NIA.

National Information Society Agency (NIA). (2007). *2007 Informatization White Paper* Seoul, Korea: NIA.

National Information Society Agency (NIA). (2008). *2008 Informatization White Paper* Seoul, Korea: NIA.

National Information Society Agency (NIA). (2009). *2009 Informatization White Paper* Seoul, Korea: NIA.

National Information Society Agency (NIA). (2010). *2010 Informatization White Paper* Seoul, Korea: NIA.

National Information Society Agency (NIA), & Ministry of Information and Communication (MIC). (2006). *IPv6 Status Report 2006*. Seoul: NIA (in Korean).

Noh, H.-W. (2008, May 18). Illegal CCTVs used for monitoring illegal activities (in Korean). *Hankyoreh Shinmun*.

Noumba UM, P., & Dinghem, S. (2004). *Private Participation in Infrastructure Projects in the Republic of Korea*. Washington, DC: World Bank.

OECD-World Bank Institute. (2000). *Korea and the Knowledge-based Economy: Making the Transition*. Paris, France: OECD.

Oh, H. M. (2004). Forming the East Asian Community: "Cultural Translation" as an Alternative of *Dongdosoegi* (in Korean). *New Asia, 11*(4): 86–115.

Open Net Initiative (2011). Access Controlled. Retrieved August 30, 2011, from http://www.access-controlled.net/

Organization for Economic co-operation and Development (OECD). (1996). *The Knowledge-based economy*. Paris, France: OECD.

Organization for Economic co-operation and Development (OECD). (2000). *Regulatory reform in Korea*. Paris, France: OECD.

Organization for Economic co-operation and Development (OECD). (2007). *OECD Economic Surveys: Korea*. Paris, France: OECD.

Organization for Economic co-operation and Development (OECD). (2010). *OECD Information Technology Outlook 2010*. Paris, France: OECD.

Organization for Economic Co-operation and Development (OECD). (2010, June). OECD Broadband Statistics (Publication. Retrieved 10 May, 2011, from OECD: www.oecd.org/sti/ict/broadband.

Organisation for Economic Co-operation and Development (OECD). (2011) OECD. StatExtract. Available at http://stats.oecd.org

Park, B.-G. (2008). Uneven development, inter-scalar tensions, and the politics of decentralization in South Korea. *International Journal of Urban and Regional Research, 32*(1), 40–59.

Park, C.-S. (2007, August 29). NEIS, suspected by the massive leaking of students' information to the companies (in Korean). *Hankyorae Shinmun*.

Park, W.-I. (2007). Privacy Issues and Public Opinion in Korea. *KyongHee Beophak (KyongHee Law Review), 42*(2): 305–26.

PBS. (2006). The Net @ Risk. On *Moyers on America* [Television program]: PBS.

PBS, (2007, October 18). Moyers on America: The Net @ Risk. Retrieved August 30, 2011, from http://www.pbs.org/moyers/moyersonamerica/net/neutrality.html

PBS. (2008). Growing Up Online. *Frontline* [Television program]: PBS.

PBS. (2010). Digital Nation. *Frontline* [Television program]: PBS.

People's Solidarity for Participatory Democracy. (2009, October 21). UN Special Rapporteur Faced "Ironic Korea" IT Power but Freedom of Opinion and Expression Oppressed. Retrieved May 25, 2011, from http://blog.peoplepower21.org/English/20876.

People's Solidarity for Participatory Democracy. (2003, February). Revise SOFA! No more death! Retrieved May 23, 2011, from http://blog.peoplepower21.org/Peace/10344.

People's Solidarity for Participatory Democracy. (2003, June 26). Human Rights Activists in South Korea start Hunger Strike against National Education Information System (NEIS) Retrieved May 12, 2011, from http://blog.peoplepower21.org/English/10335.

Phillips, D. J. (2003). Beyond privacy: Confronting locational surveillance in wireless communication. *Communication Law and policy, 8*(1): 1–23.

Picot, A., & Wernick, C. (2007). The role of government in broadband access. *Telecommunications Policy, 31*(10–11): 660–74.

Pieterse, J. ([1995] 2005). "Globalization as Hybridization," 626–57 in G. Durham and D. Kellner (Eds.) *Media and Cultural Studies: Keyworks.* Revised ed. Malden, MA: Blackwell Publishers.

Pirie, I. (2006). Social injustice and economic dynamism in contemporary Korea. *Critical Asian Studies 38*: 211–43.

Poster, M. (1990). *The Mode of Information: Poststructuralism and Social Context.* Chicago: The University of Chicago Press.

Poster, M. (2004). The information empire. *Comparative Literature Studies, 41*(3): 317–34.

Poulantzas, N. ([1965] 2008). Study of Hegemony in the State. In J. Martin (Ed.), *The Poulantzas Reader: Marxism, Law, and the State* (74–119). NY: Verso.

Poulantzas, N. ([1978] 2000). *State, Power, Socialism.* London and New York: Verso.

Presidential Commission on Policy Planning (PCPP). (2008). *The National Education Information System (NEIS).* Seoul: PCPP.

Privacy International, (2007). PHR2006 – Republic of (South) Korea. Retrieved August 30, 2011, from https://www.privacyinternational.org/article/phr2006-republic-south-korea

Privacy International. (2011). PHR2006 – Republic of (South) Korea. Retrieved May 12, 2011, from www.privacyinternational.org/article.shtml?cmd%5B347%5D=x-347–559490.

Public Infrastructure Division, NIA, (2006, December): unpublished paper.

Raley, R. (2004). eEmpires. *Cultural Critique, 57*: 111–50.

Relyea, H. C. (2002). Homeland security and information. *Government Information Quarterly, 19*(3): 213–23.

Reporters Without Borders (2011). *Enemies of the Internet: Countries under Surveillance.* Retrieved May 20, 2011, from http://en.rsf.org/IMG/pdf/Internet_enemies.pdf.

Ro, T.-S., & Kim, J.-C. (1996). Evolution of the communications industry in advanced countries: Implication for the policy direction of Korea. *Telematics and Informatics, 13*(4): 199–211.

Robertson, R. (1990). "Mapping the Global Condition: Globalization as the Central Concept," 15–30 in M. Featherstone (Ed.) *Global Culture: Nationalism, Globalization and Modernity*. London: Sage.

Robins, K., & Webster, F. (1999). *Times of the Technoculture: From the Information Society to the Virtual Life*. London: Routledge.

Robinson, W. I. (2005). "What is a Critical Globalization Studies? Intellectual Labour and Global Society," 11–18 in R. P. Appelbaum, & W. I. Robinson (Eds.) *Critical Globalization Studies*. London: Routledge.

Roediger-Schluga, T. (2007). Public–Private R&D Partnerships: Current Issues and Challenges. In J. Mahlich, & W. Pascha (Eds.), *Innovation and Technology in Korea* (pp. 115–26). Berlin/Heidelberg: Physica-Verlag.

SaKong, I. (1993). *Korea in the world economy*. Washington, DC: Institute for International Economics.

Samsung (2010). Samsung Profile 2010. Retrieved September 1, 2011, from http://www.samsung.com/au/aboutsamsung/corporateprofile/ourperformance/samsungprofile.html

Sassen, S. (2005). "The Many Scales of the Global: Implications for Theory and for Politics," 155–66 in R. P. Appelbaum, & W. I. Robinson (Eds.) *Critical Globalization Studies*. London: Routledge.

Sassen, S. (2006). *Territory, authority, rights: From medieval to global assemblages*. Princeton, NJ: Princeton University Press.

Sassen, S. (2007). Introduction: Deciphering the Global. In S. Sassen (Ed.), *Deciphering the Global: Its Scales, Spaces and Subjects* (pp. 1–18). New York: Routledge.

Sawhney, H. (1993). Circumventing the centre: The realities of creating a telecommunications infrastructure in the USA. *Telecommunications Policy, 17*(7): 504–16.

Schaefer, R. J. (1995). National information infrastructure policy: a theoretical and normative approach. *Internet Research: Electronic Networking Applications and Policy, 5*(2): 4–13.

Schiller, D. (1999). *Digital Capitalism: Networking the Global Market System*. Cambridge, MA: The MIT Press.

Schiller, D. (2001). World Communications in Today's Age of Capital. *Emergences: Journal for the Study of Media & Composite Cultures, 11*(1): 51–68.

Schiller, D. (2007). *How to Think about Information*. Urbana and Chicago: University of Illinois Press.

Schiller, D., & Mosco, V. (2001). Integrating a Continent for a Transnational World. In V. Mosco, & D. Schiller (Eds.), *Continental Order? Integrating North America for Cybercapitalism* (1–34). Lanham, MD: Rowman and Littlefield.

Schiller, H. I. (1981). *Who Knows: Information in the Age of the Fortune 500*. Norwood, NJ: Ablex Publishing Corp.

Schiller, H. I. (1984). *Information and the Crisis Economy*. Norwood, NJ: Ablex Publishing Corp.

Scott, J. (1991). Networks of corporate power: A comparative assessment. *Annual Review of Sociology, 17*: 181–203.

Seo, E.-K., & Kim, J.-H. (2009, April 12). Young South Koreans become the "880,000 Won Generation." *Reuter*, Seoul, Retrieved 25 May, 2011, from www.taipeitimes.com/News/bizfocus/archives/2009/04/12/2003440846.

Shaviro, S. (2002). Capitalist monsters. *Historical Materialism, 10*(4), 281–290.

Shelley, B. (2001). Protest and globalization: Media, symbols and audience in the drama of democratization. *Democratization, 8*(4): 155–74.

Shim, D. (2002). South Korean Media Industry in the 1990s and the Economic Crisis. *Prometheus, 20*(4), 337–350.

Shin, C., Byung-il, C., & Seon-Kyou, C. (1996). Restructuring the Korean telecommunications market: Evolution and challenges ahead. *Telecommunications Policy, 20*(5): 357–73.

Shin, D.-H. (2007). A critique of Korean National Information Strategy: Case of national information infrastructures. *Government Information Quarterly, 24*(3), 624–45.

Shin, J.-S., & Chang, H.-J. (2003). *Restructuring Korea Inc.* London: Routledge.

Shin, J.-S., & Park, Y.-T. (2007). Building the national ICT frontier: The case of Korea *Information Economics and Policy, 19*(2): 249–77.

Shin, K. Y. (1998). The Political Economy of Economic Growth in East Asia: South Korea and Taiwan. In E. M. Kim (Ed.), *The Four Asian Tigers: Economic Development and the Global Political Economy* (pp. 1–31). San Diego, CA: Academic Press.

Shin, K.-Y. (2006, March 25). *Globalization and social polarization.* Paper presented at the Korea Social Forum 2006, Seoul, Korea.

Sinclair, J. (1999). *Latin American Television: A Global View.* Oxford: Oxford University Press.

Siochru, S. O. (2004). Will the Real WSIS Please Stand Up?: The Historic Encounter of the 'Information Society' and the 'Communication Society'. *Gazette, 66*(3–4): 203–24.

Skocpol, T. (1979). *States and Social Revolutions: A Comparative Analysis of France, Russia, and China.* Cambridge, London: Cambridge University Press.

Soja, E. W. (1996). *Thirdspace: Journey to Los Angeles and Other Real-and-Imagined Places.* Oxford, UK: Blackwell.

Sreberny, A. (2005). The Global and the Local in International Communication. In G. Durham, & D. Kellner (Eds.), *Media and Cultural Studies: Keywords* (Revised ed., pp. 604–25). Malden, MA: Blackwell Publishers.

Statistics Korea, (2010). Korean Statistical Information Service (KOSIS). Available at http://kosis.kr/

Statistics Korea, (2011). Korean Statistical Information Service (KOSIS). Available at http://kosis.kr/

Straubhaar, J. (1991) "Beyond Media Imperialism: Asymmetrical Interdependence and Cultural Proximity," *Critical Studies in Mass Communication, 8*: 39–59.

Straubhaar, J. (1997). World Television: From Global to Local.

Straubhaar, J., & S. Hammond (1998). "Complex Cultural Systems and Cultural Hybridization," a paper presented to the Intercultural and Development Communication Division of the International Communication Association, Jerusalem, Israel.

Strover, S. (2000). The first mile. *The Information Society, 16*(2): 151–4.

Synott, J. (2007). The Korean Teachers and Educational Workers Union: Collective Rights as the Agency of Social Change [Electronic Version]. *International Electronic Journal for Leadership in Learning, 11* Retrieved May 20, 2011, from www.ucalgary. ca/iejll/vol. 11/synott.

Taylor, C. (2006, June 14). The future is in South Korea. *Business 2.0.* Retrieved 1 June, 2011, from http://money.cnn.com/2006/06/08/technology/business2_futureboy0608/ index.htm.

Tcha, D.-W., Park, J. S., Chang, S.-G., & Song, K. H. (2000). Korean telecommunication industry in transition. *Telecommunication Systems, 14*: 3–12.

Telecommunications Council. (1994). *Reforms towards the Intellectually Creative Society of the 21st Century.* Tokyo: Ministry of Posts and Telecommunications.

Tomlinson, J. (1991). *Cultural Imperialism: A Critical Introduction.* London: Pinter Publishers.

Townsend, A. (2004, May 31). Big in South Korea. *New Statesman*, xxxi–xxxii.

Urry, J. (2000). "Mobile sociology," *British Journal of Sociology*, *51*(1): 185–203.

Urry, J. (2007). *Mobilities*. Cambridge: Polity Press.

Urry, J. (2005). The Complexities of the Global. *Theory Culture Society*, *22*(5), 235–54.

US Central Intelligence Agency (CIA, 2011). Retrieved May 1, 2011, from https://www.cia.gov/library/publications/the-world-factbook/geos/ks.html.

US Central Intelligence Agency (CIA, 2011). Retrieved May 1, 2011, from https://www.cia.gov/library/publications/the-world-factbook/geos/kn.html.

US Department of Education. (1997, June 27). E-Rate overview. Retrieved 5 May, 2011, from www.ed.gov/Technology/overview.html.

Våge, L. (2004). *China's search engine censorship continues* (Publication. Retrieved April 27, 2008: www.pandia.com/sw-2005/09-china.html.

Varis, P. (1984). *Global Traffic in TV Programming*, 144–52 in G. Gerbner, & M. Siefert (Eds.) *World Communications: A Handbook*, New York: Longman.

Venturelli, S. (2002). Inventing e-regulation in the US, EU and East Asia: Conflicting social visions of the Information Society. *Telematics and Informatics*, *19*(2): 69–90.

Virilio, P. (1997). *Open Sky*. London, Verso.

Virilio, P. (2000). *The Information Bomb*. London and New York: Verso.

Visser, J. (2003). Unions and unionism around the world. In J. Addison, & C. Schnabel (Eds.), *The International Handbook of Trade Unions* (pp. 366–413). Chelteham, UK: Edward Elgar.

Wade, R. (1990a). *Governing the Market: Economic Theory and the Role of Government in East Asian Industrialization*. Princeton, NJ: Princeton University Press.

Wade, R. (1990b). Industrial Policy in East Asia: Does It Lead or Follow the Market? In G. Gereffi, & D. L. Wyman (Eds.), *Manufacturing Miracles: Paths of Industrialization in Latin America and East Asia* (231–66). Princeton, NJ: Princeton University Press.

Wallerstein, I. M. (1979). *The Capitalist World-economy: Essays*. Cambridge: Cambridge University Press.

Watts, J. (2003, February 24). World's first Internet president logs on: Web already shaping policy of new South Korean leader. Retrieved May 23, 2011, from Guardian: www.guardian.co.uk/technology/2003/feb/24/newmedia.koreanews.

Weiss, L. (1998). *The Myth of the Powerless State: Governing the Economy in a Global Era*. Cambridge, UK: Polity Press.

Weiss, L., & Hobson, J. M. (1995). *States and Economic Development: A Comparative Historical Analysis*. Cambridge, UK: Polity Press.

White, G., & Wade, R. (1988). Developmental States and Markets in East Asia: An Introduction. In G. White (Ed.), *Developmental States in East Asia* (pp. 1–29). New York, NY: St. Martin's Press.

World Bank. (1993). *The East Asian Miracle: Economic Growth and Public Policy*. Oxford, England: Oxford University Press.

World Bank. (2005). *World Development Report*. Washington, DC: World Bank.

World Bank. (2006). *Korea as a knowledge economy: Evolutionary process ad lessons learned*. Washington, DC: World Bank.

World Bank. (2009). The Knowledge Assessment Methodology (KAM). www.worldbank.org/wbi/kam

World Bank. (2010). *The Little Data Book – South Korea*, Washington, DC: World Bank.

World Economic Forum (WEF). (2007). *The global competitiveness report 2007–2008*. Geneva, Switzerland: World Economic Forum.

Yang, I.-M. (2006). Searching for Japanese identity in Asia Discourses on the East Asian

Community in the 21st century Japan (in Korean). *Today's Oriental Thoughts, 15*: 151–68, 282–3.

Yang, S. C., & Olfman, L. (2006). The effects of international telecommunication investment: Wireline and wireless technologies, 1993–1998. *Telecommunications Policy, 30*(5–6), 278–96.

Yonhap News Agency. (1998, February 25). Kim Dae Jung's inauguration speech. Retrieved May 30, 2011, from http://news.bbc.co.uk/1/hi/world/monitoring/59967.stm.

Yonhap News Agency. (2003, June 19). The MEHR argues, "Most local schools went with the NEIS" (in Korean).

Yoon, C.-H. (1999). Liberalisation policy, industry structure and productivity changes in Korea's telecommunications industry. *Telecommunications Policy, 23*(3–4): 289–306.

Youm, K. H. (1986). Press Freedom under Constraints: The Case of South Korea. *Asian Survey, 26*(8): 868–82.

Youm, K. H., & Salwen, M. B. (1990). A Free Press in South Korea: Temporary Phenomenon or Permanent Fixture? *Asian Survey, 30*(3): 312–25.

Yurtoglu, B. (2007). Corporate Governance and Investment in R&D in South Korea. In J. Mahlich, & W. Pascha (Eds.), *Innovation and Technology in Korea* (pp. 71–86). Berlin/Heidelberg: Physica-Verlag.

Zuboff, S. (1988). *In the Age of the Smart Machine: The Future of Work and Power*. New York: Basic Books.

Index

Page numbers in *italics* denote tables, those in **bold** denote figures.